Elizabeth Wood

Play, Learning *and the*
Early Childhood Curriculum

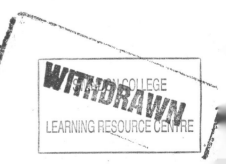

3rd Edition

Elizabeth Wood

Play, Learning *and the* Early Childhood Curriculum

Los Angeles | London | New Delhi
Singapore | Washington DC

Los Angeles | London | New Delhi
Singapore | Washington DC

SAGE Publications Ltd
1 Oliver's Yard
55 City Road
London EC1Y 1SP

SAGE Publications Inc.
2455 Teller Road
Thousand Oaks, California 91320

SAGE Publications India Pvt Ltd
B 1/I 1 Mohan Cooperative Industrial Area
Mathura Road
New Delhi 110 044

SAGE Publications Asia-Pacific Pte Ltd
3 Church Street
#10-04 Samsung Hub
Singapore 049483

Editor: Marianne Lagrange
Assistant editor: Kathryn Bromwich
Production editor: Nicola Marshall
Copyeditor: Gemma Marren
Proofreader: William Baginsky
Indexer: Martin Hargreaves
Marketing manager: Catherine Slinn
Cover design: Naomi Robinson
Typeset by: C&M Digitals (P) Ltd, Chennai, India
Printed in Great Britain by MPG Printgroup, UK

Library of Congress Control Number: 2012947266

British Library Cataloguing in Publication data

A catalogue record for this book is available from the British Library

MIX
Paper from
responsible sources
FSC
www.fsc.org   FSC® C018575

ISBN 978-1-84920-115-5
ISBN 978-1-84920-116-2 (pbk)

This book is dedicated to the new master players in my family: Joshua and Liam, Blake and Summer, Bella and Dolly

CONTENTS

LIST OF FIGURES

ABOUT THE AUTHOR

Elizabeth Wood is Professor of Education at the University of Sheffield. She teaches on a range of post-graduate programmes and runs in-service courses for teachers and early years practitioners. She has worked on a number of collaborative research projects with teachers in early years and primary schools. Elizabeth co-directed two ESRC funded research projects with Neville Bennett: Reception Teachers' Theories of Play (1995–1997) and Progression and Continuity in the Early Years (1999–2000). She has authored books and articles based on her research interests in play, young children's learning, early childhood pedagogy, equity and equality, policy critique and collaborative action research.

PREFACE

The third edition of this book builds substantially on the previous two editions, which were jointly authored by myself and Jane Attfield. Jane's career has taken her to working overseas, but I remain indebted to her research that was carried out during the Dorset Play Project. Jane also sustains her profound belief in the value of play through her own teaching practice, in spite of the attempts within successive government policies to capture and tame play.

There have been many developments since 1996, some positive and some less so. The field of play scholarship continues to thrive, with research emerging from many different countries where early childhood education systems are undergoing rapid development. Much research reveals the influence of Euro-American theories and definitions, but there is also evidence of more attention to variations in play, based on dimensions of diversity such as gender, social class, ethnicity and disabilities. Much of this research challenges dominant Western ideologies and practices, and challenges researchers and practitioners to think critically and ethically about our work with children and families. This research is included in the book to demonstrate changes in theory and practice.

Another arena for significant change is in the field of early childhood policies, which vary in their focus across the age range from birth to seven or eight years. As many countries develop their early childhood provision, national policies are driving unprecedented changes for different purposes: expanding provision, improving quality, aligning pre-school with primary schooling, driving up standards and improving children's life chances. Early childhood education is at the heart of policy-making agendas in the four UK countries (England, Scotland, Wales and Northern Ireland), and in many other developed and developing countries. These policy interventions have been a mixed blessing for play, especially with the influence of international research on the effectiveness of pre-school education and the characteristics of high quality provision. While play is endorsed as a valuable means of learning and development, the trends are towards educational versions of play, in which planned and purposeful play are privileged. Thus it will be argued in this book that policy versions of 'educational play' are distinct from the diverse understandings that are evident in play scholarship, and the aspiration to understand play in all its complexities.

Fortunately play scholarship continues to thrive, with the addition in 2012 of a new *International Journal of Play*, which brings together research from different disciplinary perspectives. Contemporary research studies are challenging in their foci, innovative in their methods and contentious in the eclecticism of their theoretical frameworks. Play scholars are likely to draw on the work of Foucault rather than Froebel, Deleuze rather than Dewey and there are some interesting ways in which post-structural and post-modern theories are being developed. The field remains open to debate, discussion and argument regarding the role and value of play in learning and development and across the human life span. There have been many outcomes from research that are of direct relevance to practitioners.

The third edition reflects these trends and draws substantially on academic and practitioner research to illustrate key ideas and debates. Guided by feedback from readers, this edition maintains a strong integration between theory and practice. The first four chapters focus on different ways of understanding learning and development, the benefits of different forms of play and a rationale for integrated curriculum and pedagogical approaches in early childhood settings. The second half of the book develops the theme of creating unity between playing, learning and teaching, focusing on the practicalities of curriculum planning, pedagogical practices, observation and assessment. Each chapter highlights ongoing issues, questions and dilemmas that practitioners encounter, and provides practical examples to show how these have been addressed in different contexts.

This edition presents the practice-based evidence from my own research and from the work of early childhood practitioners who have been involved in in-service and modular degree programmes, or who welcome me into their classrooms to observe, discuss and theorize play. I have been privileged to work with dedicated practitioners, who form a resilient core of enthusiastic advocates for play, and active resisters of policy directives that are not in tune with how young children learn. Thanks are due especially to Joanna Cook, Amanda Kersey, Charlotte Rowland, Diann Cudmore and Jaqui Bamford for their observations and analyses of children and adults at play.

I hope that this third edition will inform and inspire practitioners and researchers, provoke debate and encourage reflection and critical engagement. I also hope that the book will remind readers of the importance of lifelong playing and learning.

A NOTE FROM THE AUTHOR

I have worked in early childhood education for all of my professional life, and have seen many changes, not least in my own thinking and practice as a teacher, researcher, writer and advocate for critical engagement with play. The mysteries and complexities of play continue to intrigue and challenge my thinking. I remain optimistic about the future of play from the perspective of the immense diversity of play scholarship across international contexts. I am somewhat pessimistic about the future of play in education settings, given the content of dominant policy discourses and the ways in which these are interpreted. I was once told by a local authority adviser that they would not use me for professional development because I was 'off message' (that is, not compliant with policy discourses about play). I took that as a compliment. I am privileged to work with students, teachers and practitioners who are, and continue to stay, 'off' the kinds of messages that diminish children's play.

I have argued that policy frameworks have proved to be a mixed blessing, because they define educational entitlements, but can be interpreted as straitjackets. Finding a 'best fit' between the orderliness of these frameworks and the complexities of play is problematic. But this does not mean that we should tolerate diminished versions of play. Our ethical and pedagogical endeavours need to focus on holding this complexity against policy discourses, and stay 'on message' and in tune with children's, and our own, play and playfulness. Henricks (2006) expresses eloquently the indefinable essence of play:

> For play is the laboratory of the possible. To play fully and imaginatively is to step sideways into another reality, between the cracks of ordinary life. Although the ordinary world, so full of cumbersome routines and responsibilities, is still visible to us, its images, strangely are robbed of their powers. Selectively, players take the objects and ideas of routine life and hold them aloft. Like wilful children, they unscrew reality or rub it on their bodies or toss it across the room. Things are dismantled and built anew. (2006: 1)

Free online material to accompany the book

 To gain free access to specially selected SAGE journal articles related to key topics discussed in this book please visit: **www.sagepub.co.uk/wood**

CHAPTER 1

UNDERSTANDING PLAY: COMPLEXITY AND CHALLENGE

The aim of this introductory chapter is to review contemporary debates about play, focusing on the ideologies and theories that inform the ways in which play is defined. You will understand some of the key issues and challenges in:

- Defining play
- Debating the status of play
- Exploring lifelong playing and learning
- Making a distinction between play in and out of 'educational' settings
- Developing critical perspectives on play

The ideological tradition

Early childhood education is underpinned by an ideological and theoretical tradition which regards play as essential to learning and development. The eclectic mix of ideas from this tradition ranges from the rhapsodic to the pragmatic, regarding the value of play, the nature of childhood, the purposes of education, the rights of the child and adults' roles and responsibilities. Central to this tradition are the educational and psychological theories of Johann Pestalozzi, Freidrich Froebel, Rudolf Steiner, John Dewey, Maria Montessori, Margaret and Rachel McMillan, Susan Isaacs, Anna Freud and David Winnicot. Their ideas were innovative and transformational: they generated new ways of understanding childhood and how children should be treated in society. Until the nineteenth century, childhood was seen as an immature form of adulthood and children from all social classes had little status and few legal rights or protection. For many, childhood was cut short by the need to work in the home or in factories, often for long hours and in dangerous conditions, leading to exploitation and abuse. The concept of original sin meant that children were regarded as naturally sinful, and needed to have moral rectitude instilled in them by whatever means adults thought acceptable, whether in the home, school or workplace. The child's mind was seen as an empty vessel, or a blank slate, which could be filled with the knowledge, skills and behaviours deemed valuable by society. Froebel and Pestalozzi took the opposite view: children's natural goodness could be harnessed through nurture, care, play and appropriate education. Along with social reformers such as Charles Booth and Charles Dickens, the early pioneers changed attitudes towards children and developed better provision for their development, care and education, where freedom to play and learn could be combined with appropriate nurturing and guidance. Intrinsically bound with this movement were ideals about social justice and a more egalitarian society.

The pioneer educators established the concept of childhood as a distinct stage in human development, and emphasized children's natural affinity for play. However, they did not demonstrate consistent agreement in their principles or practices. Although play was valued differently by each of the pioneers, they harnessed its educational potential in different ways (Saracho, 2010). The Romantic, child-centred ideology advocated the enabling of children to follow their natural development through free play and structured activities. Although the pioneers recognized that play allows children to express their inner needs, emotions, desires and conflicts, in terms of their educational recommendations it was not always the dominant activity. Montessori did not believe that children need to play, and did not value play as a creative force in itself. In designing special child-sized environments, she was not directly stimulating imaginative role play, but encouraging practical independence and autonomy. She had an instrumental view of play as a means to cognitive, social, moral and emotional development. The curriculum models devised by Froebel and Montessori were based on specific materials to be used in particular sequences, in carefully structured environments and sometimes with adult guidance. The curricula designed by Margaret and Rachel MacMillan and Susan Isaacs included pragmatic adult-directed elements such as sense-training, language and speech training, self-discipline, orderliness, cleanliness and the formation of good habits and dispositions (Boyce, 1946).

These curricula were socially, culturally and historically situated: they were designed with reference to particular values and purposes within rapidly changing societies. For example, the Progressive movement, which developed in the USA at the turn of the twentieth century, criticized the programmes of Froebel and Montessori as being highly structured, formal and ritualized. Montessori's emphasis on sensory training, individualism and academic learning was considered to be at odds with notions of freedom, creativity, play, fantasy and self-expression. We might also consider whether Romantic notions of childhood freedom and innocence remain relevant in contemporary society: a Reception class teacher questioned why she taught nursery rhymes when children know all the words, actions and dance routines of the latest pop idols.

These ideologies and theories melded with those of the Progressive movement in early childhood and primary education, which emerged in the early twentieth century, informed by the work of John Dewey, Jean Piaget, Susan and Nathan Isaacs and their followers. Progressivism rejected the formality and instrumentalism of established approaches, and argued for child-centred approaches and greater autonomy for children by enabling them to play and follow their interests through topics or projects. Progressivism created new ideas about the nature of childhood, how children learn and develop and the developmental processes of building knowledge. Education was conceptualized not as something that is done to the child, but as a complex process within which the child is an active participant, through agency, choice, control and ownership of play and project work. This orientation was theoretically seductive, because it reflected powerful notions of choice, freedom, autonomy and empowerment through education, all central tenets of the social and educational reform movements. These assumptions were a direct challenge to established behaviourist and instrumental discourses which positioned the child as a blank slate or empty vessel.

The work of the early childhood pioneers influenced a psychological view of play, which in turn laid the foundation for 'educational play'. The work of Jean Piaget (described in Chapter 2) has been influential in early childhood education, partly because his theories of play were interpreted alongside the ideals of Progressivism, and resonated with the liberal ideas of the 1960s. Thus a 'universal discourse' was created which positioned play as essential to children's learning, as a developmental need and as a fundamental right. Within this discourse, key ideas about child-centred education, choice and freedom, hands-on activities, exploration and discovery, and the primacy of play were taken up with enthusiasm but with little critical engagement (Bennett, Wood and Rogers, 1997).

Activity

O'Brien (2010) poses some challenging questions about play, which prompt us to think critically about these 'universal discourses' and whether these serve to marginalize or include children who have disabilities. Consider

(Continued)

(Continued)

these questions in relation to your own experiences of play as a child/ adult, and in your professional practice:

> Can *all* children play? *Should* all children play? Do all children *learn* from play? And if they do learn, *what* do they learn? *Must* all children play in order to develop fully? Is, in fact, access to play one of children's *rights*? And, if many of the most prominent researchers in the field of child psychology ... have viewed play as endemic to the human species, why did they so rarely address children who appear to be outside the parameters of typical development? (O'Brien, 2010: 183)

Although many of these theories remain part of the discourse of early childhood education, there have been significant changes in the field, with play now being validated within many national policy frameworks (Broadhead, Howard and Wood, 2010; Brooker and Edwards, 2010; Pramling Samuelsson and Fleer, 2009). However, policy versions of play are explicitly educational, because play is expected to lead towards (or at least contribute to) the learning goals or outcomes in curriculum frameworks. In Chapter 3 we will see that 'educational play' has its own purposes, but throughout this book research from the field of play scholarship will show that there are different ways of understanding the complexities of play, which reflect children's purposes and meanings. This is because play is a distinctive form of human activity which has its own rules, rituals and cultural practices, and is not always amenable to overly structured forms of social control within the educational/pedagogic gaze.

The purposes of play

In spite of positive endorsements from different theoretical perspectives, the definitions, purposes and value of play continue to be debated. These debates have had positive outcomes because they have kept play high on educational agendas in policy, research and practice. These trends can be seen in different countries as national policy frameworks are extended to early childhood provision with the aim of laying foundations for learning, improving children's life chances and raising achievement. Play continues to be taken seriously in the academic community, as evidenced by the scope of play scholarship across the human life span (Holzman, 2009; Hughes, 2010; Kuschner, 2009; Smith, 2010), across different contexts such as hospital and therapeutic play, and across different academic disciplines (Henricks, 2006; Saracho, 2012). Play and playfulness are considered to be lifelong activities: far from tailing off towards the end of childhood, play continues to develop in complexity and challenge

(Broadhead, 2004). Thus in order to understand these complexities, this book will draw on the international field of play scholarship and on different theoretical perspectives. The first question to be addressed is how can we define play?

Defining play

In defining play, there are different emphases on functions, forms, characteristics and behaviours. Two questions continue to challenge the research and practitioner communities: what is play? And what does play do for the child? Chazan (2002: 198) takes a broad and positive view of the functions of play:

> Playing and growing are synonymous with life itself. Playfulness bespeaks creativity and action, change and possibility of transformation. Play activity thus reflects the very existence of the self, that part of the organism that exists both independently and interdependently, that can reflect upon itself and be aware of its own existence. In being playful the child attains a degree of autonomy sustained by representations of his inner and outer worlds.

This definition indicates the potential variation and complexities of play as a social and cultural practice. Play activities involve a wide range of behaviours, actions and interactions, which may have multiple meanings for the players. Play can be regarded as deeply serious and purposeful, or trivial and purposeless. It can be characterized by high levels of motivation, creativity and learning, or perceived as aimless messing about, as shown in the following vignettes.

 Case study

Neill and Jamel: Play is serious or trivial?

Neill and Jamel (both aged five) did not settle immediately to a maths activity, but began play-fighting, using their pencils as swords. Their play was not aggressive, but as it became more noisy they fell off their chairs, were reprimanded by the teacher and separated for the rest of the session. In contrast, deep and serious play can be respected and encouraged by teachers. In a nursery, some boys were playing with Duplo™ and made a large layout on the floor. As the complexity of their play developed, they used other resources to create a town, including Playmobil™ figures that were used to act out various scenarios. The teacher realized the need to 'go with the flow' of their ideas and asked other children not to cut across their space or take away their equipment. The children were not interrupted to join in with mid-session circle time as their play continued to evolve over two hours. At review time they proudly explained their layout to the whole class, and dismantled it only after it had been shown to parents and caregivers.

It is not surprising that there are ambiguities about the definitions of play. Hutt et al. (1989) argue that play is a jumbo category that encompasses a multiplicity of activities, some of which are conducive to learning, but many of which are not. Garvey (1991) suggests that not everything that young children do together can be classified as play: there is a continuous moving back and forth among different activities with different modes of action, interaction and communication. Garvey regards play as an attitude or orientation that can manifest itself in numerous ways, according to what children play with, what they can play at, and the imaginary worlds and scenarios they create. These possibilities expand as new areas of experience are encountered, and as children's skills as players develop through childhood and into adulthood. Thus what play is, and what play does, cannot be constrained by theoretical or temporal definitions. Smith (2010: 4–5) identifies three ways of looking at play. In the functional approach, researchers focus on what the purpose of the behaviour is, or appears to be, and what are the potential benefits. In the structural approach, researchers focus on the behaviours themselves, the ways in which they are organized and sequenced, and what distinguishes play from non-play activities. The third approach is criteria-referenced, and is based on the observer's perspective for defining whether a behaviour sequence is play or not play. The more criteria that can be identified, the more likely it is that the activity or behaviour can be seen as play. In each of these approaches, play is defined by the researcher from a theoretical position, and not from the children's perspectives or the play context.

Meckley (2002) has drawn on Garvey's definition of play characteristics to provide qualitative descriptors of play, taking into account children's perspectives and the influence of the play context. Meckley's ideas are elaborated in Figure 1.1 to make links between what play is, what players do and what purposes play serves.

---

1 *Play is child-chosen*

Before children play, they have ideas about what they want to do and who they want to play with. As children start to play, they choose materials, activities and other players. Although children are in control of their play, they must cooperate and negotiate with others to play together. Because children choose their play and playmates, they are usually successful, even though the activities may include a lot of argy-bargy (Factor, 2009). They feel satisfied and proud of their accomplishments. Within a child's own play, no one but the child determines what is the right way or the wrong way because the child makes the rules for play within the framework of what is acceptable at home or in school. Children learn the most from play if it belongs to them. If adults choose children's activities or assign children to play areas, children consistently report that, from their perspective, this is work and not play (Dockett and Meckley, 2007; Howard, 2010). It follows that adults cannot plan children's play for them, but they plan for play by providing access to space, time and resources.

2 *Play is child-invented*

Play is not only chosen by children but also invented by them through their play cultures. Children are always creating something new when they play, such as a new construction or a new idea. To an adult, the construction may not be new because it may look just like another child's construction; to the child it is new because they tried and completed something that *they* never did before. In play, children are the inventors and experimenters: they take risks as they try out new activities and combinations. They create and solve problems and develop metacognitive capabilities (being aware and in control of their plans, thoughts, actions and behaviours) (Whitebread, 2010).

3   *Play is pretend but done as if the activity were real*

Children learn a great deal in pretending with activities and ideas that are like real events but are not real. They develop understanding of cognitive, social and emotional concepts by playing with their working theories and funds of knowledge in new ways. They develop perspective about people, events, social relationships and rules through playing about them. Children use play to make sense of their everyday social and cultural experiences, but at the same time use those experiences to inform and develop their play. Play involves pretence: the 'what if' and 'as if' qualities of play make it distinctive from other activities.

4   *Play focuses on the doing (process not product)*

Play is the leading activity in early childhood (Vygotsky, 1978). The process or activity of play is where learning occurs. Communication is essential to play, through language, body movement, gestures, signs and symbolic representations. In play children use more complex language than in conversations with adults. Children frequently make their first attempts at reading and writing when they are playing, by acting as if they are competent readers and writers. The benefits of play may not always be visible or immediate, but may become clear and may be cumulative over time (Smith, 2010). Children may choose to create products in their play, which are often of immediate use or relevance (such as props that convey pretence).

5   *Play is done by the players (children) not the adults (teachers or parents)*

Play is what children choose and manage for themselves. Because children learn through the process of playing, they need plenty of time, open-ended materials and co-players (Broadhead, 2004; Broadhead and Burt, 2012). Adults cannot plan children's play, but they can help to plan for play, and to support children's own plans and activities. Adults provide the play/learning environments, the support, the rules, the safety, so that children can obtain the maximum benefits from playing. Adults can be co-players if they are invited to do so by the children, and if they can play on the children's terms.

6   *Play requires active involvement*

Because children's bodies, emotions and minds are active in play, they can learn about their own limits and set their own challenges. Given a choice, they often choose a task which is more challenging than one chosen by an adult (Whitebread, 2010: 173), which may require different approaches to learning. Play is where the activity of childhood is occurring: playful children develop their own play in their own ways and on their own terms. Play is done for its own sake and children can become deeply immersed in the mood or spirit of play. They see the world from the perspective of play, creating their own meanings, symbols and practices, which are imbued with cultural significance and result in self-development and self-actualization (Wood, 2010a). Play helps to sow the seeds of confidence (Dowling, 2010), including self-esteem, self-efficacy, positive dispositions and the ability to manage the everyday hurly-burly of making/breaking friendships, making up/falling out, leading/following, cooperating/contesting.

7   *Play is fun*

Play is typically fun and enjoyable because children choose their activities and playmates, and draw on their own motivation and ideas. However, play may not be fun or enjoyable if children cross the agreed boundaries of 'play' and 'not play'. Sutton-Smith (1997) cautions that we need to be alert to the occurrence of 'dark play' and 'cruel play', where children may engage in teasing, bullying and other forms of social aggression. These forms of play may be interpreted in different ways, according to the child and the context. Some children may not feel safe (emotionally, psychologically and physically), while others may develop emotional resilience and coping strategies.

Figure 1.1   The characteristics of play

Research studies that use play functions, behaviours and characteristics tend to reduce complex activities to component parts in terms of what play is and what play does. However, play is complex, variable and paradoxical, and always depends on the context in which it takes place. Play can be orderly and rule-bound or free and spontaneous; it can appear chaotic, but there can be rules and patterns within the activities that emerge over time. The purposes and goals of play often shift as children manipulate play and non-play situations because they understand implicitly that, in certain contexts, different types of behaviour are permitted, whereas others, such as rough and tumble and play-fighting, are often banned. Play does not take place in a vacuum: everything that children play at, or play with, is influenced by wider social, historical and cultural factors, so that understanding what play is and learning how to play are culturally and contextually situated processes. There are family, cultural and personal variations in approaches to learning (Chen, Masur and McNamee, 2011), and to play choices and activities which add another layer of complexity to defining play.

Given that play is varied and complex, can definitions help us to solve the problem of what play is and what play does for the child? Pellegrini (1991) and Saracho (1991) define play in terms of dispositions that players bring to events and activities (Figure 1.2).

- Play is personally motivated by the satisfaction embedded in the activity and is not governed either by basic needs and drives or by social demands.
- Players are concerned with activities more than with goals. Goals are self-imposed and the behaviour of the players is spontaneous.
- Play occurs with familiar objects or following the exploration of unfamiliar objects. Children supply their own meanings to play activities and control the activities themselves.
- Play activities can be non-literal.
- Play is free from rules imposed from the outside and the rules that do exist can be modified by the players.
- Play requires the active engagement of the players.

Figure 1.2   Dispositions in play

These definitions indicate how play activities are qualitatively different from non-play activities. Although Pellegrini's definition states that play is free from rules imposed from the outside, this is not the case with play in educational settings. It is the imposition of adults' rules that makes 'educational play' different from child-initiated play in everyday contexts, because of the ways in which policy frameworks position play and the various constraints within pre-school and school settings. These definitions agree with Fromberg (1987: 36) that play is:

Symbolic, in that it represents reality with 'as if' or 'what if' attitude.

Meaningful, in that it connects or relates experiences.

Pleasurable, even when children engage seriously in an activity.

Voluntary and intrinsically motivated, whether the motives are curiosity, mastery, affiliation or others.

Rule-governed, whether implicitly or explicitly expressed.

Episodic, characterized by emerging and shifting goals that children develop spontaneously.

These criteria can be used differentially to categorize children's behaviour as a continuum from pure play to non-play:

> As a result, play can be categorized as 'more or less play', not dichotomously as 'play or not play'. Behaviours meeting all criteria might be categorized as 'pure play', whereas behaviours with fewer components are 'less purely play'. Simply put, acts should not be categorized as 'play' or 'not play': they should be related along a continuum from 'pure play' to 'non-play'. (Pellegrini, 1991: 215)

The concept of a continuum from pure play to non-play is developed by Broadhead (2004; 2010), and is useful for early childhood practitioners for several reasons. First, not everything that children do in their self-chosen activities can, or should, be classified as play. Second, children step in and out of play in order to provide a framework for their activity and to maintain flow and direction. They may interrupt their play to find or make props, or to get assistance from peers or adults. Third, practitioners often adopt playful orientations to teaching and learning, for example by animating stories and providing imaginary scenarios for solving mathematical or technological problems (Worthington and Carruthers, 2003). They also model humour and playfulness in order to encourage engagement, involvement, interest and enjoyment. Finally, there are many different forms of play including: role play, socio-dramatic play, heuristic play, constructive play, free-flow play, structured play, rough-and-tumble play, technological play, all of which involve a wide range of activities and behaviours (as described in Chapter 2). Therefore when striving to understand play, we need to consider the varied contexts for play and play as a socio-cultural activity: the message that 'this is play' is fundamental to playful engagement and participation between peers, and between adults and children, in homes, communities and education settings.

Much attention is given to proving that play is useful for children's learning and development and is, therefore, educationally purposeful. There is sub-stantial evidence that different forms of play promote a range of skills, learn-ing processes and outcomes. For example, socio-dramatic play involving characters, roles and imaginary events is considered to be a complex form of play because it encourages representational thinking and symbolic actions (making one thing stand for something else) (Broadhead, 2004). Outdoor play with loose parts (tyres, crates, straw bales, fabrics, wood offcuts, planks, logs and branches) and den building helps to develop social cooperation, flexibility and creativity (Brown, 2003; Knight, 2011a; 2011b). Constructive play involves mathematical and technological concepts, while sand and water play provide opportunities for learning scientific concepts (Carruthers and Worthington, 2011; Worthington and Carruthers, 2003). For older children, playful approaches to learning can include developing historical imagination through authentic activities such as museum visits, investigating artefacts and dramatizing factual events. Therefore, definitions of play should take into account different contexts as well as the cultures, interests, affective states and preferences of children at different ages: what counts as play will vary according to who is playing, the choice of play activity, and the knowledge and dispositions that children transfer from their home cultures and everyday experiences. Any play activity (particularly role play) is not one event, but many different multi-layered events. Therefore analyses of play need to capture the ways in which children's funds of knowledge are connected, how power relations operate and what other possibilities and events are conjured into the mix.

As these different definitions indicate, play is varied and complex. What adults want or choose to see in children's play may not be consistent with children's purposes and meanings, because these may not be immediately visible or accessible. This is because much play takes place 'in the mind', and symbolic activities are embedded in children's cultural and imaginative experiences. Play represents cognitive, affective, cultural, temporal, historical, social and physical interconnections, involving dialogue between:

- reality and imagination
- everyday worlds and play worlds
- past, present and future
- the logical and the absurd
- the known and the unknown
- the actual and the possible
- safety and risk
- structure and flexibility
- chaos and order.

In summary, Holzman (2009) argues that the focus on behaviour in play reflects a predominantly psychological approach, which leads to play being separated into constituent parts. Moreover, play behaviours and characteristics do not take account of play contexts, the variability of play and players, or the intentions, purposes and meanings of the players. Qualitative descriptions of play indicate its wholeness and complexity, particularly where children's purposes and meanings are foregrounded. In addition, children have their own definitions of play.

Children's definitions

Children's definitions of play focus on their choices (rather than adults' choices), their activities (rather than adults' instrumental objectives) and their freedom (rather than adults' expectations and directions) (Dockett and Meckley, 2007; Factor, 2009). Children have their own distinctions between work and play: they often associate work with adult-directed activity rather than free choice and child-initiated activity, and with sitting down rather than being active (Howard, 2010). The following comments from children aged six to seven reflect a range of views: they were recorded after a morning of play activities organized by post-graduate student teachers:

- 'No, we haven't been working this morning because we could choose.'
- 'Play is what you do when you choose, like Lego and things, but work is what the teacher tells you to do like reading and writing things down.'
- 'I think we've been playing and working. It was hard work making that go-kart because it kept falling to bits.'

Ethnographic studies of play capture the meaning and purposes of play from children's perspectives and reveal patterns and layers of complexity (Corsaro, 2004; Edmiston, 2008; Kelly-Byrne, 1989). In order to establish mutual awareness of play and non-play situations, children create roles, use symbols, redefine objects, transform ideas and determine the action through negotiation and shared meanings. Children play to detach themselves from reality but, at the same time, they get closer to reality: pretending to be frightened of a monster enables them to experience fear, but typically in an emotionally safe context. Their enactments of play themes and stories, or their creation of play scripts, reveal far more subtleties than academic definitions can capture. Moreover, play is not just about fantasy or pretence: children continuously weave in and out of play, transferring funds of cultural knowledge, skills and understanding from their interests and experiences, including popular culture and on-line play worlds (Edwards, 2010; Hedges, 2011a; Marsh, 2005; 2010). Play is rich with meanings that children create for themselves, and may want to keep hidden from the regulating gaze of adults because they are subverting or challenging adults' rules (Wood, 2013). Thus agency is central to understanding play from children's perspectives because play incorporates their desires to act in the world, to act on the world, and to see 'what happens if' and 'what happens when'. This is consistent with Sutton-Smith's discussion of the rhetoric of power within children's play: he argues that children always seek to have their own separate play culture, and within that, resistance against adult power and conventions is a hidden transcript of childhood (1997: 125). Similarly, Henricks (2011: 212) argues that in playful modes, self-interest (and the possibility of subterfuge from others) is to be expected, along with the willingness of players to exploit situations when they can.

Educational and psychological definitions do not capture the spirit and essence of play, especially where play is fractured into behavioural 'units of analysis'. Other ways of defining play draw on philosophical idealism and humanitarianism, sociological and anthropological perspectives. Henricks sees play as 'the laboratory of the possible':

> To play fully and imaginatively is to step sideways into another reality, between the cracks of ordinary life. Although that ordinary world, so full of cumbersome routines and responsibilities, is still visible to us, its images, strangely, are robbed of their powers. Selectively, players take the objects and ideas of routine life and hold them aloft. Like wilful children, they unscrew reality or rub it on their bodies or toss it across the room. Things are dismantled and built anew. (Henricks, 2006: 1)

Play has been credited with romantic, spiritual and existentialist dimensions: play is a mode of existence, a state of mind and a state of being (Henricks, 2006; Sutton-Smith, 1997). For Holzman (2009) children (and adults) are always in a state of being and becoming: in play children can be who they are, who they are not and who they want to be, by imagining and pretending. They can detach themselves from time, space, contexts and material conditions, in order to create new possibilities and invent new meanings. Children have inner power and potential which can be realized and revealed through play. Developing the capacity to play, and being in a state of play determines what players do, and enables them to be open to the spontaneous development of ideas, roles and opportunities. However, a paradox of play is that freedom does not mean that children can do anything they want to do, at any time, and with no concern for the consequences of their actions. As children learn and develop, they set the boundaries of their own play activities, and create ethical spaces in which they come to understand complex social issues such as power, authority, oppression, control, responsibility and altruism (Edmiston, 2008). Play does not have to include externally observable behaviours and actions. The spirit or essence of play can be invoked at any time and in any place. The following vignette exemplifies 'instant play' – the 'in the moment' playfulness of the human mind.

     Case study

Paul: A practical joke

The science theme in a Year 2 class was life processes and living things. The children had investigated eggs, learning the difference between the albumen and yolk. They had also incubated eggs and were waiting for them to hatch. Paul (aged six years and seven months) was fascinated by this topic. One day he brought in an egg to show his teacher. Unknown to him, Paul's father (a keen ornithologist) had 'blown' the content of the egg, leaving a hollow shell. Paul showed the egg to his teacher, carefully concealing the holes:

Paul: Can you guess what's inside this egg?
Teacher: I guess there's some transparent albumen, and a yellow egg yolk.
Paul: No, you're wrong (crushes the egg in his hand). This is an egg joke!

The teacher was taking the pedagogical opportunity to reinforce factual knowledge, which perhaps makes Paul's punch-line all the more amusing. He successfully manipulated the play/not play situation by setting up the serious question, and he understood the ritual and structure of playing a practical joke.

Given its enormous diversity, there is little wonder that play defies precise definitions. However, despite its complexity and potential, and the breadth of play scholarship, the status of play remains problematic.

The status of play

Although play has an idealized status in early childhood, there are competing discourses inside education, and more widely in society, which challenge this viewpoint. Play is often seen as a trivial activity, which is for leisure, fun and relaxation. When we say that something is 'child's play', we mean that something is easy and requires little effort. But the richness and diversity of play scholarship indicates the very opposite: play is complex, challenging and dynamic, and often makes high cognitive, social and emotional demands on the players. While many play activities do support learning and development, the 'outcomes' are often not visible or measurable. This goes some way to explaining why play occupies an ambiguous position in the 'educational play' discourse. On the one hand, early childhood professionals are encouraged to provide play because it is often promoted as *the* way of learning and can fulfil educational purposes. On the other hand, they are encouraged to provide play because it supports the free and natural expression of children's needs and interests. Thus practitioners have to struggle with educational and policy-centred versions of 'purposeful' play, as well as ideological versions of free play and free choice. The tensions between the rhetoric and reality of play remain a consistent theme in research and practice.

Rhetoric and reality

The tensions between rhetoric and reality create one of the main challenges for practitioners and remain a theme in much research on play in early childhood settings (Brooker, 2011; Martlew, Stephen and Ellis, 2011; Sherwood and Reifel, 2010). These tensions provided the impetus for a study of the relationship between teachers' thinking and classroom practice in a Reception class (four- to five-year-old children) in England (Bennett, Wood and Rogers, 1997). Nine teachers were studied for one year, with a focus on their beliefs and theories about the role and value of play, how they planned for play in the curriculum, and what factors enabled or constrained play in their classrooms. The teachers analysed videotaped episodes of play to discover whether their intentions were realized in practice. The evidence challenged the teachers' theories and beliefs, and revealed some of the reasons for the rhetoric–reality divide. Although there was common agreement that play is child-chosen and child-initiated, play was structured by time, resources, the learning environment, the planned or anticipated learning outcomes and downward pressures from the National Curriculum. Free play sometimes became noisy and disruptive, with children following their own, rather than the teacher's, agenda. Many of the activities the teachers planned enabled children to engage with curriculum content in playful ways, but work was sometimes disguised as play. Although they valued play as a medium for learning, other curriculum priorities meant that they did not involve themselves as co-players, and they spent little time assessing or understanding learning through play. Therefore play did not readily provide evidence of progress and achievement, because the teachers did not have time to observe, discuss and reflect, and feed their understanding into subsequent planning. One teacher described the complexities of managing play as 'spinning plates'. Other factors such as classroom layout, resources, class size and insufficient adult support also intervened between teachers' theories and practice so that their beliefs about play could not always be put into practice. In spite of these constraints, the teachers provided some interesting models of how they integrated play into the curriculum. The study demonstrated that achieving good quality play is resource-intensive and requires high levels of pedagogical skill and organization, as well as time and expertise to observe, assess and interpret children's meanings and intentions.

The rhetoric–reality problem is also enmeshed in wider societal perceptions. Play can have a life of its own because it belongs to the private worlds of children and is often invested with a mystique that is integral to childhood. Sutton-Smith (1997) notes the disagreement among Western philosophers as to whether play is basically orderly and rule-governed, or a chaotic, violent and indeterminate interaction of forces. The latter view of play is problematic in educational settings because it may threaten adults' control, disrupt their choices, challenge their values or provoke concerns about risks and hazards. Within the dominant 'play as education' discourse, policy frameworks require practitioners to ensure that play is purposeful and educational in that it results in defined learning outcomes, a theme that will be explored in Chapter 3. The 'quality' of play is evaluated in relation to pedagogical effectiveness, rather than the more complex processes discussed in this chapter. Play continues to be seen as preparatory to 'real' learning in school and may not be valued or understood by parents or colleagues. While policy discourses emphasize the need for 'more challenging work', there is no acknowledgement of children's needs (and their rights) for more challenging play. In addition, frequent 'media panics' and the 'toxic childhoods' discourse are based on adults' concerns about the changing forms of play in contemporary childhoods.

Contemporary forms of play

The historical development of children's play reveals continuities and changes, with ongoing debates about the value of 'free' versus 'structured' play. These debates often reflect adults' value judgements about what is 'good' and 'bad' play in relation to the potential outcomes, or its perceived social value. However, play has its own purposes and value, because it belongs to children's private or secret worlds and is often invested with a mystique that is truly child-centred and therefore not accessible to adults. Because play can be chaotic, anarchic, subversive and unpredictable, adults try to control and manipulate play both inside and outside the home. Taming play is about taming children. Allowing children to make choices and decisions may be theoretically seductive, but can be threatening to adults' control. Thus play is not just the natural and spontaneous activity of childhood, but sites in which power relationships are played out in many different ways. As Henricks (2010: 198) argues, players wish to do more than reassure themselves about their own powers: they wish to know what the world will do when it is provoked. Implicated in these power relationships are strategies for including and excluding peers on the basis of gender, ethnicity and special needs (Blaise, 2005; 2010; Jarvis, 2007; Skånfors, Löfdahl and Hägglund, 2009), themes that will recur throughout this book.

Children still enjoy many 'traditional' activities such as construction, den-building, sand and water, and creating secret spaces and places (Moore, 2010) (see Chapter 6). But they are also engaging in contemporary forms of play in on-line and virtual communities, with ever-expanding opportunities for where, when and how they play (Marsh, 2010). These trends have provoked debates around the influence of popular cultures, the amount of 'screen time' spent on computer games and social networking sites, the reduction in outdoor and physical play and the rise in childhood (and adult) obesity. Children's natural tendencies to play provide a lucrative market in popular culture, which influences children's choices and activities. They are exposed to many different media influences, and readily use 'pester power' to demand the latest must-have collectable toys, computer games and other spin-offs that are tied to 'product placement' films and television programmes. There are different viewpoints about these trends: educators and parents may resent this commercial and economic exploitation, and may question the educational value and quality of these products. Marsh and Millard (2000) note that possibly the single most overriding adult objection to popular cultural texts is the prevalence of violence, especially in superhero sagas, cartoons, action–adventure films and programmes, comics, magazines and computer games. In contrast, Cohen (1993) argues that toys and characters from television programmes and films can provide rich 'springboards for fantasy'. This raises the question of who is providing the springboards and controlling the fantasies – adults or children? Marsh and Millard (2000) argue that children are not passive recipients of shifting and often transient trends in popular culture: they both accept and reject the products offered, and create their own cultural practices based on their experiences in their home, community and friendship groups. Research studies reveal the creative potential of contemporary forms of play in virtual spaces and with technological media (Marsh, 2010; Wohlwend, 2009). Thus there are arguments for practitioners using rather than ignoring children's popular culture as a means of building on children's interests and experiences, and enabling them to experiment with different forms of representation (Edwards, 2010; Wolfe and Flewitt, 2010).

There are other influences in society that question the status of play and reflect some of the paradoxes of post-modern life. In their leisure time, children may be channelled into clubs and activities that some parents see as having higher status and lower risk than traditional forms of play. Fears for children's safety and inadequate time and space have reportedly reduced opportunities for outdoor play (Bilton, 2010; Knight, 2011a; 2011b; Tovey, 2010) and physically active play (Brady et al., 2008; Kapasi and Gleave, 2009). Physical play may be seen as part of a health and fitness regime (under adults' control) rather than freely chosen outdoor play with its greater potential for risk, adventure and challenge. Decreasing levels of physical activity have given rise to concerns about increasing levels of obesity in childhood, again linked to the amount of 'screen time' that children are allowed. Thus the media panics and toxic childhoods discourse lead to the conclusion that there are almost as many 'dangers' in home play environments as there are outdoors, and a more balanced perspective on these issues needs to be debated in relation to lifelong play.

Lifelong playing and learning

If playing and growing are synonymous with life itself, then lifelong playing can be seen as an important aspect of lifelong learning and well-being. In the educational play discourse, play becomes less relevant to children beyond the age of five, although it may be allowed in 'choosing time' in Key Stage 1. By

Key Stage 2, play in school tends to become a distant memory except as organized games and outdoor playtime. This is ironic given that toy and games manufacturers have perceived the inherent need for play to change and progress from childhood into adulthood, with new forms of technological play leading the way. For example, Lego™ provides a carefully sequenced range of construction kits from Duplo™ for pre-school children, to the more complex LegoTechnik™ and computer programs for older children.

Beyond childhood, the status of play is enhanced when it contributes to productivity and effective working practices. Adults are encouraged to use their leisure time productively in playing games to maintain health and fitness. Role-play techniques are used in training programmes in business and industry for enabling people to deal with difficult situations, rehearse strategies and cope with emotional responses (Holzman, 2009). Firefighters, police officers, para-medics and the armed forces use invented scenarios and virtual environments to learn techniques and strategies, and to act out their feelings in difficult situations. Play is used as an incentive and reward for successful performance in business: there are companies that specialize in organizing 'executive play' breaks, including white-water rafting, health and beauty weekends, rally driving and bungee jumping. A stroll around a toyshop reveals a wide range of board games for adults and increasingly sophisticated electronic games that can be played at home or on the move. Many virtual-reality computer games are based on role-play scenarios where players take on a character and work out strategies and actions in response to problems. Players can connect virtually from any time zone or region of the world and create their own play communities

---

Playful contests (such as beauty pageants and drinking games).

Carnivals, circuses and parades.

Festivals and feasts.

Playgrounds and theme parks.

Community and national celebrations.

Games and sports, including national and international contests and championships (for example the Olympics).

Extreme sports that involve high levels of challenge and risk (bungee jumping, white-water rafting, sky diving).

Theatrical performances (music, dance, drama, comedy acts, pantomime, films).

Clubs and leisure activities.

Travel, exploration and adventure activities.

Mind play (dreams, fantasies, word games, puzzles, mind games).

Figure 1.3   Different forms of play

and cultures. We are encouraged to adopt a 'use it or lose it' approach to our brains and bodies as we age: doing crosswords, playing games such as bridge and bingo, and remaining physically and socially active can maintain mental, emotional and physical health. Far from play being an exclusive occupation of childhood, human beings are lifelong players.

In a scholarly review of play research, Sutton-Smith (2001) describes many different forms of play and play contexts that span childhood and adulthood, including those that represent expert levels of skill (such as in sport) and bring high rewards and social status (Figure 1.3). Play and playfulness are thus deeply embedded across the lifespan as cultural activities that have a wide variety of meanings and significance. Different forms of play serve many different purposes, from the individual mind at play in a game of chess, to whole communities at play in carnivals and festivals.

Linking play in childhood and adulthood

There are lifelong links between children's play worlds and subsequent adult roles, identities and occupations. The imaginary worlds that are constructed in childhood can develop into adulthood and become more elaborate and structured (Cohen and MacKeith, 1991). For example, the architect Frank Lloyd Wright played with Froebelian building blocks and acknowledged the influence these had on his later career. The musicians Jacqueline and Hilary du Pré grew up in a playful musical world, with a mother who was an inspiring co-player:

> From as early as I can remember, Mum entertained us with music. She was always singing, playing the piano, clapping and stepping rhythms, making shapes in the air according to the phrase shapes. We curled into the tiniest forms when the music was soft, and burst out jumping in the air when it was loud. We tiptoed and crouched for creepy music and skipped to dotted rhythms. We had to convey ferocity or tragedy and all as a spontaneous reaction to her playing. (du Pré and du Pré, 1997: 29)

Their mother wrote tunes especially for Jacqueline because there was nothing suitable for a young budding cellist. The tunes were illustrated with drawings and stories of everyday events such as a visit to the zoo, as well as fantastical tales about witches and elves. In contrast, the formative years of the writers Charlotte and Emily Brontë could not have been more different. Their mother was often ill; their father was stern, aloof and absorbed in his work. The children found escape from a gloomy and lonely childhood through inventing and acting out plays which often drew on their knowledge of famous characters in history. Their brother Branwell's box of toy soldiers provided the props for the stories. By the age of 13, Charlotte Brontë was an avid writer of tales, dramas, romances and poems, which were written in minute handwriting in their 'little magazines'. Not surprisingly, escapism was a recurring theme in their tales of adventure, shipwreck and creating new societies in far-off islands. These examples show how children's play worlds can influence their subsequent pathways into adulthood. It is always interesting to ask students and teachers how they played and what they played with as children. Almost invariably there is a lot of 'school play' involving toys, peers, siblings and sometimes adults.

Playfulness, imagination and creativity are inextricably linked in our playing and working lives. Increasingly in adulthood we engage in different forms of play; for example playing with ideas, roles, words, media, meanings, and with relationships between events, people, concepts, materials and systems. Young people have one foot in childhood and the other in adulthood – they too are playfully being and becoming. They gradually play their way into the next stage of their lives by projecting images and adopting roles that are often influenced by the media and popular culture. The dressing-up box of childhood becomes the wardrobe of adulthood, whether it is a suit for work, the latest fashions for going out clubbing, a hi-tech outfit for a sports activity or a fancy-dress outfit for a party. For many adults, play is still a deeply enjoyable experience and maintains the possibilities for change and transformation identified by Chazan (2002). For example, a group of girls and boys played energetically for two hours on a beach, digging holes and burying each other, building sand castles and sand sculptures and creating a miniature Neolithic stone circle which closely resembled Stonehenge. Their playfulness flowed between rough and tumble, construction, teasing and joking. Between the playful banter these young people (who were 17–18 years old) discussed their forthcoming exam results, their preparations for going to university and their hopes and fears for the future. Play is riddled with paradoxes: children and adults often work quite hard at their play in terms of effort, motivation, concentration and outcomes. Children play at being adults, while adults continue to enjoy playing in the sand. Play in childhood is seen as trivial: play in adulthood can have high status and bring rich rewards, even though this might involve the drudgery of practice, the discipline of training and endless competitions to maintain status. Creating a continuum between lifelong playing and learning is perhaps even more critical in the twenty-first century as economic success relies on people who are creative, flexible, innovative, imaginative and playful in the workplace.

Summary

The general mistrust of play in educational contexts arises from three sources:

1   The lack of a precise operational definition of play.
2   The persistent view that play is the opposite of work.
3   The fear of play as subversion.

From an educational view, play is less likely to produce either tangible evidence of learning or contribute to the learning outcomes that are valued in curriculum frameworks. Practitioners therefore have to tame play in order to justify its contribution to 'effective' teaching and learning. However, there are different constructs of 'effectiveness' and 'quality' in early childhood education, and the pragmatic educational discourse needs to be balanced alongside different theoretical perspectives, which are the focus of Chapter 2.

Activity

Think about your own play life as a child, including your choices, activities and preferences.

In a group, make a time line that is divided into age bands, starting with your earliest play memories. Make a note of what forms of play you engaged in, who you played with and where. Discuss these as a group; note any trends, similarities or differences and how these can be explained.

Discuss what rules were imposed on your play by adults (think about the home, community and school contexts). Now discuss the ways in which you broke or subverted those rules and whether there were any consequences.

Discuss what forms of play you engage in now and the extent to which technological tools and media are part of your play lives.

Further reading

Bennett, N., Wood, E. and Rogers, S. (1997) *Teaching Through Play: Teachers' Thinking and Classroom Practice*, Buckingham: Open University Press.

Brooker, L. (2011) 'Taking children seriously: an alternative agenda for research?', *Journal of Early Childhood Research*, 9 (2): 137–149, http://ecr.sagepub.com/cgi/reprint/9/2/137.

Hedges, H. (2011a) 'Rethinking SpongeBob and Ninja Turtles: popular culture as funds of knowledge for curriculum co-construction', *Australasian Journal of Early Childhood*, 36 (1): 25–29.

Henricks, T. (2006) *Play Reconsidered – Sociological Perspectives on Human Expression*, Urbana, IL: University of Illinois Press.

Holzman, L. (2009) *Vygotsky at Work and Play*, East Sussex: Routledge.

Marsh, J. (2005) *Popular Culture, New Media and Digital Literacy in Early Childhood*, London: RoutledgeFalmer.

Marsh, J. (2010) 'Young children's play in online and virtual worlds', *Journal of Early Childhood Research*, 8 (1): 23–29, http://ecr.sagepub.com/cgi/content/abstract/8/1/23.

O'Brien, L.M. (2010) 'Let the wild rumpus begin! The radical possibilities of play for young children with disabilities', in L. Brooker and S. Edwards (eds), *Engaging Play*, Maidenhead: Open University Press, pp. 182–194.

 To gain free access to specially selected SAGE journal articles related to key topics discussed in this book please visit: **www.sagepub.co.uk/wood**

CHAPTER 2

UNDERSTANDING CHILDREN'S LEARNING: CONTEMPORARY THEORETICAL PERSPECTIVES

This chapter reviews some of the main trends in play theory and research, along with their implications for understanding the purposes of play for children. Four key themes are addressed:

- Why do children play?
- What are the main forms of play in early childhood?
- What do children play with and what do they play at?
- What does play do for the child?

This chapter examines research from the thriving international community of play scholarship, drawing on a range of studies, with diverse research designs, methods and theoretical orientations. There have been some significant advances in theory and practice for understanding the purposes of play (Smith, 2010), and the meanings that children create in their play worlds (Broadhead and Burt, 2012; Brooker and Edwards, 2010; Pramling Samuelsson and Fleer, 2009). Inevitably the outcomes of play scholarship are varied and not always in agreement, which is understandable given the challenges of defining play discussed in Chapter 1. Because the field of play is so broad, many play scholars have chosen to focus on types of play (such as role play); areas of learning (such as literacy); groups of children, for example those with additional or special educational needs and disabilities, or specific age groups.

Early childhood education has traditionally been reliant on psychological theory and research, with a particular emphasis on how play contributes to development and learning (Fromberg and Bergen, 2006; Hughes, 2010). However, studies that draw on sociology and socio-cultural theories provide a broader understanding of play in theory and practice. In addition, play is now contested as much as it is validated: research that draws on critical and post-structural theories has challenged some of the long-standing assumptions about play that derive from the ideological tradition and from developmental psychology (Blaise, 2005; Grieshaber and McArdle, 2010). These different perspectives make play scholarship a fertile site for engagement, but do not align with the neat solutions or policy prescriptions that increasingly dominate practice (as described in Chapter 3). From the perspective of play as education, it is important to maintain an expansive view of play in all its complexities and variations, in order to engage critically with the constraining influence of policy discourses.

Why do children play?

Theories of play have changed over time, and there are different emphases according to the disciplinary focus of play research (psychological, biological, sociological, anthropological, educational). Figure 2.1 summarizes classic

---

Play allows children to express ideas, emotions and feelings. Play can be seen as emotionally and psychologically cathartic and provides a safe outlet for tensions and anxieties. Children consciously express, and may exaggerate, emotions (for example fear, anger, aggression) in order to learn how to handle these more rationally.

Play provides opportunities for relaxation and recreation, allowing children to regenerate energy expended during work-based activities.

Play enables children to use surplus energy.

Play enables children to practise for the next stage of development, including adulthood, for example through role reversal (child becomes parent, pupil becomes teacher).

Play enables children to engage in a wide range of problem-solving activities (cognitive, manipulative, social), and contributes to intellectual growth.

Play facilitates learning across the three domains of development – cognitive, socio-affective, psycho-motor.

Play facilitates learning relevant processes such as rehearsing, practising, repeating, imitating, exploring, discovering, revising, extending, problem-solving, combining, transforming, testing.

Play contributes to the development of learning dispositions such as intrinsic motivation, engagement, perseverance, positive social interactions, self-esteem, self-confidence and 'can-do' orientations. Play thus contributes to mastery of learning.

Figure 2.1   Theoretical perspectives on why children play

theories (Hughes, 2010: 22–23) and contemporary theories about why children play.

As these multiple theories indicate, play can serve different purposes across children's learning careers: different forms of play appear to be of immediate value and for future learning, although it is sometimes difficult to establish these connections. There has been a distinct change in emphasis from theories that describe play as a biologically predetermined activity (a natural, instinctive way of promoting optimal development) to those that focus on the role of play in the social, emotional and cultural adaptation of children in different societies. In the field of educational play, scholars have provided evidence of links between play and the subject disciplines such as literacy and numeracy, and the different contexts in which play occurs (described in more detail in Chapters 4 and 5 on curriculum and pedagogy). There is also a critical distinction between play as play, and play in educational settings, because the latter is constrained by the expectations in policy frameworks that play will contribute to defined developmental and learning outcomes.

What are the main forms of play in early childhood?

Many researchers have distinguished between different forms of play and have defined their characteristics or qualities. Because Piaget's theories about play and learning have been so influential in early childhood, a brief summary is given here.

Piaget (1962) defined three categories and stages of play (Figure 2.2) which have been challenged and refined. Smilansky (1990) added a fourth category of *constructive play* because of its dominance in early childhood. Constructive play is characterized by the manipulation of objects to build or create something, involving symbolic, spatial and multi-dimensional constructions and representational forms, based on small or large blocks and other constructional equipment, as well as playdough and collage materials.

- *Practice play* – sensori-motor stage: exploratory play based on physical activities (birth to two years).
- *Symbolic and construction play* – pre-operational stage: pretend, fantasy and socio-dramatic play, involving the use of mental representations. When play becomes representational (making one thing stand for something else), it is regarded as intellectual activity (two to seven years).
- *Games with rules* – concrete operational stage: games with predetermined rules (from six or seven years upwards).

Figure 2.2   Piaget's categories and stages of play

Piagetian perspectives on play, learning and development

Piaget (1962) was interested mainly in the origins of logical, mathematical and scientific thinking and aimed to establish the relationship between biological and cognitive development. Piaget's theory of cognitive development placed action and self-directed problem-solving at the heart of learning and development: by acting in and on the environment the learner discovers how to control tools and materials, and understand the consequences of actions. Piaget's image of the child as a scientist is based on children's abilities to work actively to construct knowledge and understanding through discovery, active learning, experience and social interaction. The emphasis on internal construction of cognitive structures or schemas is the basis for his constructivist theories of learning. Piaget conceptualized learning as a series of transitions through age-related stages, in which forms of thinking progressed from immature to mature, from simple to complex, and from concrete to abstract. These stages are linked to the concept of *readiness* – critical periods when a child has developed the capacity and readiness to learn and to progress to a new level of understanding. Interventionist teaching which ran ahead of these stages could not facilitate development or learning and, in Piaget's view, could actively prevent children from learning something for themselves.

Piaget proposed that three processes are important in learning and development because they enable adaptation to take place – assimilation, accommodation and equilibration. Assimilation involves incorporating new information into existing cognitive structures (or schemas), and can include imaginative processes such as symbolic transformations. Accommodation involves modifying or extending existing cognitive structures (or schemas), to suit external realities. When children encounter new experiences, concepts or knowledge, their existing internal schemas (or forms of thought) must adapt or change, which can cause a state of disequilibrium or cognitive conflict. Disequilibrium motivates new learning until a state of equilibration is reached, and adaptation or change occurs.

Piaget argued that children's play promoted assimilation rather than accommodation, thereby consolidating newly learned behaviours, but not provoking new learning. Therefore playing was not the same as learning but could facilitate learning by exposing the child to new experiences and new possibilities for acting in and on the world. Thus play was not seen as a leading source of learning and development, but could actively contribute to these processes. Piaget's theories melded easily with the work of the early pioneers, and the ideologies of the Progressive movement, because of his emphasis on discovery and exploration and child-centred views of learning. His theories were interpreted to imply that educators should create environments in which children could be active learners, free to explore, experiment, combine different materials, and create and solve problems through their self-chosen, self-directed activities. Through these processes, development would lead learning. The role of the teacher was interpreted as enabling and facilitating these processes, responding to children's initiatives, and identifying cognitive concerns, but not teaching through direct instruction. In contrast, contemporary studies that develop schema theory show that children's schemas need to be supported with worthwhile content and appropriate assistance from adults who can enable children to extend their range of experiences (Meade and Cubey, 2008; Nutbrown, 2011).

Piaget's work has influenced much subsequent research on the important developmental questions of 'what develops?', 'how does development occur?', 'what are the main mechanisms for developmental changes?', and 'what interventions support development?' While these are relevant questions to ask, they do not always provide the forms of knowledge that are useful to practitioners in education settings (Wood, 2013). Many Piagetian theories have been interpreted and challenged in subsequent research (DeVries, 1997). For example, Meadows (2006) challenges notions about 'ages and stages', and argues that the development of performance is age-related, but being stage-like in the sense of being clearly discontinuous, cohesive, synchronous or even across tasks requires stronger evidence than is available in most areas. The three stages and categories of play proposed by Piaget implied a developmental progression that reflected his 'simple to complex' and 'concrete to abstract' orientations to cognitive development. However, play does not seem to fall consistently into such categories, and the consistent logic of the mental operations that Piaget studied (for example in mathematics) is not the same as the internal logic of play, which is based on imaginative and symbolic transformations that make sense only in play contexts, from the perspective that 'this is play'.

Research shows that children combine different forms of play in outdoor and indoor environments (Broadhead and Burt, 2012), which may be of particular significance for children's social competence. Dunn (2004) provides evidence of playful interactions between children from the first few months of infancy. She highlights the importance of gazing, observing and imitating as the foundations for intimacy, intersubjectivity and friendships. Sensori-motor and exploratory play may be the dominant forms of play in infancy, but continue throughout childhood. With experience, children build repertoires of play skills and knowledge so that they move from epistemic (exploratory or practice) play (what does this object do?), towards more ludic or creative play (what can I do with this object?) (Hutt et al., 1989) (Figure 2.3). *Epistemic play* involves acquiring knowledge, using discovery, exploration and problem-solving so that children find out 'what does this object do?' (the term 'object' can include all the material affordances in the environment such as tools, artefacts and machines). Epistemic play promotes learning: children are aware of what they are making or doing, and their activities lead to higher levels of competence and control. *Ludic play* has symbolic/fantasy elements, is characterized by pretence and is dependent on mood states. In ludic play, children find out 'what can I do with this object?' Ludic play may promote learning indirectly, or may serve different

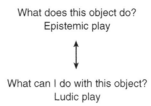

What does this object do?
Epistemic play

What can I do with this object?
Ludic play

Figure 2.3   Play and creativity

functions, such as enhanced creativity, self-efficacy and mastery orientations to learning. When combined with socio-cultural theories about the importance of tools, the concepts of epistemic and ludic play can be extended to include personal, cultural and social/environmental tools.

Young children (between 12 and 36 months) have been shown to engage in symbolic and imaginative play, for example using sounds and vocalizations to represent a car, animal or toy (Cohen, 2009) and in the active creation of their peer cultures (Engdahl, 2011; Löfdahl, 2006). Solitary and parallel play may serve children's motives and purposes, such as observing what is happening with a view to creatively imitating the activities, or learning the skills needed to join the play. They are already combining 'tools for use', 'tools and use' as they master their social worlds (see Figure 2.4).

Smilansky (1990) questioned Piaget's categories of play on the basis that both dramatic and socio-dramatic play develop in parallel to other forms of play, beginning at around two and continuing beyond the early years, when spontaneous play may take on the characteristics of drama. For example, Elizabeth had a collection of cotton reels which, from around 18 months, were variously transformed into food, goods to load on a train wagon, people, items

TOOLS FOR USE
(what does this do?)

Personal tools: cognitive, social, emotional, physical.
Cultural tools: symbol systems, artefacts, disciplined ways of learning e.g.
technology, literacy and numeracy.
Social and environmental tools: all the the human and material resources that are
available to support learning and development.

TOOLS AND USE
(what can I do with this?)

Figure 2.4   Tools for use, tools and use

of shopping and naughty children in school. She transformed the symbolic meaning of the cotton reels and communicated new meanings in the context of exploratory, symbolic and dramatic play forms. As the next section shows, research studies of children's dramatic and socio-dramatic play reveal how they construct their own internal rules and reflect the rules embedded in their social and cultural worlds.

Dramatic and socio-dramatic play

Much research has focused on the significance of dramatic and socio-dramatic play as a means for learning, particularly in the socio-affective domain. Smilansky distinguishes between these two forms of play (Figure 2.5).

Both forms of play involve imitation, rehearsal, pretence, imagination and creativity, symbolic activity and communication, interpreting social and cultural rules, taking on and acting in role, sustaining the theme and sequence of a play episode, motivation, involvement and engagement. As Smilansky argues, both make complex and often high cognitive and socio-affective demands on children:

> Children derive satisfaction not only from the ability to imitate but also to form make-believe play, which provides unlimited access to the exciting world of adults ... Make-believe in dramatic and socio-dramatic play, as opposed to other circumstances where it serves as a means of escape from the real world, extends the scope of the imitative activity and provides a comprehensive and comprehensible context that increases the realism of the behaviour. (Smilansky, 1990: 20)

There are six elements of dramatic and socio-dramatic play:

1 Role play by imitation
2 Make-believe with objects
3 Make-believe with actions and situations
4 Persistence in the role play
5 Interaction
6 Verbal communication

- *Dramatic play* involves pretending to be someone else, role taking, imitating a person's speech actions and patterns, using real and imagined props, using first- and second-hand experience and knowledge of characters and situations.
- *Socio-dramatic play* involves cooperation between at least two children: the play develops on the basis of interaction between players acting out their roles, both verbally and in terms of the acts performed.

Figure 2.5   Dramatic and socio-dramatic play

Each element incorporates different play skills and play knowledge. The richness of the play depends on the extent to which these various elements are used and developed. For example, communication in children's socio-dramatic play can be complex, multi-modal and purposeful, as they:

- set the scene for speaking
- make behaviour understandable
- provide proper interpretation and direction for the activity
- provide the means of management and problem-solving reflecting child-reality and child-interaction. (Smilansky, 1990: 20)

Children use metacommunicative and metacognitive skills and processes as they step in and out of the play frame to communicate symbolic transformations, comment on past and present conversations, and to clarify, maintain, negotiate and direct social and pretend play (Sawyer, 2003). The multi-modal qualities of play include facial expressions, gestures, mime, body movement, especially for babies and young children (Johansson and Emilson, 2010; Rutanen, 2007; White, 2009). Children use artefacts such as tools, drawings and constructions to create symbolic meanings, and communicate these in increasingly sophisticated ways, showing their funds of knowledge and representational capabilities (Carruthers and Worthington, 2011; Wood and Hall, 2011).

Contemporary studies challenge deficit notions of children's thinking as immature forms of adult cognition. Rather than progressing in stages from concrete to abstract modes of thinking, children move along a continuum. Between the ages of two and three, children develop a 'theory of mind' which involves understanding that other people have emotions, beliefs, intentions and desires that may be different from one's own (Meadows, 2010). As children begin to understand these ideas, they can adapt their behaviour accordingly, which is particularly useful in the context of imaginative play activities, where pretence adds another layer of complexity. These 'mind-reading' skills are evident when children construct and share dramatic and socio-dramatic play, which involves engaging in quite sophisticated activities, such as stepping into a role, acting in role, imagining different feeling states and developing empathy (seeing things from another's perspective). Children have to simultaneously hold a dual perspective in play – what something is (e.g. a plastic screwdriver) and what something isn't (e.g. a sonic screwdriver that can open doors) (Wood, 2013). Joe's playful drawing (Figure 2.6) shows that he knows he should draw himself with two legs, but he chooses to draw four. He also lets his teacher know that he is 'only joking' otherwise she might ask him to draw his picture again with the correct number of legs. Joe has already developed a good theory of his own and the teacher's mind.

Mind-reading skills can serve different purposes in play contexts. As Naerland and Martinsen (2011: 362) argue, young children become increasingly focused on playing with their peers and on what other children say and do. They have a large influence on each other and dominance and status are established from

I am Joe.

I am only joking
I don't really have 4 legs.

Figure 2.6   'I'm only joking'

an early age. In a study of children's withdrawal strategies in Swedish pre-school settings, Skånfors, Löfdahl and Hägglund (2009) reveal the agency of young children (aged two to five) as they find their own places and spaces for withdrawal as a means of contesting adults' rules and of excluding peers. Similarly Alcock (2010) studied three- to four-year-old children in New Zealand early childhood centres and documents the power roles that the children take up and the ways in which the power balance changes in different contexts. In a study of young children's theory of mind, Newton and Jenvey (2011) state that a high frequency of social-interactive peer play was associated with social competence, because these contexts afford opportunities for children to develop the skills of cooperation, interaction and sharing. While the qualities of communication, togetherness and reciprocity are common features of children's play, so too are struggles for status, power, leadership and control. These themes will be revisited in Chapter 6.

Children do not just play with objects and materials: they also play with emotions, meanings, ideas, roles, rules and relationships, and can make significant cognitive leaps and transformations (see Figure 2.7). The ability to think in quite sophisticated, abstract ways is an undervalued aspect of children's play. This is because imitation, make-believe and symbolic activity are complex cognitive, emotional and social processes which are not always understood by practitioners in terms of their relationship to learning. As Kelly-Byrne (1989: 212) argues, these complex forms of play may be a neglected resource:

> it is the excitement and compulsion of a personal agenda that motivates much self-initiated and self-directed play in the lives of children ... In the privacy of a space of their choosing and among friends, the dramatic play of children is an alluring and incredibly complex kind of behaviour that is likely to encompass most, if not all, of a child's resources and integrate them into a whole. The value of tapping its momentum and power, in the child's own terms, should be obvious to those of us concerned with facilitating children's communication and their sense of their own power.

For younger children, action tends to arise more from things: therefore they tend to be more absorbed in assigning roles and arranging props. In solitary dramatic play, children may use self-speech or out-loud thinking to communicate the pretence (often using different voices), and provide a commentary on the action as they play in role. Themes that are rehearsed in this way may be

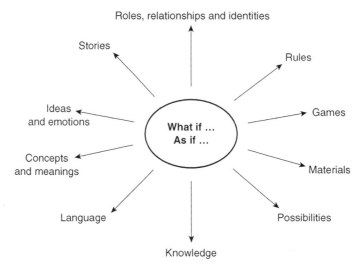

Figure 2.7   What do children play with?

transferred to socio-dramatic contexts as children gain confidence in their skills as players and progress to more complex forms of social/cooperative play. Although it may appear chaotic, children's dramatic and socio-dramatic play reveals patterns and consistencies. In an ethnographic study of play with six- to seven-year-old children, Meckley's observations show that each play event had distinct, consistent and predictable patterns of actions, objects and players: there was always a set sequence of actions for each play event which identified a specific event to the children enacting the event, and to those engaged in other activities in the room. Sustained and systematic observation allowed Meckley to interpret the meaning of play in the children's own terms as they communicated and interpreted their individual and collective social realities:

> Shared knowledge of the subjective and collective realities of child participants in this social culture can also be known by the adult participants through attention to metacommunicative signals which regularly occur during the play period. These signals include, but are not limited to gaze or watching, body orientation or movement, specific actions with objects, specific sequences of action, imitation, language, and voice change. These actions reveal information about the play events and players' understandings about these events. (Meckley, 1994: 47)

When children organize socio-dramatic play, they may recall what has been previously played in terms of characters, plot and sequence of activities. These actions and play memories provide some direction and internal consistency to the actions and interactions (the 'what if' and 'as if' qualities of play). Consistency is often sustained by rituals that begin the play, and the play script, which reveals children's knowledge of plot, characterization and sequence of events. Thus in creating a play frame and a psychological frame, children draw on a wide repertoire of cognitive, social and emotional dispositions in order to sustain the flow. Players can make transformations and reversals, and create real/not-real paradoxes so that a wide variety of imaginary situations can be played into the action. Imagination and creativity are essential as children invest objects and actions with new meanings and intentions that have to be accepted and understood by the players. As the play develops they may revise, repeat or extend previous themes, combine and recombine ideas, negotiate rules and perhaps accommodate new players with different perspectives and contributions. Children step in and out of play to reformulate or elaborate plans, renegotiate rules, reconstruct the plot, reason about cause and effect, direct actions and behaviour, rehearse dialogue and roles. Such transformations involve sophisticated levels of thinking and action as children communicate multiple meanings through language, gestures, symbolic and iconic representations.

With age and experience, action arises from ideas: children become increasingly adept at negotiating the play and determining the actions and interactions. As experienced players, older children readily formulate goals, which they realize through cooperation and reciprocity (Broadhead, 2004; Broadhead and Burt, 2012). Children become more skilled at exercising and controlling their will, in order to engage in successful, sustained play. Such control is dependent on the skills, dispositions and mood states of the group of players. The benefits of successful play are inclusion, enjoyment, shared control, peer-group identity and self-efficacy. Gradually they learn to understand and integrate the perspectives of others: in taking on or assigning roles, they interpret how other people behave and coordinate each other's perspectives. They build their play skills and their play knowledge (what is involved in being a successful player). However, as we have already seen, these processes involve struggles for status, power and control, which highlights the notion that play is not just the natural, spontaneous activity of childhood. Edmiston (2008) argues that play creates authoring spaces for children's identities, through these complex socio-cultural activities. They are developing the capacities and capabilities to play, as shown by Abigail in her creative imitation of being a pupil, being a teacher.

 Case study

Abigail: 'Fingers on lips!'

Abigail (aged four) loved reading. In this episode she demonstrated her knowledge about the functions of print, how books work and her interpretation of learning contexts both in and out of school. She sat on a stool with a favourite *Meg and Mog* book and announced to her grandma, mother and aunt that she was going to read the story. Because they were chatting she said, in a teacher voice, 'Fingers on lips', and didn't start until they were all quiet. When her aunt put her hand down, Abigail said sternly, 'I don't remember telling you to take your finger off your lips. Put it back.' She read the title of the book and asked her audience what they thought the story was about. She held the book the right way up and turned the pages in sequence. On each page she asked questions such as 'And *where* are Meg's shoes? Are they *on* the bed? Are they *under* the bed? What do you think is going to happen next? Will Mog fall *off* the broomstick?' She picked out the words 'Meg' and 'Mog' by recognizing the capital M, but did not differentiate between them. She followed the words from left to right with her finger, and pointed at specific parts of the picture when asking questions. Abigail was behaving as a competent reader; she reproduced a schooled version of literacy by emphasizing the prepositions and using a teacherly voice to establish order and engage the adults. She was also demonstrating playful enjoyment of sharing books in a social context, making connections between learning at home and school.

Children's creativity and imagination direct, influence and generate complexity. The roles that children create involve feeling and mood states that link affective and cognitive processes. Children use stories as a powerful means of making sense of everyday and imaginary experiences, and play with a wide range of emotions such as love, hate, fear, anger, jealousy. These are often played out as opposing forces – good and evil, cruelty and kindness, strength and weakness, protection and abandonment, friendship and enmity. Such powerful moral and affective themes are often drawn from children's popular culture, as well as their everyday experiences (Anning and Ring, 2004; Marsh, 2010; Wohlwend, 2011). The driving forces for play are intrinsic and extrinsic motivation, the pleasure afforded by play and the ability to take control and exercise power in an adult-dominated world.

Dramatic and socio-dramatic play involve dynamic, unifying activities that integrate many areas of learning across the curriculum, which will be explored in greater detail in Chapters 5 to 7 (see Figure 2.8). These forms of play are also evident in constructive and tough-and-tumble (R&T) play.

- Language and communication
- Planning and organization
- Developing social and cooperative skills
- Acquiring social knowledge
- Acquiring discipline-based knowledge
- Relating to peers and adults
- Understanding self and others
- Developing empathy and mind-reading skills
- Creativity and imagination
- Representation and symbolization
- Creating plots, themes, stories, routines
- Developing and using play knowledge

Figure 2.8   Integrating learning across the curriculum

Constructive play

Constructive play involves the manipulation of objects and materials to build or create something, using natural and manufactured materials such as blocks and constructional kits, as well as playdough, junk and collage materials, loose parts, sand and water. Different forms of constructive play may be combined with socio-dramatic and dramatic play because children often enjoy making props to support their play, and playing with what they have created. Constructive play involves exploration and discovery, tactile stimulation, problem-solving, social interaction, engagement and concentration, and attention to processes and outcomes. Children represent their ideas, knowledge and interests in multi-modal ways such as layouts, buildings, plans, drawings, sculptures and collages, as shown in the following examples.

Case study

Robert: Designing and building a castle

Robert (aged six, Year 1) played alone, making a large castle from the blocks. During the early stages he was involved in selecting materials for the task, designing, and making decisions about where to place each block for strength and stability. He was representing his thought processes as he talked to the teacher/observer about a holiday visit to castles in Wales.

In the second stage, he combined Playmobil™ figures with his castle, and introduced fantasy elements, thus flowing into dramatic play. Robert allowed other children to join in and explained the different parts of the castle, and what the game would be (a siege between the English and Welsh). In the final stage, they decided as a group to build a tall look-out tower in the centre of the castle, and played cooperatively, using problem-solving skills to combine height with strength and stability. Finally the tower collapsed noisily and the castle was broken up. This was an energizing, satisfying episode of play in which the children used a repertoire of social and manipulative skills. Their dialogue revealed everyday knowledge about castles and structures, and enabled the teacher to assess their skills, knowledge and understanding.

Case study

Martin: Building a racing car

Martin (aged four, Nursery) built a racing car with hollow blocks and, for a while, was content to sit behind the steering wheel by himself making engine noises. Other friends joined the activity and negotiated with Martin to extend the size of the car and include extra seats. They went for a long drive, visiting different places on the way, stopping for petrol and oil. At some point Martin felt that he was losing control of his original intentions because he told the others to leave: the car was really a Grand Prix racing car and could only take one person. He removed the extra seats, returned to his solitary play and put a blanket over his head to signify a helmet and/or the cockpit, and to exclude other children. This sequence incorporated constructive, manipulative, symbolic and socio-dramatic play. It was also rule bound: the children negotiated the rules and maintained them in order to sustain the pretence. They displayed their everyday knowledge and understanding of social conventions. They also deferred to Martin's ownership and control, partly because he had made the car. This was a common pattern in the collaborative play of this group of four-year-old boys. Martin was popular, articulate, inventive and capable of directing imaginative play sequences. His friends usually accepted his leadership because he was a skilled player and they enjoyed inclusion in his games.

These episodes demonstrate some of the conditions that support children's learning through different forms of play, particularly allowing sustained periods of time for play to develop; providing open-ended materials that can be combined in different ways; enabling children to assess potential hazards so that they can take some risks.

Constructive play can be extended in outdoor environments to incorporate challenge and extension. Where children have access to loose parts, they can engage with larger, heavier materials such as old tyres, planks and blocks of wood, crates, plastic pipes and guttering, hay bales, driftwood, tree stumps, lengths of fabric and rope (Broadhead and Burt, 2012; Brown, 2003). Constructive play with loose parts tends to provoke cooperation, such as lifting, carrying and organizing the materials, creating dens, 'cubbies' and secret spaces (Moore, 2010). Children benefit from a diverse range of opportunities for open-ended play and for taking manageable risks, which contrasts with the design of outdoor spaces in educational settings, where fixed equipment is popular.

Rough-and-tumble and superhero play

Rough-and-tumble and superhero play provoke debates among practitioners as they strive to reconcile their personal values about what forms of play can be allowed, tolerated or banned (Holland, 2003; Jarvis, 2010). Adults often have clear ideas about what is 'appropriate play' (taking into account safety factors), but at the same time struggle with their commitment to nurturing children's interests and play themes when these include play-fighting or war games. Real conflicts occur in many forms of play, especially where children lack the skills of cooperation, sharing, negotiation and turn-taking. Practitioners report that play-fighting can develop into real fighting if children either do not understand, or deliberately transgress, the real/not-real boundaries. It follows that not all play is fun, because some children use play spaces to engage in bullying and social aggression, showing 'the dark side of play' (Sutton-Smith, 1997). As a consequence, R&T and superhero play are often banned (but may still occur in spaces away from the gaze of adults). Inevitably gender issues come to the forefront, because these forms of play are typically, but not exclusively, dominated by boys and involve a lot of physical activity such as chasing, running, jumping, wrestling, rolling, crawling, as well as dramatic gestures and actions that imitate fighting and martial arts (Jarvis, 2010). So what can research tell us about the benefits and problems in superhero and rough-and-tumble play?

As noted in Chapter 1, these forms of play are often related to children's popular culture and are accessed through many different media – television, computers, videos, films, games, comics, books, toys and dressing-up clothes. Superheroes are not a recent social and cultural phenomena: there is a long tradition of myths, legends, folk tales and stories that portray struggles between heroes and villains, good and evil, right and wrong. Sports personalities and adventurers are portrayed as heroic and often take on the same iconic, almost mythic status of legendary gods and warriors. Children's literature portrays children, not just adults, as heroes and villains: for example in J.K. Rowling's series of books about Harry Potter, the children have magic powers which enable them to fight the forces of evil, as well as bullying from their own peer group. Superhero play is often combined with R&T as children engage in play-fighting.

There are ongoing debates about whether these forms of play enable children to work through difficult emotions and behaviours and control difficult feelings such as fear, anxiety, aggression, anger and powerlessness. Fromberg and Bergen (2006) provide a detailed analysis of the research that shows the behaviours of different children within rough-and-tumble play, and their impact. Children often feel a sense of agency, control and excitement as they imitate their superheroes, which may contrast with feelings of powerlessness in adult-controlled situations. They may also use these forms of play to deal with the real and often disturbing images they see of war, conflict and violence in the media, and possibly in their own communities, such as families who are refugees and asylum seekers (Hyder, 2005). Jarvis argues that rough and tumble creates positive emotional engagement among the players, in which they voluntarily manage their physical contact and often swap roles, for example from chasing to being chased (2010: 62). Alternatively, children may use role models from popular culture to learn how to be aggressive, and use violence to solve problems or establish dominance and control over others. The central theme of superhero programmes is that the 'good guys' (they are almost always male) triumph over the 'bad guys', usually through conflict and might rather than through dialogue and moral reasoning. This arguably offers children limited role models and few choices about how they resolve conflict in their own lives. Edmiston (2008) takes a contrasting perspective of these forms of 'mythic play'. Reporting an ethnographic study of his son's play, and child–adult interactions, Edmiston argues that play creates social aesthetic spaces in which children and adults create moral dilemmas, based on themes such as oppressive and constructive uses of power:

Monsters are monstrous because they want all the power for themselves. They take what they want and often use violence. They ignore the effects of their actions on their victims. Heroes are heroic because they want to redirect power to the powerless. Heroes act on behalf of victims to stop monsters, to speak the unheard protests of oppressed people, and to mitigate victims' pain. Peoples' deeds lie between the extremities of monsters and heroes. People can become monstrous or heroic at times but are rarely in situations where they are faced with moral choices that have monstrous consequences for others. (Edmiston, 2008: 192)

Taking into account these concerns about violence and aggression, are prac-titioners always right to ban these mythic forms of play? Marsh and Millard

- Children are attracted by the discourses of power, which serve as a counterpoint to the dominant rules and regulations imposed by adults.
- Children can explore complex realities and role models (good/evil, male/ female, right/ wrong) rather than accepting these as bipolar concepts.
- Children are attracted to the dressing-up clothes and props that characterize the different superheroes.
- Girls as well as boys engage in superhero play, and may challenge its masculinist nature.
- Superhero play can have powerful effects on children's motivation to engage in literacy practices where practitioners consciously incorporate this into their role-play areas and themes.
- Superhero play is a potential site for language development, and is particularly strong for bilingual children. Because English is most often the language in which superhero narratives are experienced, children may use key words and phrases in their play.
- Practitioners can use these forms of play to build critical discourses with older children, in which they learn to challenge the images and messages that they convey. (Marsh and Millard, 2000: 51–52)

Figure 2.9   The benefits of superhero play

- Reciprocal role-taking helps to sustain play as children alternate between hero and villain, chaser and chased, aggressor and victim.
- Bouts of rough-and-tumble play often lead to other forms of social play, such as cooperative games. This is more typical for popular children, but for rejected children often leads to further real (rather than mock) aggression.
- Rough-and-tumble play develops from around the age of three to four, peaks at around the age of seven and declines by around the age of eleven, so it has its own particular place in children's development.
- More boys than girls engage in rough-and-tumble play and their play tends to be more vigorous, particularly after long periods of sedentary work.
- Children engage in social problem-solving and experiment with different social roles (but again this is more typical of popular rather than rejected children).
- Children learn to encode and decode emotions, which contributes to their social competence.

Figure 2.10   The benefits of rough-and-tumble play

(2000) take a positive view of the potential benefits of superhero play (see Figure 2.9). Pellegrini and Blatchford (2000) also identify many benefits of rough-and-tumble play (Figure 2.10), but highlight that these benefits may not be the same for all children. Rough-and-tumble play may have positive benefits for some children, but not for others. Where children understand the boundaries of rough and tumble, their play scripts and themes can develop over time, becoming increasingly organized and coordinated. These play events share the positive features of dramatic and socio-dramatic play: they provide opportunities for developing social relationships, creating stories and events and engaging the players socially and emotionally. Children can also remain sensitive to the comfort and safety of other players while playing vigorously (Broadhead, 2004), and can reason about their perspectives and experiences. Similarly Edmiston (2008) argues that, over time, play contributes to exploring possible selves and co-authoring ethical identities.

Activity

What are your own beliefs and values regarding R&T play? Why do you hold these beliefs? How do they influence your practice?

Is R&T play gendered?

Much naturalistic research on free play indicates gendered preferences, with boys typically choosing R&T. It is all too easy to see gender as determining stereotypical play choices. When boys and girls play together or in same-gender groups, they often have different agendas and narratives which influence their play repertoires. These variations are documented with older children (aged six to eleven) with girls being less physically active than boys in outdoor play in the school playground (Pearce and Bailey, 2011). In studies of R&T play, Jarvis (2007: 185) notes an intricate web of inter- and intra-gender cooperation and competition, particularly in games of chase. Girls and boys have ways of controlling specific areas and exercising power with and over their peers. Some boys may do this visibly and audibly with guns, bombs and sticks. Some girls may do this more covertly with magic wands, potions and secret symbols to control who can and cannot join the play.

Activity

What differences have you noticed between boys and girls in R&T play? What do you think are the reasons for any differences? Is gender the main category for understanding differences in R&T play? What have you noticed about children with special educational needs and disabilities and about cultural diversity in R&T play?

The variability of play

Research on children's play consistently reveals the variability of play and of the players (Sutton-Smith, 2001). The imaginative content of children's play is driven by emotional agendas and the need to generate excitement, danger, threat and disruption, which is why they often include monsters, naughty animals, super-heroes, good and bad characters such as robbers and pirates, witches and wizards. By creating these characters, children can introduce concepts of danger and safety, strength and weakness, bravery and fear, winning and losing, and opportunities for dealing with threats, which may include explosions, volcanoes, floods, earthquakes, kidnapping, being killed/frozen and coming alive, being locked up and escaping, and all kinds of magical events such as spells, potions, and incantations. They use logic and reasoning to sustain the pretence and the narrative. Dangerous creatures (dogs and sharks seem to be particularly popular) occupy a special place in children's play for different reasons. First, they can create threat and chaos, which evokes the need to tame and control the creature. Taming and controlling can include an ethic of care: giving the creature treats and attention, taking care of wounds and making sure it does not get into trouble. Second, when children act in role, for example as a dog, they cannot be treated as if they are a child. Behaving 'as if' they are dogs gives them permission to challenge adults' rules. For example, in a Nursery class, the rule was that only four children could play outside without an adult present. However, five children were outside on one occasion, two of whom were naughty dogs. When the teacher reminded the children of the rule, they said that the two dogs did not count because they were dogs and not children, and anyway they could not come out of the playhouse because there were too many children on bikes and the dogs would get run over. This reminds us that we need to understand the logic of play from children's perspectives and respect (wherever possible) their efforts at subverting classroom rules. In the 'what if' and 'as if' modes of play, what children play with has endless potential.

Themes derived from folk tales, fairy tales, television programmes and popular culture influence children's play worlds (Edwards, 2010; Marsh, 2010). Through these themes they make sense of events and concerns in their own lives in ways that go beyond emotional catharsis, such as rules, power, conflict, control, coercion, jealousy, anger, punishment, justice, care and concern, and self-determination. From a sociological perspective, Henricks argues that because many aspects of the world are too vast or too powerful to be played with, play usually involves an attempt to place these matters into much narrower situations over which individuals can exercise some measure of control (2010: 202).

- The child's origin and identity
- The battle between good and evil
- The testing of her powers and weaknesses
- Her relationships with parents, peers, males and females
- Strong women rescuing men who were weak and abandoned
- The upgrading of her own supposedly inferior status as a girl by performing super feats
- Understanding the polarities of smartness versus dumbness
- Sorting out differences between good and bad mothering
- Making sense of her own sexuality
- Exploring the power of language to posit worlds and transform situations. (Kelly-Byrne, 1989: 211)

Figure 2.11   Themes in Helen's play life

Similar themes are revealed by Kelly-Byrne's study of the play life of six-year-old Helen, which was a 'mass of diffuse yet intricately patterned symbols, structures and rhetoric' (1989: 209). Helen's home was the naturalistic setting for the fieldwork and included both solitary and peer-group play. Kelly-Byrne involved herself in Helen's play, at her request and under her direction. Helen's preferred mode of play was make-believe, with themes derived from myths and legends, television characters (including Wonderwoman) and her everyday life at home and school. These themes were interwoven with immense complexity and were further elaborated and transformed by Helen's creativity and imagination. The predominant play themes included are listed in Figure 2.11.

Helen's preoccupation with powerfulness and powerlessness was explored in her Wonderwoman play, reflecting her position as a child and her interpretation of gender socialization processes, especially those relating to images of women portrayed in the media. Kelly-Byrne was struck by Helen's deep involvement, abundant energy levels and intense excitement during play sequences, and argues that this evidence challenges the 'wishy-washy' and idealized views adults often hold about children's play:

> Helen learned that play is a special kind of medium for packaging life's contradictions, for ordering confusion, and for destroying and transforming patterns and realities that are disliked; and, moreover, for doing so with a spirit of involvement, happy abandon, madness and festival. The materials she used in shaping her imaginary worlds were provided by the culture and motivated by her inner conflicts and agenda. She also had a sense of the spirit of play, one that was in keeping with the negative cultural state that play holds in our society. Therefore her play was often irrational, exuberant, combative, unbridled, and grotesque in its moments of intense passion. (Kelly-Byrne, 1989: 216)

Contemporary theories highlight the role of play in the transmission of culture through social interaction and communication. These processes contribute to children's social cognition – their understanding of roles, rules, relationships, values, beliefs, how society is organized and their own place in the world. There is substantial evidence of children learning through peer-group interactions in play, and the ways in which they create and express their identities. In Broadhead's (2004) ethnographic study of children's social and cooperative play, the children used symbolic, abstract forms of thinking and communicated these to each other in quite sophisticated ways, including signs, symbols, gestures, facial expressions and body language. Broadhead's research demonstrates that we need to attend to the content of children's play, particularly the subtleties of language and behaviour, in order to understand their thinking and learning.

In terms of what play does for the child, the studies reviewed here show that play offers many benefits for learning, and as a motivating force for development. However, reflecting on contemporary concerns with equity and diversity, the same or similar benefits are not necessarily available to all children, because different forms of play are not equally accessible (Grieshaber and McArdle, 2010; O'Brien, 2010). For example, children with autistic spectrum disorders may find dramatic and socio-dramatic play incomprehensible, but they have other resources and interests that can be developed (Kangas, Määttä and Uusiautti, 2012). Children with physical disabilities may have difficulties participating in rough-and-tumble play. In culturally diverse communities, home-based child-rearing practices may not be consistent with developing independence and self-management strategies in play. Children from some ethnic minority communities may be disadvantaged by these approaches, because they encounter different expectations and behaviours in schools. Children who have not been enculturated into Western forms of 'educational' play experience early childhood settings as limiting rather than enabling their participation, accessing the curriculum or negotiating childhood and classroom cultures (Brooker, 2010; Levinson, 2005). Because play is valued differently in many cultures, some children experience different home-based play themes and patterns that may not transfer readily into pre-school and school settings, if practitioners do not understand the cultural funds of knowledge that children bring with them (Brooker, 2006; 2011). These issues are addressed in more detail in Chapters 4, 5 and 6. Rather than privileging the universal discourse of play as intrinsically valuable for all children's learning and development, practitioners need to understand the potential that exists for cultural distance and dissonance as children move between the cultures of home, pre-school and school.

The problems with play

In the first two chapters, we have seen that play has many different forms and serves different purposes. Because play is so diverse, and so complex, the task of understanding play is challenging, and even more so when practitioners need to make connections between this vast research and knowledge base and the expectations of play in practice. There remains a general mistrust of play in educational contexts, which arises from two sources: the lack of a precise operational definition of play and the persistent view that play is the opposite of work. Therefore play is less likely to produce either tangible evidence of learning or the learning outcomes that are valued by parents and politicians. Research evidence shows consistently that while play may be encouraged in early childhood, the boundaries between work and play are clearly drawn in the primary school, often from Reception class onwards. Beyond early childhood play is undermined because there is relatively little research to inform practitioners how children's play progresses as they get older and how the school curriculum can support progression.

Summary

This chapter has identified four significant trends:

1   Contemporary research has moved play beyond the seductive principles of the early pioneers towards a more secure evidence base, which identifies some of the complexities and dilemmas of play.
2   Studies of play have moved out of the experimental frameworks of developmental psychology and into more naturalistic settings such as children's homes, communities and pre-school/school. Understanding the child as player/learner and the child in playing/learning contexts is valuable in terms of understanding the role and value of play, and providing recommendations for practice that reflect the forms of 'educational play' that they encounter in pre-school/school.
3   There has been a shift away from broad-scale theories towards more detailed descriptions of the characteristics, patterns and processes of children's learning and development, with greater attention to social and cultural diversity (which will be outlined in more detail in Chapters 4 and 5). Piaget's theories have become part of the 'universal' discourse of learning and development which is applied in many countries in spite of their Western, Euro-centric orientation. However, contemporary theories contest this discourse and provoke critical engagement with play and diversity.
4   Theory and research in early childhood can inform practitioners' understanding about the relationship between play and learning but, at the same time, they create their own knowledge about play, taking into account the complex contextual variables in their settings. This involves developing personal theories, values and beliefs, and questioning how these influence their practice, and what aspects of their thinking and practice need to be changed, as exemplified in studies by Bennett, Wood and Rogers (1997), Broadhead and Burt (2012) and Carr et al. (2009). There is no single definition, and no single theory, which can explain the role of play in children's learning and development.

Activity

Look at Figure 2.1 – Theoretical Perspectives on Why Children Play. Think about a few episodes of play which you think illustrate these different purposes and modes of play. Drawing on your own knowledge and experiences, can you add more justifications for why children play? Discuss these purposes in a group: are there any variations according to dimensions of diversity such as gender, ethnicity, social class, sexualities, culture? From your perspective, what explains any variations, and how are these variations manifest in children's play repertoires?

Further reading

The following authors provide a range of perspectives on play and learning across early childhood and primary education, making links between theory and practice.

Broadhead, P. (2004) *Early Years Play and Learning: Developing Social Skills and Co-operation*, London: RoutledgeFalmer.

Broadhead, P. and Burt, A. (2012) *Understanding Young Children's Learning Through Play: Building Playful Pedagogies*, Abingdon: Routledge.

DeVries, R. (1997) 'Piaget's social theory', *Educational Researcher*, 26 (2): 4–17, http://edr.sagepub.com/cgi/reprint/26/2/4.

Edmiston, B. (2008) *Forming Ethical Identities in Play*, Abingdon: Routledge.

Edwards, S. (2007) 'From developmental-constructivism to socio-cultural theory and practice: an expansive analysis of teachers' professional learning in early childhood education', *Journal of Early Childhood Research*, 5 (1): 83–106, http://ecr.sagepub.com/cgi/reprint/5/1/83.

Holland, P. (2003) *We Don't Play with Guns Here: War, Weapon and Superhero Play in the Early Years*, Maidenhead: Open University Press.

Hyder, T. (2005) *War, Conflict and Play*, Maidenhead: Open University Press.

To gain free access to specially selected SAGE journal articles related to key topics discussed in this book please visit: **www.sagepub.co.uk/wood**

CHAPTER 3

PLAY IN NATIONAL POLICIES: INTERNATIONAL PERSPECTIVES

The aims of this chapter are to:

- Describe the main trends in policy and practice in early childhood curriculum frameworks in the United Kingdom
- Outline the version of play that has emerged in the Early Years Foundation Stage (EYFS) in England
- Consider the research findings that underpin 'educational play' and the challenges they create for practitioners
- Provoke reflection and critical engagement with policy discourses

Play and national curriculum policies

This chapter leads from broad understandings of play to the forms of 'educational play' that are embedded in early childhood policy frameworks. Since the previous editions of this book were published in 1996 and 2005, early childhood education has undergone many changes, notably from intensive policy interventions that have aimed to integrate services and provision for children and families across education, health and social care. These changes have been informed by international research evidence that high quality pre-school provision can make a difference to children's learning and development, especially for those in low-income families. Furthermore, those benefits can be sustained in high quality primary education alongside family support services (Lowenstein, 2011; Sylva et al., 2010). Policy developments in many countries have been driven by increased funding, improving the quantity and quality of provision and raising expectations for children's progress and achievements. However, these investments have come with certain conditions. In England successive government policies from the 1990s onwards have pushed towards more prescriptive approaches to curriculum and pedagogy, defining educational standards for curriculum goals and outcomes, and the training and qualifications of the workforce, creating inspection frameworks for monitoring and regulation, and linking effectiveness with narrow outcomes and a focus on 'school readiness'. The validation of play in these frameworks has been welcomed by early childhood practitioners, but at the same time creates some tensions because play has been captured within these neo-liberal policy discourses. So what has happened to play and what are the key directions in national policy frameworks?

As we have seen in Chapters 1 and 2, the powerful discourse of play-based learning is linked to the concepts of play-based curriculum (Chapter 4), play-based pedagogy (Chapter 5) and play-based assessment (Chapter 7). The tenuous status of play beyond the pre-school phase has remained a consistent theme in research (Broadhead and Burt, 2012; Wood, 2010a). Debates continue about the role of adults in children's play and the efficacy of free versus structured play (Brooker, 2011; Stephen, 2010), and the challenges of developing progression and continuity beyond the early years (Walsh et al., 2011). The research evidence is not consistent in supporting the claims being made for learning through play, in relation to planning for defined learning outcomes and obtaining evidence of children's progression and achievements. As a result, play has been exposed in the context of neo-liberal policy agendas that emphasize educational accountability and performance. This is for the reasons outlined in Figure 3.1:

Play does not always bear a resemblance to what it leads to.

Progress in play does not always equate to progress in curriculum areas of learning.

The capabilities, skills and knowledge that children use in their play are not always transferred into other contexts.

Play has particular purposes and meanings that are unique to play.

Freely chosen, open-ended play may serve children's and not adults' purposes.

Figure 3.1   Play and the policy–practice interface

Capturing play in policy frameworks

Successive attempts to capture play within policy frameworks have produced versions of educational play, which can be seen across UK and international policy contexts (Carr et al., 2009; Grieshaber and McArdle, 2010; Lillemyr, 2009; Nuttall, 2013). These trends have been influenced by research on pre-school and school effectiveness (Sylva et al., 2010) and by international measures of children's performance at different ages (typically in Mathematics, Science and Language/Literacy) that are used to construct 'league tables' for comparing the performance of education systems in different countries. The ideological emphasis on free play has gradually been eroded in favour of play that is planned, structured and purposeful, in order to align play with curriculum goals and outcomes. The vulnerability of play (especially free play) has not been caused by prescriptive policies, but has undoubtedly been exacerbated by these trends.

Table 3.2 describes the policy frameworks in the UK (England, Scotland, Northern Ireland and Wales), and their positions on curriculum content and play.

Country	England	Scotland	Northern Ireland	Wales
Government department	Department for Education (DfE)	Learning and Teaching Scotland (LTS)	Council for Curriculum, Examinations and Assessment (CCEA)	Department for Children, Education, Lifelong Learning and Skills (DCELLS)
Policy title	Early Years Foundation Stage	Curriculum for Excellence	Foundation Stage	Foundation Phase
Age range	Birth to 5	3–6	4–6	3–7
Areas of learning	*Prime areas* Communication and language; Physical development; Personal, social and emotional development. *Specific areas* Literacy; Mathematics; Understanding the world; Expressive arts and design.	Expressive arts; Health and well-being; Languages; Mathematics; Religious and moral education; Sciences; Social studies; Technologies.	The Arts; Language development; Early mathematical experiences; Personal, social and emotional development; Physical development and movement; The world around us.	*Seven areas of learning* Personal and social development, well-being and cultural diversity; Language, literacy and communication skills; Mathematical development; Welsh language development; Knowledge and understanding of the world; Physical development; Creative development.
Assessment	Developmental check at age 2 Early Learning Goals at age 5	Ongoing teacher assessment, levels of learning at age 6	Ongoing teacher assessment of characteristics and skills in each area	Teacher assessment of Foundation Phase Outcomes at age 7

| Position on play | Play must be planned and purposeful. Curriculum must be delivered through play. Mix of adult-led and child-initiated activity. | Active learning is learning which engages and challenges children's thinking and ... takes full advantage of the opportunities presented by spontaneous and planned and purposeful play. | Children should experience much of their learning through well-planned and challenging play. | Children follow their own interests and ideas through free play.

Play should be valued by and structured with clear aims for children's learning. |

Figure 3.2   Play in UK early childhood education policies

Play in the Early Years Foundation Stage (England)

This section examines policy trends, focusing mainly on England.

The Early Years Foundation Stage has undergone four changes between 1997 and 2012. In 2010, a review of the EYFS was led by Dame Clare Tickell. Over the two-year consultation period, several reports were produced, culminating in the publication of the 2012 statutory framework for the EYFS (DfE, 2012a). This version reflects a commitment to educational play as one of three key characteristics of effective teaching and learning:

Playing and exploring: children investigate and experience things, and 'have a go'.

Active learning: children concentrate and keep on trying if they encounter difficulties, and enjoy achievements.

Creating and thinking critically: children have and develop their own ideas, make links between ideas, and develop strategies for doing things. (DfE, 2012a: 7)

The EYFS takes an instrumental view of play as 'the route through which the areas of learning should be delivered' (DfE, 2011: 28):

> Each area of learning and development must be implemented through planned, purposeful play and through a mix of adult-led and child-initiated activity. Play is essential for children's development, building their confidence as they learn to explore, to think about problems, and relate to others. Children learn by leading their own play, and by taking part in play which is guided by adults. There is an ongoing judgement to be made by practitioners about the balance between activities led by children, and activities led or guided by adults. Practitioners must respond to each child's emerging needs and interests, guiding their development through warm, positive interaction. (DfE, 2012a: 6)

This pedagogical position is also validated in the international literature on 'educational play' because there is a broad consensus that play/learning environments (indoors and outdoors) can be planned intentionally to achieve defined outcomes or curriculum goals (Frost, Wortham and Reifel, 2005; Johnson, Christie and Wardle, 2005; Saracho, 2012). Even within democratic pedagogical approaches (for example in Scandinavian countries) it is accepted that some structures are necessary to support and enhance learning through play (Lillemyr, 2009; Pramling Samuelsson and Fleer, 2009; Sandberg and Ärlemalm-Hagsér, 2011). Johnson, Christie and Wardle (2005: 251) argue for a combination of curriculum-led play and play-led curriculum: practitioners can be involved in play through their pedagogical framing, decisions and actions which include organizing the environment; planning for play/learning activities; playing alongside children; observing and assessing play. A critical distinction is that practitioners cannot plan children's play, but can plan for play, and interpret the outcomes that emerge from play.

When we look at these curriculum and pedagogical processes from within a statutory policy framework such as the EYFS, play becomes intrinsically bound with the contemporary politics of education, because it is subject to regulation and managerial processes such as target setting, teacher/practitioner performance, inspection regimes and standards. In contemporary critical discourses, these concepts are seen as problematic (File, Mueller and Wisneski, 2012) because these techniques produce versions of early childhood curricula in which macro-level policy guidance assumes that the complexities and paradoxes of play can not only be managed, but neutralized to produce defined learning outcomes. So there is a difference between the emergent/responsive approaches to play that are advocated in research and the transmissive/directive approach in the EYFS (Wood, 2010a). The latter approach privileges adults' provision for play and their interpretation of children's outcomes in line with defined developmental indicators, curriculum goals and the school readiness agenda.

The Wales Foundation Phase also promotes play and active learning and, by focusing on children aged three to seven, extends these approaches into the Primary school:

> There should be opportunities for children to follow their own interests and ideas through free play. Children's learning is most effective when it arises from first-hand experiences, whether spontaneous or structured, and when they are given time to play without interruptions and to reach a satisfactory conclusion. (DCELLS, 2008a: 5)

The combination of freedom and structure is similar to the EYFS:

> Play should be valued by all practitioners and structured with clear aims for children's learning. It should be structured in such a way that children have opportunities to be involved in the focus, planning and setting up of play areas both indoors and outdoors, as this will give them ownership of their learning. (DCELLS, 2008a: 7)

In order for play to deliver educational outcomes, there are common caveats within these policy documents which state the pedagogical conditions under which play can and should happen, including informed adult involvement and intervention; planning and organization; well-resourced environments (indoors and outdoors); sustained periods of time for play; adult observation and assessment of play. Theoretically, there is some confusion across the practice guidance documents. For example, in the Wales Foundation Phase, assessment is based on the traditional Piagetian 'developmental stages of play', but with the proviso that children develop at different rates according to their previous experience (DCELLS, 2008a; 2008b). Similarly, the discourse of planning for individual development and needs is embedded in the EYFS (DfE, 2012a), even though 'outcomes' in play are likely to be achieved through collective, relational activity.

The four UK frameworks have their own versions of 'educational play', which have strengths and limitations. On the beneficial side of the argument, children do benefit from participating in play environments and activities that are provided in pre-school and school settings, especially where they do not have access to resources at home such as large construction kits, challenging outdoor equipment and the opportunities to play with children in large and small groups. In contrast, if play is overly directed and controlled children may not experience the full potential of play. Play is also diminished if it is allowed only during 'choosing time' or if children have to 'earn' time for play as a reward for good behaviour (as happens in 'Golden Time', see p.143). From this perspective, play is used to tame children through behaviour management routines, just as play has been tamed by dominant discourses of outcomes, quality and effectiveness.

Play, quality and effectiveness discourses

Developments in the EYFS and the Wales Foundation Phase have been supported by the findings from the British government-funded study on the Effective Provision of Preschool Education (EPPE), and its related studies, which have located play within a discourse of educational effectiveness (Sylva et al., 2010). From intensive case studies of 'effective settings', the following characteristics of effective pedagogy have been defined:

> Effective pedagogy in the early years involves both the kind of interaction traditionally associated with the term 'teaching', and also the provision of instructive learning play environments and routines.

> A good grasp of pedagogical content knowledge is a vital component of effective pedagogy.

> There is an equal balance between teacher-initiated group work and freely chosen yet potentially instructive play activities. (Siraj-Blatchford et al., 2002; Siraj-Blatchford and Sylva, 2004: 38)

Practitioners are expected to use different pedagogical approaches, which include adult-led and child-initiated activities, as well as 'free' and 'structured' play. Adult-led activities include defined learning intentions that are applicable to the whole class or to groups. However, there are varying degrees of flexibility for children in how tasks are presented and what responses are expected. While the EPPE findings regarding 'potentially instructive' and 'planned and purposeful play' indicate proactive roles for practitioners, these are open to misinterpretation in practice and raise questions about whose notions of instruction and whose plans are privileged. If it is those of the adults, then the activity will not really be play (though it may retain some playful elements such as positive affect, imagination and flexibility). In child-initiated play, children do not always accept adults as co-players, particularly if they wish to maintain some secrecy or privacy (Moore, 2010). Children consistently make their own demarcations between work (adult-directed/controlled) and play (freely chosen, child-directed activities), a position that is evident in England (Howard, 2010; Roberts-Holmes, 2012), Australia and the USA (Dockett and Meckley, 2007; Factor, 2009). These tensions will be explored in more detail in Chapters 4 and 5 on curriculum and pedagogy.

The emphasis on 'purposeful play' carries the opposite assumption that without pedagogical framing, play would be purposeless and less likely to pay into curriculum goals. The implication here is that adults' pedagogical plans and purposes are privileged. Moreover, in terms of power relationships, practitioners control what forms of play are allowed, how much ownership and control children have, and what limitations are placed on time, space and resources for play. Such a focus distorts the more complex meanings and purposes of play that are evident in research, including the ways in which children exercise power, agency and control (Ryan, 2005; Wood, 2013), how they make and communicate meanings through symbolic activity (Carruthers and Worthington, 2011), how they author their identities (Edmiston, 2008), and how they create spaces for intellectual play through different media such as drawings and plans (Hall, 2010; Wood and Hall, 2011). Moreover, the concept of 'balance' between child- and adult-initiated activities cannot be prescribed in policy terms, because this is likely to vary for individuals and groups of children, across age ranges, across time and space (such as indoors and outdoors), and in response to dimensions of diversity (Figure 3.3).

Dimensions of diversity include age, ethnicity, cultural values, beliefs and traditions, language, religious affiliation, ability, social class, sexualities, and additional or special educational needs and disabilities, home-based learning experiences and child-rearing practices, home-based expectations of children's activities in pre-school.

Dimensions of diversity intersect in ways that enable or constrain children's repertoires of participation in play.

Figure 3.3   Dimensions of diversity

The terms 'well-planned' and 'structured' play can have different meanings, depending on how they are interpreted in practice. For example, structure can imply a tight (and possibly restrictive) curriculum framework that focuses on defined learning outcomes and 'approved' forms of play. Alternatively, structure can imply a more open framework which ensures that play activities potentially lead to a variety of purposes that are controlled by the children and not solely by adults, and allow time and space for children to involve adults in activities such as making props for play or being a co-player.

Within the EPPE study, play is used as an umbrella term, even though children's choices include a range of activities that cannot be classified as play. These recommendations assume that all children have (or will acquire) the necessary skills to access play activities in ways that enable them to engage with curriculum goals, and that curriculum goals can be achieved through play. In the EYFS (DfE, 2012a) practitioners are required to create enabling environments, with positive images that challenge children's thinking and help them to embrace differences in gender, ethnicity, language, religion, culture, special educational needs and disabilities. However, there is little consideration for how dimensions of diversity intersect and how this influences children's abilities to learn curriculum content through play. In relation to linguistic diversity, the emphasis is on ensuring that 'children have sufficient opportunities to learn and reach a good standard in English language during the EYFS, ensuring children are ready to benefit from the opportunities available to them when they begin Year 1' (DfE, 2012a: 6). The EYFS does not foreground more complex principles of democracy, social justice, inclusion, community, voice and identity that underpin the models that are described later in this chapter.

The EYFS recognizes that 'Children learn in different ways and at different rates' (DfE, 2012a: 3) as reflected in the age bands when children are typically expected to achieve the early learning goals. In contrast to the policy discourse, research shows a more complex understanding of diversity: Sutton-Smith (1997) identifies wide variations among players, and among forms of play, with the implication that practitioners need to construct local explanations for local variations by developing knowledge about children, their families and their home and community cultures. This is because play, learning and development are culturally situated processes: children engage in different repertoires of play activities and develop different approaches to learning (Chen, Masur and McNamee, 2011; Guttiérez and Rogoff, 2003). Constructs of 'effective' practices within the EYFS age bands will vary, because play serves contrasting purposes and children's skills, choices and preferences vary across contexts. Moreover, play is not just about acquiring curriculum knowledge: through play, children gradually gain authority over their own worlds, and those of adults, which they express through pretence, social communication and relationships (as discussed in Chapters 1 and 2). The qualities of play include resistance, nonconformity and subversion, which do not align easily with the transmissive/directive curriculum in the EYFS.

In summary, many different factors have been shown to influence the ways in which play is constructed as a complex relational and political space, not just the natural activity of young children (Ryan, 2005; Wisneski and Reifel, 2012). Thus policy-driven recommendations for 'effective practice' do not consistently reflect deeper concerns with equity and social justice, or with contemporary views of children as competent social actors and decision-makers; as active participants/drivers in their learning and development; and as deserving of autonomy and freedom. O'Brien (2010) argues that play and inclusion are problematic constructs, because of the deficit views that are held of children with disabilities and the pedagogical urge towards managing behaviour. Play becomes part of the pedagogical imperative to provide highly structured tasks and routines that contribute to learning atomized skills and fill the missing gaps in curriculum goals. For O'Brien, these practices do not help children to develop fully in terms of their capacities and potential. They may need more time for play, more opportunities for practice and consolidation and more finely tuned provision to support their learning and participation. A critical issue (which is addressed more fully in Chapter 6) is how to make play areas safe without stifling children's choices, creativity, imagination and need to be powerful? (O'Brien, 2010: 188). As we have seen in Chapter 2, these concepts are central to developing critical engagement with policy and practice. Another contentious area that warrants critical scrutiny is how the EYFS, and other curriculum frameworks, conceptualize progression in learning and play.

Activity

Consider the statements about the purposes of play in the curriculum frameworks that you are currently using in your practice. Do you agree with these statements? To what extent do they enable or constrain your planning and provision for play? To what extent do they enable or constrain free play and free choice?

Taking a critical perspective on policy frameworks, in what ways do you think they contribute to taming play and taming children? What rules operate in settings (your own or settings that you have observed) and what are the purposes of these rules?

Play and progression – EYFS to Key Stage 1 (birth to seven)

Although play is valued within the EYFS, there remain concerns about transition to Key Stage 1. Many local authorities in England have a single point of entry to Reception class (aged four to five) in September (Roberts-Holmes, 2012) which means that young four-year-old children receive full-time education within a primary school setting. Many early childhood specialists argue that the Foundation Stage should be extended upwards into Key Stage 1, to make it less like the Key Stage 2 model and improve progression and continuity from birth to seven years.

From a policy-compliant perspective in the EYFS, pedagogic progression in play is framed as a transition from a balance between adult- and child-initiated play to formal, adult-initiated activities, which reinforces the point that play is valued not for what it is, but for what it leads to:

> As children grow older, and as their development allows, it is expected that the balance will gradually shift towards more activities led by adults, to help children prepare for more formal learning, ready for Year 1. (DfE, 2012a: 6)

The EYFS model of pedagogic progression is informed by the EPPE research findings and its related qualitative study on Researching Effective Pedagogy in the Early Years (REPEY) (Siraj-Blatchford et al., 2002; Siraj-Blatchford, 2009). Educational play serves age-related developmental purposes, but is gradually phased out during the Reception year in order to ensure 'school readiness'. This model is based on Vygotskian theories about the transition from playing to learning as the leading activity, specifically from following the child's own agenda to following the school agenda as the social situation of development changes between pre-school and school (Bodrova, 2008: 362). However, there are some problems with these concepts and the ways in which they have been interpreted in the EPPE research. In Vygotskian theories of progression, transitions between pre-school and compulsory school occur at six to seven years. This means that young four-year-old children in England are making this transition up to two years earlier than anticipated in Vygotskian theories. Transition points vary between five and seven years in different countries, which means that there is at least a two-year span during which children are expected to become 'ready for school' and orientate towards the changes from child-initiated to adult-led pedagogical approaches. For this transition to occur in England during the Reception year remains a problematic aspect of the EYFS.

Play as a leading activity

The concept of play as a leading activity is theoretically complex. First, it does not mean that play is the main activity in early childhood (although this is a common misinterpretation). The concept of leading activities defines the processes and contexts (social and cultural situations for development) involved in transforming existing ways of thinking and learning into increasingly complex forms of psychological functioning. These emerge from and interact with social situations, which change over time, with activities in one period of life preparing children for the next period. Edwards (2011) uses the metaphor of leading activity as a bridge that supports children's transitions from one psychological activity to another. In Vygotskian theory, it is only when all play elements are fully developed into social make-believe play that this becomes the leading activity of pre-school and kindergarten age children (Bodrova, 2008: 363) which, in Vygotskian terms is defined as up to seven years of age. This age span enables children to develop mature forms of play, characterized by an imaginary situation, social roles and relationships between people, and rules that are based on the logic of real-life situations. On this basis, if play is phased out during the Reception year, children are denied the full potential benefits of play.

Figure 3.4   Play as a leading activity

Activity

Consider your own experiences of working with or observing children in the four to five age range. What are the different models of transition that you have seen? What do you think are good practices in preparing children for the transition to compulsory education? How do schools become ready for children to make this transition and what is the role of play in these processes?

Play is at risk within pre-school to school transitions, at whatever age this occurs, because the policy assumption is that children need less play. An alternative perspective is that children need more challenging forms of play that support progression towards social affiliation and symbolic complexity. Broadhead (2004) provides evidence to support the significance of different forms of play for children aged three to six. In a collaborative study with early years teachers, Broadhead focused on children's language, sociability and cooperation, and developed the Social Play Continuum (SPC), which identified four domains of play (see Figure 3.5).

associative • social • highly social • cooperative

Figure 3.5   Broadhead's four domains of play

The four domains are described in Broadhead (2010: 56–57) and provide a tool for observing and understanding playful learning and for evaluating areas of provision. The SPC is based on sustained observations of play and provides evidence of the meanings that children construct and communicate in their play, and how these can be interpreted within and beyond defined curriculum frameworks. Broadhead uses socio-cultural theories for interpreting children's contextually situated meanings and actions, their agency as social actors and as co-constructors of learning. Children drive their own development in play because they are often highly motivated to become, and to be seen as, more competent and to achieve mastery. The SPC challenges Piagetian notions about forms, ages and stages of play, because the evidence demonstrates increasing complexity in language, symbolic activity and behaviour as children move flexibly between the SPC domains. Therefore continuity and progression in play should incorporate the ways in which children's interests develop, and their continuing need for choice, autonomy and challenge.

A further consideration is that transition is not just an issue of different pedagogical and curriculum practices. Research shows that children learn to construct their identities in different sites, and accomplish this by learning strategies for participating in classroom life and dealing with the mixed messages that circulate in classrooms (MacLure et al., 2012: 461). In technocratic pedagogic constructions of play children may be caught between different subjectivities: pleasing the teacher through 'approved' play choices, and contesting classroom discipline, rules and routines. In these conditions, it is not surprising that play occurs under the radar of the pedagogical gaze.

Policy–practice dilemmas – Cinderella's glass slipper?

Like Cinderella's glass slipper, play does not fit neatly into policy frameworks because it does not consistently 'pay into' defined learning outcomes. From a critical perspective, the ways in which play is framed within the EYFS begs contrasting interpretations: here we have the power of the state harnessing established (but selective) truths about the power of play, but in ways that may be circumscribed by technical and managerial approaches to education. Policy frameworks typically present a version of order, stability and agreed meanings within which certain forms of knowledge (and ways of knowing) are valued and codified in the curriculum. Thus negotiating different values, beliefs and approaches is a major pedagogic challenge, because play does not align easily with these techniques of organization. The focus of 'educational play' is learning about the culture of the settings, socially valued forms of knowledge and the rules of society. The 'outcomes' relate to the learner as an individual and learning as individual acquisition. In contrast, play is about collective, relational activity, which is always culturally, socially and historically situated. The surveillance and control that policy frameworks promote is unlikely to yield the range or depth of knowledge that is needed in order to understand the complexities of play, particularly from an educational effectiveness perspective.

As indicated in Chapter 1, play as a child-centred and child-directed practice is influenced by children's play lives at home, their interpretations of their cultural experiences, their identities and their abilities to understand the 'as if' and 'what if' qualities of play. Play is ambiguous and complex, in terms of the content, social interactions, symbolic meanings, communicative languages and the environmental affordances that mediate play and playfulness. Meanings are produced dynamically, drawing on the socio-cultural–historical resources of the players and their multiple, shifting identities. There are different interpretations of what play is, and what play does for the players, according to the perspectives of educators and children (Rogers and Evans, 2008), and across dimensions of diversity (Grieshaber and McArdle, 2010; MacNaughton, 2009). From children's perspectives, play is also about subversion and inversion, order and disorder, chaos and stability, inclusion and marginalization, which is where issues of power, agency and control are played out. Thus play incorporates political and ethical issues that are not addressed in the universal assumptions about educational play in policy discourses.

Despite these tensions, a key message is that early childhood educators can integrate play into the curriculum in ways that include creativity, flexibility and responsiveness. However, the challenges and complexities involved should not be underestimated, because this requires sophisticated curriculum and pedagogical approaches (Chapters 4 and 5). Although the policy agenda validates 'educational play' as an approach to learning and as a means for curriculum delivery, practitioners should not be constrained by following policy agendas slavishly: there are other versions and other visions which can inform provision. A key challenge for practitioners is to use policy frameworks as a guiding structure rather than as a prescriptive straitjacket by developing their abilities to tune into potential outcomes, including the outcomes that children construct for themselves and co-construct with others in their play and work.

There has been much dissatisfaction with 'one size fits all' policies, with increasing interest in 'designer versions' of the curriculum that are more in tune with children, families, local communities and the professional knowledge base within early childhood education (File, Mueller and Wisneski, 2012). Practitioners need deep understanding of young children's learning, and diverse funds of pedagogical knowledge and expertise to plan a curriculum that is responsive and anticipates future developments. In the next section, we look at the principles and theories underlying different curriculum models.

Curriculum models

To create 'designer' versions, practitioners can draw on curriculum models which are described in the following section, and can be combined or adapted to individual settings. All integrate play, alongside playful and creative approaches to teaching and learning. These models continue to evolve in response to research, theory and wider social change, so they are not set in stone, but are open to skilful adaptation.

Te Whāriki curriculum (New Zealand)

Te Whāriki (New Zealand Ministry of Education, 1996) is the national curriculum statement for Aotearoa/New Zealand, for children from birth to five years in the early childhood sector. It is a bi-cultural curriculum that reflects the cultural heritage, beliefs and traditions of Māori communities, and can be adapted within different settings to reflect the multi-cultural society. Te Whāriki is informed by socio-cultural theories of learning and development, and has moved the sector away from individualistic approaches to developmentally appropriate programmes, towards recognition of the socially constructed nature of learning, and the importance of knowledgeable others in the setting, home and community (Carr et al., 2009; Carr and Lee, 2012). The metaphor of curriculum is a *whāriki*, or mat, which is woven from principles, strands, goals and learning outcomes. The four principles are outlined in Figure 3.5.

- *Empowerment*: the early childhood curriculum empowers the child to learn and grow.
- *Holistic development*: the early childhood curriculum reflects the holistic way children learn and grow.
- *Family and community*: the wider world of family and community is an integral part of the early childhood curriculum.
- *Relationships*: children learn through responsive and reciprocal relationships between people, places and things.

Figure 3.6   Te Whāriki: principles

The five strands are listed in Figure 3.7.

- Well-being – *Mana Atua:* the health and well-being of the child are nurtured.
- Belonging – *Mana Whenua*: children and their families feel a sense of belonging.
- Contribution – *Mana Tangatta*: opportunities for learning are equitable.
- Communication – *Mana Reo*: the languages and symbols of their own and other cultures are promoted and protected.
- Exploration – *Mana Aotūroa*: the child learns through active exploration of the environment.

Figure 3.7   Te Whāriki: five strands

Within each strand the broad goals relate to the overall learning environment, what the children learn and experience, and how practitioners make links between the home, community, the setting and other early childhood services. Equity goals are integral to the educational goals, based on culturally situated theories about being, becoming and belonging.

The curriculum framework specifies learning outcomes (knowledge, skills and attitudes) in the five strands, along with examples of experiences that help to meet these outcomes. The learning outcomes are summarized as working theories and learning dispositions which are indicative rather than definitive. Practitioners are encouraged to think critically about the quality of their provision and their everyday routines and practices in relation to how the outcomes are being achieved. Each of the strands links with the learning areas and essential skills of the New Zealand Curriculum Framework for primary education (New Zealand Ministry of Education, 2007). The dispositions for learning in Te Whāriki permeate the goals and strands.

Activity

Learning Dispositions

Children are being/becoming: ready, willing and able, curious, creative, playful, inventive, imaginative, resourceful, resilient, persistent, helpful, caring, considerate, cooperative, responsible, competent, capable, respectful, reflective, independent, interdependent, collaborative, cooperative ...

Think of a child in your setting and try to describe her/him in relation to these dispositions. Are different dispositions evident in different contexts (child-initiated and adult-directed)?

By focusing on children and their learning, curriculum planning is based on their interests so that skills, knowledge and understanding are embedded in activities and experiences that reflect their cognitive, emotional and social concerns. Spontaneous, free and structured play activities are valued as key learning experiences. Family involvement is encouraged through shared assessments across home and the setting, with family members contributing to children's documented learning stories (Carr and Lee, 2012). The following vignette shows how these principles work in practice:

> Vini, aged four, tells the teachers that his mother needs new slippers. He makes a pair for her (with much measuring and gluing and decorating), and when the teachers write this up their assessment emphasizes Vini's developing identity as a 'caring' and thoughtful person. His mother contributes a comment to the assessment folder that adds a reference to the technical expertise that this work illustrated: she writes that the slippers Vini made were 'unbelievable in terms of thoughtfulness and technical perfection for a little child'. (Cowie and Carr, 2004: 98)

The outcomes in Te Whāriki are broader and more process-oriented than those in the Early Years Foundation Stage. For example, in the Exploration strand, children develop:

> Spatial understandings, including an awareness of how two- and three-dimensional objects can be fitted together and moved in space in ways in which spatial information can be represented, such as in maps, diagrams, photographs and drawings. (New Zealand Ministry of Education, 1996: 90)

The outcomes are holistic in the sense that they transcend subject boundaries. In contrast, the goals and outcomes in the EYFS (DfE, 2012a) are specific and hierarchical in terms of knowledge, skills and understanding within each of the areas of learning. These two orientations reflect contrasting assumptions about children and childhood, and the purposes of education. In England, provision has been influenced by instrumental approaches to learning, and school readiness, particularly in literacy and numeracy. The socio-cultural orientation of Te Whāriki places more emphasis on the early childhood centre or classroom as a community of learners: learning is a co-constructive process that involves the child acting in context, with increasingly competent forms of participation (Carr et al., 2009).

In New Zealand, there are ongoing debates about curriculum content, and 'interests versus skills', particularly with reference to children with special educational needs (Hedges and Cullen, 2011), which reflect similar issues in the wider early childhood community. Within a predominantly interests-based approach, it is challenging for practitioners to identify specific learning goals for individual children. Within a predominantly skills/content-focused approach, too much atomization and specification of learning goals is equally problematic if teaching and learning are fragmented. A resolution to this tension is that practitioners need to ensure that children's interests are supported and extended with relevant content, based on subject knowledge and domain-specific expertise (Carr et al., 2009: 3).

A common area of agreement across international contexts is that children are competent, powerful and strong. This is reflected in the Reggio Emilia approach from Northern Italy, which has influenced practice in many countries.

The Reggio Emilia approach (Northern Italy)

This approach developed in Reggio Emilia in the years following the Second World War has gained international recognition and respect for its ethos, democratic pedagogy centred on child–adult engagement in the construction of curriculum provision, and the focus on the creative arts. The image of the child is expressed eloquently by Loris Malaguzzi, the founder of Reggio:

> Our image of children no longer considers them as isolated and egocentric, does not see them as only engaged with actions and objects, does not only emphasize

the cognitive aspects, does not belittle feelings or what is not logical and does not consider with ambiguity the role of the affective domain. Instead our image of the child is rich in potential, strong, powerful, competent, and most of all connected to adults and other children. (Malaguzzi, 1993: 10)

Malaguzzi proposes that children have a 'hundred languages' for constructing, expressing and communicating their knowledge, ideas and experiences. These can be expressed in multi-modal ways, using a variety of materials, tools and resources: drawing, painting, mark-making, printing, writing, signs and symbols (including Braille and Makaton), dance, mime, drama, facial and body gestures, puppets, shadow play, plans, maps, buildings, designs, photographs, sculptures, blocks, construction materials, natural materials, computers and ICT and many more. The children learn to use tools correctly in order to develop their knowledge, creativity and representation by engaging in authentic activities with skilled atelieristas (artists): for example, creating a sculpture garden, growing fruit and vegetables, investigations of the natural world, involvement in community projects.

The Reggio Approach (as it has become known) is founded on key principles and images of children and how these influence practice; capturing and thinking about learning experiences through observation, documentation, interpretation, reflection and a 'pedagogy of listening' (Figure 3.8).

The 'hundred languages' principle reminds us that empowerment arises through using all modes of representation so that children are engaged intellectually and emotionally in their work and play. This is valuable for children with speech and communication difficulties and those with English as an additional language. The concept of 'a hundred languages' enables practitioners to think creatively about inclusion, by ensuring that there are multi-modal opportunities for play.

So what can we learn from these principles?

Practitioners who visit Reggio settings are often impressed by the quality of the material resources, the design and layout of the spaces, the provision of ateliers/art specialists and the quality of children's representations (Thornton and Brunton, 2007). Assessment and evaluation develop through observing and 'a pedagogy of listening' (Rinaldi, 2006), which enable educators to build on experiences and activities in ways that nurture the child's interests through meaningful content, challenge and multi-modal representations. Practices in Reggio Emilia are child-centred because teachers strive to understand children's thoughts and ideas:

Ultimately the studio teacher must learn where the child is and the child must teach the atelierista what they do and do not understand and where they are willing to grow and make meaning. (Parnell, 2011: 302)

The child as protagonist: children are strong, rich and capable. They have readiness, potential, interest and curiosity in constructing their learning. They use everything in the environment to help them. Children, teachers and parents are the central protagonists in the educational process.

The child as collaborator: children grow up in communities of practice which include *more* and *differently* knowledgeable others. Learning takes place in social contexts, using the resources (material and human) within the environment. How children learn, and how they create their identities, are intimately connected with their experiences in their social worlds.

The child as communicator: many different forms of symbolic representation are valued – written and spoken language, movement, drawing, painting, building, sculpture, shadow play, collage, dramatic play, music. These 'hundred languages' enable children to represent and communicate their thinking in different ways, including what they know, understand, wonder about, question, feel and imagine. An *atelierista*, or trained artist, enables these processes.

The environment as third teacher: the design of the learning environment (indoors and outdoors) supports educative encounters, communication and relationships. Specific learning spaces are provided, with equipment and materials which may change over time as projects develop. Choice and independence are encouraged through access to materials and the opportunities that children have to combine and explore them. The environment is a motivating force in creating spaces for learning and creating a sense of well-being and security.

Teachers as co-constructors: teachers work collaboratively with children, developing and extending themes and interests. They work on short-term and long-term projects which are designed and planned collaboratively. Teachers interact in supportive ways, by listening, observing, talking and documenting children's learning journeys. In the *atelier*, or art studio, the children work with the *atelierista* on projects. By discovering children's interests and agendas, teachers can help them to make further discoveries in and about their environment.

Teachers as researchers: by developing collegial relationships, staff engage in continuous professional development, based on documenting and discussing children's progress and achievements. They draw on established theories and build their own working theories about their provision.

Documentation as communication: in common with Te Whāriki, documentation is shared with the staff, other adults in the setting and parents/families. Documentation panels (displays) and books provide evidence of children's learning through photographs, representations, transcriptions of their language and comments by practitioners. Documentation is shared with parents for joint discussions about children's interests, progress and achievements and shows children that their work is valued.

Parents as partners: participation is actively encouraged, including two-way communication about the child's experiences. Parents offer ideas and suggestions to support the child's learning and development and contribute their skills to the setting. Parents contribute to interpreting children's multi-modal representations based on their home and community cultures and experiences.

Figure 3.8   Reggio Emilia key principles

Although this approach is inspiring, it is not sufficient to 'do Reggio' by adopting surface-level practices, or acquiring 'Reggio' resources, because this approach is grounded in principles and beliefs about children, families and communities, and images of children (Parnell, 2011; Rinaldi, 2006). Therefore, practitioners need to question the extent to which the Reggio experience can be generalized or melded with technocratic models such as the EYFS. Versions of good or effective practice cannot be built from the nuts and bolts of other models, unless they are guided by their underpinning theories and principles.

If we regard children as strong, capable, resilient, competent and rich, it follows that practitioners should be seen in similar ways. Being strong and resilient in their principles, capable and competent in their provision and rich in their professional knowledge may also help practitioners to resist pressures for inappropriate practices from politicians, colleagues, parents and the media.

The High/Scope curriculum (USA)

The High/Scope curriculum originated in the USA and was based originally on Piagetian theories and developmentally appropriate practice (DAP). Subsequent revisions have foregrounded socio-cultural theories, responsiveness to social and cultural diversity, and proactive roles for practitioners (Bredekamp and Copple, 1997). Detailed guidelines describe curriculum content, planning, routines and strategies for assessment and record-keeping. Curriculum content is based on key experiences, which represent the eight areas of learning listed in Figure 3.9.

The curriculum is planned around active learning experiences that reflect children's needs, interests and ongoing cognitive concerns and can be adapted to different age groups and settings. Adult-directed activities are valued and focus on teaching specific skills and knowledge across the eight areas and providing resources to support children's interests. The approach incorporates plan–do–review (PDR), which involves children setting their own goals and choosing their activities within a structured, well-resourced environment. Children carry out their plans individually, in pairs or in groups. This element of choice does not embody a *laissez-faire* approach because practitioners structure the indoor and outdoor environments to provide key experiences in the eight areas of learning and to encourage flexibility and independence. Their roles are to support the children's decisions and plans, support their learning, and use assessments to inform further provision. Pedagogical interactions should respond to the children's activities but encourage challenge and extension.

- Active learning
- Language
- Representation
- Classification
- Seriation
- Number
- Spatial relations
- Time

Figure 3.9   Areas of learning in the High/Scope approach

There is an underlying assumption in this model that what children choose is what they need. However, this is problematic because research has shown that some children repeat what is safe and known; they may not have the knowledge, confidence or expertise to use materials and resources differently, to try out new activities, push their own boundaries, join a group of players or engage successfully in more complex forms of play (Broadhead, 2004) Alternatively, what they choose may contest the rules of the setting (Wood, 2013). In a socio-cultural model of learning/teaching, communities of learners co-construct learning through joint activity and guided participation, and responsive interactions based on children's choices of activities and their repertoires of participation. Practitioners need to identify what potential for learning is afforded by different areas of play provision, how these areas can be accessible to all children in order to support their plans and what choices are being enacted. These ideas are explored in more detail in the following section.

Plan–do–review (PDR)

In PDR activities, children are allowed to plan activities and combine materials and resources, then come together during review time to discuss what they have done, made or learned. They are encouraged to ask questions, share information and think about future challenges and extensions of their activities. When used effectively, review time can encourage the development of metacognitive skills and processes. The effectiveness of PDR depends on the size of the group and the practitioner's expertise in guiding the discussion, modelling open-ended questions, prompting thinking, providing feedback and encouraging children to engage in metacognitive processes – conscious awareness and control of their thinking, learning and activity.

Fisher (2013) draws on the principles that inform PDR and provides detailed guidance for practitioners on what adults plan, what children plan, how children can be involved in making decisions and organizing indoor and outdoor environments, and how they can develop the skills of reflecting on their activities to plan further learning. The review process can inform practitioners about children's emergent and working theories, and how these can be developed through adult- and child-initiated activities. When children plan activities such as arranging PE equipment, and organizing outdoor learning environments, they can incorporate challenge and extension, as well as attending to issues of safety and risk. These approaches are purposeful and aspirational in terms of valuing children's play and self-initiated activity, with potential for co-constructive engagement between adults and children. PDR incorporates the principles of democratic and inclusive participation, because of children's involvement in planning, designing, negotiating, deciding and organizing aspects of their settings and in co-constructing the curriculum.

In order to be implemented successfully, the PDR approach involves teaching children the psychological tools for thinking and learning, including metacognitive skills and strategies (Figure 3.10). Planning in collaboration with others helps to develop social and communicative skills; in mixed age groups, older children

What planning skills do children need to learn?

- Speaking and listening in a group
- Understanding the concepts of planning and making decisions
- Being able to implement a plan
- Selecting and knowing how to use materials and resources
- Acting independently and collaboratively
- Asking for assistance from peers and adults
- Specifying the assistance needed to implement a plan or carry out a sub-task
- Paying attention to the activity
- Creating, identifying and solving problems
- Remembering how the plan was carried out
- Reflecting on action – raising and answering questions
- Representing knowledge and experience in different ways
- Processing information and communicating the meaning and purpose of an activity
- Using conscious awareness and control of learning processes (metacognition)
- Making and sustaining relationships with peers and adults

Figure 3.10   Children's planning skills

can model the PDR processes. Ideally, PDR should be implemented throughout a school so that children develop increasing levels of competence and mastery, building incrementally on 'can-do' or mastery orientations to learning.

Originally the High/Scope model was designed for an adult–child ratio of 1:8, so implementation with larger groups can be problematic. Practitioners who use PDR have reported that planning with large groups is time-consuming (up to 20 minutes) and often results in children becoming restless. Some have reported that they use small planning groups on a daily basis so that during the course of a week all children are able to experience greater choice, autonomy and independence (see Amanda's story in Chapter 8). Practitioners need to give support for children's planned activities, drawing on appropriate pedagogical strategies and interactions (Figure 3.11).

interacting, participating, listening, observing, responding, directing, redirecting, demonstrating, modelling, open-ended questioning, praising, encouraging, advising, guiding, suggesting, instructing, imparting new knowledge, diagnosing, challenging, extending, discussing, reflecting, prompting, enriching, assisting, mediating, explaining, enabling, etc.

Figure 3.11   Pedagogical interactions

Review time

Practitioners are sometimes unsure about how to use review time constructively so that children can feed back what they have been doing in their self-initiated activities, including play. Reviews can be carried out in different ways (Figure 3.12).

- 'In the moment' reviews, in response to a child's immediate success, challenge, problem-setting or problem-solving
- At the end of a session, either within a small group (with key workers, classroom assistants or other helpers) or feeding back to a larger group
- At the end of the day
- At the end of a week
- At the beginning/end of a topic (for example, creating mind-maps of children's knowledge, interests and ideas for further learning)

Figure 3.12   Strategies for review

Plan–do–review serves different purposes for children and practitioners.

Activity

The benefits of PDR for adults and children

Look at some of the benefits of PDR. Can you identify which of these benefits are already evident in your own practice? Are there areas you would like to develop and why?

- Children can value their own and others' work.
- Children can develop a sense of agency and mastery because they make decisions, identify and solve problems as they arise.
- Practitioners can shift the balance of power in classrooms, enabling children to take responsibility for their own learning.
- Practitioners can plan some aspects of the curriculum around children's interests and funds of knowledge.
- Practitioners can use review time to understand what and how children are learning and plan further provision accordingly.
- Practitioners can value the learning that arises from children's interests and motivation.
- PDR can inform differentiation and individual plans for learning.

Summary

To summarize, policy developments in early childhood have proved to be a mixed blessing. Play has remained high on the agenda, but with greater emphasis on what constitutes 'effective' and 'good-quality' play. Greater attention is being paid to developing play-based curriculum and play-based pedagogy, which validate the role of adults in planning, supporting and extending children's learning, as well as recognizing the educationally power-ful content of children's self-initiated activities. The early childhood community has been influential in articulating the characteristics of young learners and how these should influence provision. More attention is being paid to the play repertoires of children with additional or special educational needs and disabilities, and to other dimensions of diversity. These factors reinforce the view that early childhood education is a complex endeavour, requiring highly skilled professionals (DfE, 2012b). Policy frameworks should not be used as straitjackets because they provide only limited understanding of the power and potential of play. 'Designer versions' of locally responsive curricula can be informed by theories and principles from different approaches to provide coherence and structure. These concepts will be explored in greater depth in the following chapters.

Activity

Read the eight principles that inform the Reggio Emilia approach. In what ways do these principles align with your own beliefs and practices? What images of the child do you hold? Discuss and compare these images with your colleagues. What images of the child are held in the EYFS (or other national policy documents)?

Activity

What do you understand by a 'designer version' of the curriculum? In what ways do you think you have a) created your own designer version; b) observed another practitioner's designer version? What are the benefits of creating your own designer version? What are the risks?

Further reading

Broadhead, P., Howard, J. and Wood, E. (2010) (eds) *Play and Learning in the Early Years: From Research to Practice*, London: Sage.

Brooker, L. and Edwards, S. (2010) (eds) *Engaging Play*, Maidenhead: Open University Press.

Christman, D. (2010) 'Creating social justice in early childhood education: a case study in equity and context', *Journal of Research on Leadership Education*, 5 (3): 107–137, http://jrl.sagepub.com/cgi/reprint/5/3/107.

File, N., Mueller, J. and Wisneski, D. (eds) (2012) *Curriculum in Early Childhood Education: Re-examined, Rediscovered, Renewed*, New York: Routledge.

Fisher, J. (2013) *Starting from the Child?* (4th edn), Maidenhead: Open University Press.

Grieshaber, S. and McArdle, F. (2010) *The Trouble with Play*, Maidenhead: Open University Press.

Parnell, W. (2011) 'Revealing the experience of children and teachers even in their absence: documenting in the early childhood studio', *Journal of Early Childhood Research*, 9 (3): 291–307, http://ecr.sagepub.com/content/9/3/291.

Rinaldi, C. (2006) *In Dialogue with Reggio Emilia: Listening, Researching and Learning*, New York, Routledge.

Sutton-Smith, B. (2001) *The Ambiguity of Play* (2nd edn), Cambridge, MA: Harvard University Press.

Thornton, L. and Brunton, P. (2007) *Bringing the Reggio Approach to Your Early Years Practice*, Abingdon: Routledge.

To gain free access to specially selected SAGE journal articles related to key topics discussed in this book please visit: **www.sagepub.co.uk/wood**

CHAPTER 4

PLAY AND THE CURRICULUM

The aims of this chapter are to:

- Understand the Model of Integrated Curriculum and Pedagogical Approaches (Wood, 2010b: 21) (Figure 4.2) as a socio-cultural framework for curriculum planning
- Understand the processes that link playing and learning, drawing on socio-cultural theories
- Critically explore your own values, beliefs and theories about planning for play
- Understand how to plan for progression and continuity into the Primary school

This chapter focuses on developing a continuum between playing, learning and teaching, based on a Model of Integrated Curriculum and Pedagogical Approaches developed by Wood (2010b). This model is underpinned by socio-cultural theories and research from different countries, and reflects the principle that adults cannot plan children's play, but can plan for children's play and other self-initiated activities. Practitioners can use the model to develop their practice in ways that extend beyond national policy frameworks. Play in early years settings is always structured to varying degrees, and practitioners are expected to justify play in relation to learning goals and outcomes. However, this is not the only (or even the most appropriate) way of understanding how play can contribute to 'high quality' and 'effective' provision. Practitioners can develop their own understanding of quality and effectiveness through adapting provision in ways that are responsive to social and cultural diversity, to children with additional and special educational needs and disabilities, and to families and communities. The model will enable practitioners to develop flexibility and responsiveness in their curriculum and pedagogical approaches.

Defining curriculum

As we have seen in Chapter 3, the early childhood curriculum is defined and constructed in different ways, based on images of children and practitioners, as well as principles and values such as community, citizenship and creativity in Reggio Emilia; children's rights, gender equity and education for sustainable development in Sweden.

All curriculum models reflect different beliefs and values about what forms of knowledge or areas of learning are educationally worthwhile for children's immediate and future needs and the wider needs of society. How that knowledge is organized and sequenced reflects ways of understanding progression in learning. However, knowledge is not value-free: the models described in Chapter 3 give status to different forms of knowledge, approaches to learning and to play. What links these different models is that practitioners have a professional and ethical responsibility to make informed decisions about how curricula will be created with young children through adult- and child-initiated activities, based on their interests, working theories and funds of knowledge (see Figure 4.1), and on the content defined in different frameworks. How the curriculum is experienced and interpreted will vary according to the children in the setting and will be influenced by dimensions of diversity: gender, home/family cultures, ethnicity, languages, religious affiliations, sexualities, social class, abilities/disabilities and special or additional needs. How progression is defined through curriculum content is not the same as progression in learning. Play itself does

---

The concept of funds of knowledge was developed from research by Moll et al. (1992) and González, Moll and Amanti (2005). In the context of play and early childhood education, these theories have been developed by Hedges (2010; 2011b). Funds of knowledge are conceptualized as the knowledges that are situated in everyday practices in children's homes and communities, including information, skills, strategies, ways of thinking and learning, approaches to learning and practical skills. These knowledges include 'subject knowledge' such as mathematics, literacy, technology, which are learned in everyday contexts, combining informal and formal approaches to learning through different cultural routines and practices. Children bring their everyday knowledge from their homes and communities and develop working theories about themselves and their social and cultural worlds. In the context of play, children may be taught important cultural rules and information through games, visual and creative arts, storytelling and traditional myths and legends. Children also participate playfully in activities such as shopping, gardening, cooking, caring for siblings, festivals and celebrations. The work of Hedges (2010; 2011a; 2011b), Brooker (2011) and Carruthers and Worthington (2011) indicates that children's funds of knowledge, and cultural approaches to playing and learning, may not always be recognized or valued within early years settings.

These concepts draw on Rogoff's argument (2003) that culture is not just 'out there' in our environments, but is profoundly situated within our minds, habits, beliefs, values, dispositions, behaviours, body language, interests and orientations to the world. Therefore, culturally responsive provision attends to children's deep cultural repertoires for learning and participation and not just to surface-level cultural representations.

Figure 4.1   Funds of knowledge

not constitute a curriculum, but should be integrated within the curriculum because it creates potential spaces for learning and development.

Activity

Identify a curriculum area and reflect on how your own funds of knowledge developed in home and education settings. What misconceptions did you have and how were these corrected or restructured? What funds of knowledge from home transferred or did not transfer into school?

The concept of potential spaces is quite challenging for practitioners who work with prescriptive curriculum models. However, curriculum cannot be defined only by performance goals in policy frameworks: in the Early Years Foundation Stage (DfE, 2012a) the learning goals and outcomes are expectations of what most children will achieve by the age of five, with an emphasis on 'school readiness' skills. Many children will exceed these goals and some will need further support in the transition to the Key Stage 1 curriculum. Curriculum frameworks do not define the deeper complexities of what is valuable for children to learn, particularly the ways in which they construct their unique identities, interests and dispositions. In addition, the curriculum that is experienced by children involves all the cultural practices within the setting: activities, rules and routines, how children are greeted, how the environment is organized, how they are expected to interact with peers and adults, and what behaviours and activities are encouraged, tolerated, ignored or banned. Into this mix are added children's cultural beliefs and practices from their homes and communities. So how can practitioners incorporate these complexities into curriculum planning? The following section describes a Model of Integrated Curriculum and Pedagogical Approaches which provides possible solutions to these challenges (Wood, 2010b).

Integrated Curriculum and Pedagogical Approaches

The Model of Integrated Curriculum and Pedagogical Approaches is pragmatic because it accepts that play in school is structured to varying degrees, but does not privilege the technocratic 'play as education' discourse. By incorporating flexibility and responsiveness, practitioners will be able to engage with children in planning some of their activities and to integrate ideas from different approaches (see Chapter 3).

The model is based on the concept of a continuum between work and play, as shown in the arrow that connects the two pedagogical zones (adult-directed

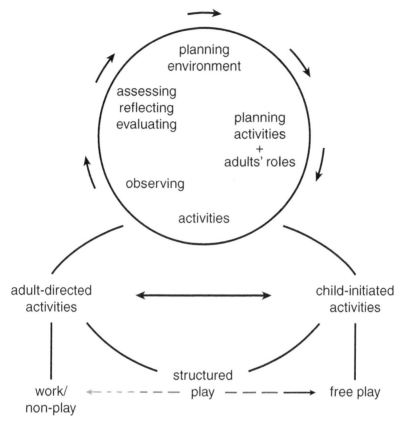

Figure 4.2   The Model of Integrated Curriculum and Pedagogical Approaches

and child-initiated). Looking at the centre of the continuum (structured play) the greater the degree of structure, the more the activity will be like work and less like play. Activities that are adult-directed may have playful and imaginative elements. The lesser the degree of structure that is imposed, the more the activity will be like play, with the recognition that 'free play' will never be truly free, but should be as free as possible within the setting. In the child-initiated zone, freely chosen activities are the closest to 'pure play' because they incorporate the qualities and characteristics of play outlined in Chapter 1. The players have choice and control; activities involve imagination and pretence, with little direction or intervention from adults; there is no pressure for 'outcomes' unless these are chosen by the children for their own purposes. Children are free to choose an adult as co-player, or refer to an adult for help; they set their own rules and possibly goals (but the goals will reflect the purposes of the play, such as building an airport or organizing props). Children may choose structured play activities, such as playing a game with rules or making a model from a plan, or activities that are more 'work-like', such as reading a story, carrying out a scientific investigation, making a sculpture or doing a mathematics game on a computer. In documenting activities in a Reggio-inspired school Parnell (2011) reports that workfulness and playfulness were indistinguishable in the children's activities and projects, but were linked by their creativity and multi-modal representational skills.

In the structured play zone, adult-directed activities can engage children in playful ways with curriculum content: there may be some elements of imagination and open-endedness, but the children's choices will be limited. For example, a practitioner may ask children to act a story with puppets or create imaginary mathematical problems to be solved. Adult-directed activities can be a precursor to play, for example taking children on community visits (vet, supermarket, fire station) and trips (Forest School, farm, zoo, local park). Adult-directed activities include introducing new equipment and resources or demonstrating technical skills, such as how to use tools and materials safely. Practitioners provide the bridge between adult-directed and child-initiated activities through interacting with and observing children, then planning with them for enrichment, challenge and extension in play, based on their emergent and working theories.

Emergent and working theories

Based on socio-cultural perspectives, the concept of emergence reflects the idea that children are always being/becoming: they are always 'ready to learn' and do not wait for readiness to develop. Emergent/responsive pedagogical approaches incorporate children's cultural practices, meanings and purposes (Wood, 2010a). They pick up snippets or fragments of knowledge and understanding in their everyday activities and interactions with people, places and things around them. From these they create working theories, which are combinations of dispositions, knowledge, skills and attitudes (Carr et al., 2009). Working theories may not be fully developed or understood conceptually, but over time they become connected and integrated as children learn to use and apply them in different contexts. Young children may not be able to 'read' in the sense of decoding symbols, but act as if they are competent readers in their play, because they understand that literacy as a social practice is purposeful, meaningful and empowering.

In the context of Te Whāriki, working theories can include making sense of the natural world, social relationships and social concepts, and social rules and understanding (Hedges, Cullen and Jordan, 2011). Working theories may constitute the gradual connections or bridges between everyday concepts and the conscious realization of scientific concepts (the concepts within the subject disciplines) that children use to transform their everyday lives (Fleer, 2010: 4). In the context of play, working theories may include understanding rules and rituals for entering play, the role of imagination and pretence, and acting with imagined competence and knowledge. Carruthers and Worthington (2011) provide many examples of the ways in which children use multi-modal mathematical graphics for communicating meaning and gradually making connections between their everyday working theories and curriculum knowledge.

Figure 4.3   Emergent and working theories

Adult-directed activities are defined as 'work' when they are tightly controlled, with focused instructional strategies, no choice or flexibility for the children, and defined outcomes. These pedagogical characteristics are associated with 'drill and skill' routines, where children may be sedentary and have to conform to regulatory practices such as sitting still, putting up their hands to answer, not calling out, taking turns or waiting to answer. There remain concerns about such formal practices, especially when children are kept in sedentary activities for long periods of time (often up to 40 minutes). This is not to underestimate adult-directed activities, because children often derive much pleasure from engaging with adults and peers in structured activities such as gardening, cooking, science investigations, mathematical challenges. However, long periods of sedentary activities often result in practitioners struggling to manage behaviour, rather than supporting learning.

This model combines two pedagogical zones which acknowledge the benefits of adult-directed and child-initiated activities, allowing for elements of playfulness and playful learning in different approaches, as recommended by Walsh et al. (2011) and Broadhead and Burt (2012). The model uses the recursive cycle of curriculum planning as described in Figure 4.4.

This model ensures flexibility and responsiveness in curriculum planning and pedagogical interactions, by allowing a flow of information and activity across the pedagogical zones. In each of the zones, there are contrasting and complementary modes of adult–child involvement and co-constructive engagement. Practitioners can move across zones to respond to children's interests, make connections between children's goals and curriculum goals, and build on their working theories and funds of knowledge. Planning can be informed by the children's play and practitioners can inspire further play by making or responding to suggestions. This model reflects contemporary interpretations of Vygotsky's socio-cultural theories about the zone of proximal development (ZPD) (Figure 4.5).

Play creates zones for potential development in which children perform 'a head taller than themselves' (Vygotsky, 1978). Play enables children to perform who they are and who they are becoming (Holzman, 2009). From these perspectives, learning leads development because learners actively seek new experiences which are within and beyond their current capabilities, to enhance their skills, knowledge and capabilities. They develop emergent or working theories, connect funds of knowledge and produce new learning through motivation, engagement and participation, and new ways of seeing themselves. Learning/teaching are co-constructive processes rather than a one-way transmission from the adult/more knowledgeable other to the child/learner. In peer play learning/teaching processes may focus on play skills – imagining, pretending, joining in, sustaining involvement, being seen as a good player.

Planning the play/learning environment

- Planning access to resources indoors and outdoors; space available for activities such as large and small construction; specific areas/learning centres for messy play, creative arts, technology, literacy, science, etc.; daily routines and activities
- Planning towards curriculum aims and objectives in adult- and child-initiated activities, including possible or potential outcomes in play. Planning for short-, medium- and long-term goals (but with an emphasis on the first two)
- Planning adult-directed activities and organizing adults' roles in one-to-one and group focus activities which may be adult-directed (teaching specific skills and knowledge in the curriculum areas; circle time)
- Planning for play and child-initiated activities

Implementing plans

- Organizing adults' roles to support play, carry out observations, monitor several areas, engage responsively with children 'on demand'
- Allowing time for play to develop in complexity and challenge
- Building on previous activities and interests, working and playing alongside children

Observing children's activities (see Chapter 5)

- Assessing, documenting, reflecting and evaluating: understanding patterns of learning, interests, working theories, dispositions
- Identifying learning outcomes from adult- and child-initiated activities
- Documenting learning to provide a feedback loop into planning and communicate with parents/caregivers
- Using evidence from all adults in the setting to evaluate the quality and effectiveness of the curriculum (see Chapter 7)

Figure 4.4   Planning for integrated curriculum and pedagogical processes

Activity

Chose two or three areas of provision (indoors and outdoors). What is the potential for learning in each area? In what ways do children extend the potential for learning through their own actions (such as combining resources?)

Within an integrated model, the concept of balance between adult- and child-initiated activities is fluid: it may change on a day-to-day basis and over time as children's play skills and friendships develop. 'Balance' may vary according to children's interests, choices and preferences. For example, because children who have autistic spectrum disorder (ASD) have difficulties with social communication, social interaction and imagination, dramatic and socio-dramatic play may be challenging. They may choose activities that are more structured and may prefer routines and repetition to challenge. However, research indicates variations in choices and activities. In an ethnographic study of five

---

Vygotsky's theory of the zone of proximal development (ZPD)

In the ZPD the novice moves from other regulation

(interpsychological)

with

skilled assistance from more knowledgeable others

(peers and adults)

in

an enabling environment

with

appropriate materials, experiences and activities

combining

social, cultural and historical influences

acquiring

tools for thinking and learning, knowledge, skills, dispositions,

sense-making capacities

leading to

self-regulation (intrapsychological)

Figure 4.5   Play as zones for potential development

children, aged six to eight years, Kangas, Määttä and Uusiautti (2012) recorded different forms of lone play and group play, although in the latter, utterances tended to be short and interactions were directed towards action, for example in technological media-based play. Children with autism develop deep interests: in their home-based study of Rosie (aged 11), Goodley and Runswick-Cole (2012) document her interests and 'passion' for Greek myths and playful engagement with popular culture. The role of practitioners is to see the potential for playful learning in these interests. Drawing on post-structural theories about how 'disability' is framed in different contexts, Goodley and Runswick-Cole argue that 'disability' is constructed and intensified when there is a gap between the ways in which an individual child functions, the demands of society and of different environments. Macintyre (2001) provides skills-based observational checklists and a developmental record for children with additional or special educational needs. These are intended to enable practitioners to track children's learning and identify areas of difficulty, but as O'Brien (2010) notes, children may demonstrate skills and capabilities in their play which do not align neatly with developmental norms or checklists. For example, children who have physical disabilities will benefit from activities that build strength, stamina or flexibility to enable them to access large equipment or outdoor play. All children have the right to play; therefore the 'need' lies with the practitioners to provide opportunities for play as they consider the balance between adult-directed and child-initiated activities.

Processes that link playing, learning and teaching

There are three levels that can be used to understand the processes that link playing, learning and teaching. First, play contributes to learning in the cognitive, affective and psycho-motor domains of development (Figure 4.6).

At a second level, the cognitive processes and dispositions that link playing and learning are relevant across ages, phases and curriculum subjects, summarized in Figure 4.7. Positive dispositions lay the foundations for lifelong playing and learning, as we encounter new tools, technologies and new opportunities for work and leisure.

At a third level, children engage with the forms of knowledge that are defined as areas of learning, or the subject disciplines in pre-school and

---

Cognitive – all the skills and processes involved in learning, thinking and understanding:

- Self-concept and identity
- Language and communication skills
- Multi-modal representations
- Positive attitudes and dispositions towards learning
- Developing metacognitive skills and processes
- Mastery and control in learning
- Developing different forms of intelligence – visual/spatial, kinaesthetic, aesthetic and creative, musical/auditory, linguistic, logical/mathematical, interpersonal, intrapersonal, physical, scientific/technological, intuitive/spiritual, social/emotional
- Social and intellectual well-being

Affective – all the skills and processes involved in learning a repertoire of appropriate behaviours and interactions:

- Making relationships with peers and adults
- Reciprocal and responsive social interactions
- Expressing and controlling emotion
- Developing a sense of self
- Empathy and understanding the needs of others
- Emotional well-being

Psycho-motor – all aspects of physical development including:

- *Fine-motor skills* – use of hands, fingers, feet, hand/eye, hand/foot coordination
- *Gross-motor skills* – large body movements such as sitting, turning, twisting, balancing, controlled movement of head, trunk and limbs. Brain–body coordination, spatial awareness
- *Loco-motor skills* – large body movements involving travelling and an awareness of space such as crawling, running, climbing, walking, hopping, skipping, jumping
- Brain–body coordination, spatial and rhythmic awareness
- Learning about the body and gaining control of movement (body awareness); communicating and expressing ideas through movement
- Gaining confidence and competence in physical coordination
- Physical and emotional well-being

Figure 4.6   Domains of development

school curricula: literacy, mathematics, technology, science, the creative arts and humanities (knowledge and understanding of the world). The curriculum models outlined in Chapter 3 integrate the subject disciplines in different ways, but reflect the principle that children enjoy learning content knowledge, skills and concepts. Skilled practitioners understand the important pedagogical concept that young children can be introduced to the subject disciplines as long as these are presented in contextually appropriate and meaningful ways.

Cognitive processes and dispositions

- Attending, perceiving, observing, recognizing, discriminating, imitating, exploring, investigating, concentrating, memorizing, retaining, retrieving and recalling information, scanning for information, integrating knowledge and experience, categorization, classification, making connections and relationships
- Making intelligent use of past experience to formulate a plan of action, reflecting on action, noticing causes and effects, using metacognitive skills and strategies – awareness and conscious control of one's own learning
- Making and testing hypotheses, predicting, innovating, combining, recombining, reasoning, transferring knowledge and skills across contexts
- Making choices and decisions, constructing knowledge, creating sense and meaning from activities. Creating, recognizing and solving problems
- Communicating ideas, meaning, knowledge and understanding in multi-modal ways: written and spoken language, gestures, mime, signs, symbols, artefacts, drawings, plans, sculptures and so forth
- Creativity, imagination, flexibility, making novel connections across areas of learning and experience
- Convergent and divergent thinking, practice, repetition, rehearsal, consolidation, interpreting, retuning, accretion, mastery ('can-do' orientations to learning)
- Developing transferability, transferring knowledge and skills between similar and different contexts

Attitudes and dispositions

- Curiosity and interest; motivation – intrinsic and extrinsic; open-mindedness, flexibility, engagement, involvement, enthusiasm, originality, creativity, independence, interdependence; willingness to take risks; ability to struggle and cope with challenge and failure; perseverance, resilience, self-efficacy ('can-do' orientations)

Influences on learning

- Mood and feeling states; child and family health; home and community cultures and experiences; parental pressures and expectations; social skills; learning environments – home, school and community; quality of relationships between children, peers and adults; child's and family's orientations to education; socio-economic status

Dimensions of diversity

- Self-systems: self-concept, self-image, self-esteem, self-worth, self-efficacy

---

Figure 4.7   Processes that link play and learning

Play in and with zones of potential development

From a socio-cultural perspective, Bodrova (2008) questions whether play and academic skills are in tension or opposition. Many of the studies referred to in this book argue that play activities support and reveal children's learning in the subject disciplines, adding depth and detail to intended, possible and actual learning outcomes. Disciplined ways of knowing and understanding contribute to children's agency and growing mastery of their social and cultural worlds. Empowerment comes through being knowledgeable, skilful, confident and competent. By building on children's emergent and working theories practitioners can ensure that learning leads development. From this perspective, learning/teaching are co-constructive processes rather than a one-way transmission. However, these are not arguments for using play predominantly as a mode of curriculum delivery. The case study of Leanne's mathematical play illustrates these principles.

    Case study

Outdoor play: hopscotch

Leanne (aged four) has chosen the chalks to draw a hopscotch grid. She measures out the grid with her feet, and counts out loud to 15. She draws the grid, writes the numerals in each square and counts backwards from 15. She runs off to look for a bike, but soon returns. 'I've no vehicle to go on.' She continues to draw the grid, counting backwards and completing the numerals in the squares: '15, 14, 13, 12, 11, 10, 9, 8, 7, 6, 5, 4 3, 2, oh no, I need another one'. She draws another square. 'There, that's one. That's all there now.'

The grid is too small for her to play hopscotch, but the drawing and counting appear to be the main purposes of the activity. Leanne enjoys mathematics, and agency is evident in her confidence, self-regulation and competence in choosing and managing similar activities. In adult-directed activities she also enjoys the daily routines of counting and calculating how many children are staying for lunch/going home. She spontaneously copies numerals when recording her calculations and enjoys sticking her record on the notice board to 'remind the teachers'. Leanne has a good understanding of mathematics as a social practice and the contexts in which it can be used. In being a mathematician, she acts with competence and confidence and enjoys using and applying her knowledge for different purposes.

Activity

Consider this case study and reflect on how play enables Leanne to demonstrate her mathematical competence and funds of knowledge. Think about the different areas of provision and discuss what opportunities they afford for children to use and apply subject knowledge.

Play as an integrating process

Looking across these three levels, play acts as an integrating mechanism for internal and external motivations. Learning leads development because children are always in a state of readiness – trying out something that is just ahead of their existing competence. As children move along the play–work continuum, they combine their everyday knowledge, skills and understanding in different activities. As we have seen in Chapter 1, learning and development depend on internal cognitive structures that are complex in their origins and are intimately shaped by children's social and cultural experiences. The processes involved in playing and learning contribute to the architecture of the brain: rehearsal and practice may lead towards pruning and editing connections; exploration, repetition and revision help to create new connections and more complex neural networks. In play children develop exploratory as well as explanatory capabilities: they actively look for patterns, test hypotheses and seek explanations, leading to increased complexity in thinking, learning and understanding (Gopnik, Meltzoff and Kuhl, 1999). Play activities enable children to impose some structure or organization on a task, make sense of their experiences and engage in ongoing rehearsal of cognitive processes (Whitebread, 2010). As children develop playful minds, they make novel connections through combining materials, objects and ideas in creative ways, which indicates the importance of open-ended environments, materials and resources. Practitioners express concern that children's play is sometimes repetitive but closer examination often reveals subtle changes in play themes and patterns as children revise and extend what has previously been played at and played with. Where play is repetitive, practitioners can help to stimulate interests and ideas by offering new materials with creative potential.

Progression in learning is supported socially and collectively when children can connect their funds of knowledge across the play–work continuum. For example, exploration, enquiry and discovery are the building blocks of science; looking for patterns and relationships is fundamental to mathematics; history involves empathy and an informed imagination; technology and the creative arts involve planning skills as well as imagination, flexibility and spontaneity. Children's learning is enriched by the subject disciplines, including their distinctive methods of inquiry, skills, conceptual frameworks, and their powerful 'tools for use'. Playful orientations (playing with ideas, rules, relationships, materials) support learning within and beyond the subject disciplines.

The three levels of understanding playing, learning and teaching provide a framework for curriculum design, which takes into account breadth, balance, differentiation, inclusion, progression and continuity across phases. Planning the learning environment (indoors and outdoors) is integral to high quality provision.

The playing–learning environment

High quality environments support unity between playing, learning and teaching, and ensure access and inclusion for all children. Open access to materials and to indoor/outdoor spaces supports children's choices but some restrictions may be necessary (no sand and water near computers). Practitioners can either restrict or enable children's activities, as the following example shows.

 Case study

Restricting or enabling children's choices?

In a private nursery, the practitioners had a rotating pattern of resources that were put out for the children on a daily basis. The children could not choose other resources or move them from one area to another. After attending an in-service course, the leader of the setting realized that they were constraining children's choices and learning opportunities. She acknowledged her own 'obsession' with tidiness, and was concerned about the mess that would be created and how long it would take for the adults to tidy up. Following some staff development work on the concept of affordance, the practitioners decided to allow the children more freedom to choose their own resources and use them in different areas. They were taught to take responsibility for tidying up and taking care of the resources. The practitioners noticed that the children extended the affordance of the resources and their play repertoires. Combining small-world resources with large construction equipment extended the children's imaginative play, by using hollow blocks to build towns, zoos, parks, space ships and developing role play with Lego™ and Playmobil™ figures. Small construction equipment was used in many different ways in role-play activities: Cuisenaire rods became chips in the cafe; small blocks became gold and jewels in the pirate ship; play people were used in the sand and water trays in dramatic scenarios of flooding, burying, drowning, getting lost and being rescued. The practitioners identified the increased complexity of children's creativity and symbolization, through new opportunities for playing and learning.

Activity

Consider the potential for children's choices in your own setting or in a setting that you have experienced. What factors enabled or restricted children's choices? Could some of the restrictions be overcome and with what potential benefits for the children?

The concept of affordance

Carr (2000) uses the concept of *affordance* to describe the relationship between learners and the setting (including people, spaces, places and materials). Affordance refers to the:

- perceived and actual properties of resources in the environment (people, objects, artefacts and tools)
- how these are used (this links with the idea of *tools for use*)
- how these might be used (this links with the idea of *tools and use*)
- how these may help or hinder learning.

In the Reggio Emilia approach, the underpinning philosophy is that children should have access to 'high affordance', intelligent resources to provoke learning (Thornton and Brunton, 2007). The specialist practitioner (*atelierista*) acts as the more/differently knowledgeable other, who helps children learn how to use authentic 'tools of the trade' in, for example, design, architecture, planning and a wide range of arts and crafts (Parnell, 2011). Following a visit to Reggio Emilia settings, Parker (2001) describes how she used familiar resources in different ways to support children's learning. These resources afforded opportunities to extend children's thinking and creativity with representation and mark-making, and particularly their language: talking, exchanging ideas, reflecting on home experiences, making connections between areas of learning, and playing with words and concepts.

The concept of affordance aligns with the socio-cultural theories that highlight the role of the 'more (or differently) knowledgeable other', and the concept of 'scaffolding' as a learning/teaching approach.

The concept of scaffolding

The concept of scaffolding is a popular metaphor for describing adult–child and peer interactions that support learning. Developed from the socio-cultural theories of Vygotsky, contemporary interpretations include a focus on joint problem-solving, reciprocal engagement and inter-subjectivity. The focus can be on teaching children how to use the tools and resources in their home and school communities, and providing optimum levels of challenge as they become more experienced and expert in their use.

Scaffolding has been interpreted in different ways and can imply a one-to-one relationship in which the teacher, expert or more knowledgeable other remains in control of what is to be learned and how the teaching will be carried out (Smidt, 2006). This underpins a transmission model and is not consistent with Vygotsky's ideas about learning leading development, the importance of mastering tools and the relationship between intra- and inter-psychological processes. Tools are psychological (ways of thinking, learning, memorizing, being and becoming) as well as material (games, computers, loose parts). The interpretation given by Bruner, Jolly and Sylva (1976: 24) is that the critical function of scaffolding the learning task relates to the ways in which the 'tutor' (a peer or adult) makes it possible for the child to internalize external knowledge and convert it into a tool for conscious control (tools for use/tools and use, as described in Chapter 2). The child's own activities and dispositions help to co-construct the interactions through reciprocal engagement. Scaffolding includes collective and culturally situated activity. There are cultural scaffolds that reflect the knowledges valued in different communities; collective scaffolds that reflect how peers teach each other about their play cultures and practices; and there are individual scaffolds that reflect personal interests, dispositions and identities.

Learning environments that have high-affordance tools, artefacts and materials can scaffold children's skills and abilities as they become real-world mathematicians, designers, artists, technologists and scientists.

Practitioners can support these processes by:

- teaching children how to use tools safely, correctly and with increasing competence
- providing tools and resources that are varied, of good quality and are maintained or replaced regularly (blunt scissors cause frustration and young children are remarkably safe with glue guns and drills)
- creating time to play with resources so that children learn to use them in creative ways and create their own problems and challenges.

Practitioners can extend the affordance of activities and resources for children with special educational needs in order to support access and inclusion. Dycem mats in the role-play area and tabletop activities provide a secure, non-slip base. Some musical instruments can be hung on the wall so that children with physical difficulties can use them. Visual props and puppets can be used to dramatize stories and encourage role play and multi-modal communication. The following sections demonstrate how practitioners can create unity between playing, learning and teaching through curriculum planning. The examples are related to the areas of learning in curriculum frameworks and illustrate the connectedness of children's experiences and activities.

Playing with literacy

The links between play and literacy have become clearly established in research, with strong justifications for planning literacy-rich play environments that include information and computer technologies and children's popular cultures (Marsh, 2012; Wolfe and Flewitt, 2010). Children use a wide variety of literacy skills, concepts and behaviours in their play and show interest in, and knowledge of, the many functions and purposes of print. When engaging in playful literacy, children are not just pretending to read and write; they are acting as readers and writers. This is a fundamental distinction which enables children to see the meaning and relevance of such activities. In Vygotskian terms, they are performing ahead of their actual level of development: their emerging capabilities and working theories anticipate future/potential progress, as shown in the four examples of children's writing (Figure 4.8)

Socio-dramatic play creates contexts for literacy practices because of the connections between story-making and telling, pretence, imagination and symbolic activity. In the case study on *Where the Wild Things Are* that follows Figure 4.7, a Year 1/2 teacher created a continuum between adult- and child-initiated activities, using a co-constructive approach which incorporated plan–do–review (described in Chapter 3).

I am haling
a lavlee
Tim at ee   Tomum
The beach
Love   10 sant mar
From   tins road
  Aidan

telephone   messages

HellO mrs
Parja Son
I am at
the Park

rr989

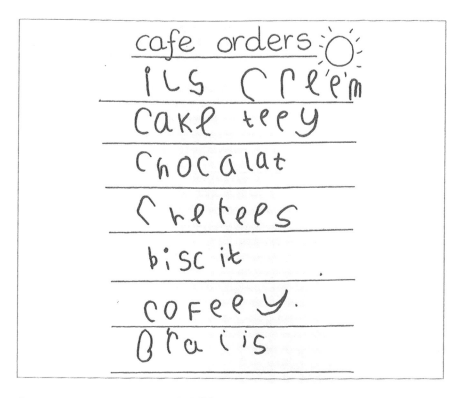

Figure 4.8   Four examples of children's writing

Case study

Where the Wild Things Are (Sendak, 1963)

Nicola decided to develop the children's role play through stories. The children chose *Where the Wild Things Are* by Maurice Sendak, which tells the story of how Max travelled to the island where the Wild Things lived, and enjoyed a wild rumpus party. The children planned to divide the role-play area into two sections – one for Max's house and one for the Wild Things' house. The children planned the area, making or bringing in props and resources. They made up names and characters for the Wild Things and represented their ideas through writing, drawing and painting. They extended the story by projecting themselves into different roles and scenarios and making up adventures. They talked and wrote about imagining the reaction of their parents to their absence, or what would happen if they brought home a Wild Thing to live with them. Salah described how he would teach him good manners and not to eat the cat. Jelika planned to make her own puppet, which she took home every day, and involved her family in writing stories and scripts that she shared with friends. One group made up a menu of Wild Things food and then planned a wild rumpus party, which involved many mathematical activities.

The children used geographical literacy: they drew maps of the land where the Wild Things live and the routes from their homes. They acted out their stories in the role-play area, which the teacher extended in dance and drama sessions (moving in the characters of the Wild Things, acting the wild rumpus). Materials and resources were always available in the writing corner and the children made books to record their stories, which became a shared resource for the class. As the children's interests developed, the teacher provided stories and poems about mythical creatures and lands, which reflected the multi-cultural community. Teacher-directed and child-initiated activities were integrated along a work–play continuum, with children having multi-modal opportunities for representing their ideas. The range of activities enabled all children to be included and to participate according to their abilities and interests.

This example demonstrates how role play can count as authorship because children co-construct play frames, scripts and texts, and understand the features of plot, characterization, sequencing, scripting and editing the dialogue and interactions to direct the course of the play. Such narratives interweave every-day funds of knowledge and imagination, drawing on their social and cultural knowledge. Play narratives can be inspired by stories (both fact and fiction) that adults tell to children, and stories that children invent.

As play progresses in complexity, children organize and structure their role play by sharing the creations of their imaginations through the following activities:

- Using story elements to structure their ideas
- Creating new worlds of meaning
- Communicating meanings explicitly to others
- Stimulating lateral thinking
- Playing out problems and possibilities
- Inventing, elaborating and extending themes
- Combining experience and creating knowledge
- Gaining new experiences
- Making connections between written and spoken language (Booth, 1994)

Linking play and literacy involves flexible planning, varied resources, engaging with children to value their activities, providing an appreciative audience, and supporting their developing skills and confidence. Marsh and Millard (2000) provide examples of how practitioners can use children's popular culture in the classroom, including comics, magazines, websites, computer games, television and films and popular music. They argue that comics can provide opportunities for supporting playful approaches to literacy, such as:

- analysing story structure
- understanding characters and how they change over time
- identifying playful uses of language such as puns, alliteration, assonance and onomatopoeia
- being critical of texts – identifying and challenging stereotypes
- making links between comics, websites, games and other 'spin-off' products.

Literacy is a social practice in which children can participate with increasing knowledge and competence. To ensure access and inclusion, books should incorporate different textures, noises that are activated by buttons, and communication systems such and Braille and Makaton. Information and computer technologies enable children to participate in structured games, as well as open-ended activities such as painting and drawing. Touch screens enable access to a wide variety of creative computer programs for children who have restricted mobility and movement.

Playing with numeracy

Children become mathematicians by participating in everyday practices in different contexts – home, community and school. Before they start school, many children demonstrate funds of mathematical knowledge and competences, but research shows that this richness and complexity is not always recognized in pre-school and school settings. Children invent their own strategies that enable them to solve a variety of addition and subtraction word problems, and develop their own systems for representing their calculations such as tallying and idiosyncratic notations (Carruthers and Worthington, 2011; Worthington, 2010). These strategies are evident in play contexts as children encounter problems and develop their own solutions.

Practitioners can build on children's invented strategies and create contexts in which they move through different stages of representation, learn the inter-relationships among ideas, and link their own informal strategies to the more formal symbol system of mathematics. From a socio-cultural perspective, Fleer (2010) argues that progression in learning happens when children make the links between everyday knowledge and scientific knowledge. But this is not the whole picture: as children become more experienced learners and players, they integrate cultural and social knowledge and, as the following example shows, demonstrate metacognitive awareness of the rules and conventions of play.

 Case study

Making a board game (Attfield, 1992: 85–87)

Linking everyday cultural and scientific knowledge, Jenny, Betty, Lee and Paul (aged between six and seven) decided to make a board game after discussion, initiated by the teacher, about the toyshop needing some more toys. The children went to a quiet area to discuss their ideas.

Betty:	Well we could have a race track.
Jenny:	Or we could have the first one to get home like a frog jumping on lily pads.
Lee:	In a jungle, in a jungle.
Jenny:	And you've got to go in your home in a jungle.
Betty:	Or you could have quite a big one and on one side have a race track. You've got to go round the race track the right way and then you get into the jungle.
Jenny:	Or what we could do is a little game for young children and put like sums on lily pads and they've got to add up the sums and they've got to jump on the next lily pad.
Lee:	I like Jenny's idea.

Paul:	It could be just like Jenny's but ... you could go along with a dice and a counter and you throw the dice and if you land on a square that's got writing on then you've got to do what it says.
Jenny:	That sounds good, like forfeits.
Betty:	I think Paul's is quite good cos it's fun.
Jenny:	What happens if it's really shy children, they might begin to cry with forfeits.
Paul:	We could have easy sums like 1 + 1.
Lee:	Easy peasy.
Jenny:	That's easy for you but not for little children.
Betty:	They put two fingers up and count with them.
Lee:	Why don't we have both ideas on it?
Betty and Paul:	Yes.
Jenny:	Why don't we have sums and forfeits? And what did you say about the jungle, Lee?

These children were skilled learners and communicators, using language for different purposes: explaining their ideas, reasoning, reflecting and sharing information. After presenting their ideas to the teacher, she extended their thinking by helping them to reflect on the design.

Teacher:	Before you start, so you've got it clear in your heads what the players can and what they can't do, there's something you need to do. How will the players know what to do?
Jenny:	Rules.
Teacher:	Right, you need some rules. How many people can play?

With further discussion and teacher participation the children clarified their ideas and decided to abbreviate the rules. In Jenny's list of rules (Figure 4.9) she is writing for a purpose: communicating the rules in order for the game to be successful. The children plan to have a pond at the end of the game as 'home' and hit another design problem.

(Continued)

(Continued)

Betty:	We'll stick the pond on the end here.
Lee:	Cut the pond about that big, turn it over and stick it here.
Jenny:	Yes, but what happens if the game breaks and that bit falls off and you can't find it and it isn't very nice in the game, you can't play it any more.
Lee:	Have it round here.
Betty:	Wait a minute. I think we should plan it before we draw.
Lee:	On this piece of paper. We don't have to put one enormous pond.
Jenny:	I know, we could have four ponds a different colour.
Paul:	Yes, red and blue.
Jenny:	The people with the green counters have to go to the green pond.
Betty:	Yes and red counters for the red pond, and yellow for the yellow pond and what's left?
Lee:	The blue one.

This case study illustrates several theoretical concepts that underpin an integrated approach to curriculum planning. The activity was initiated by the children and was scaffolded collectively: the teacher provided skilled assistance at the right moments, by responding to the problems identified by the children. Their metacognitive skills included joint recall of previous games (successful and unsuccessful), knowledge of social and cultural conventions in playing games, empathy and theories of mind (understanding the younger children's minds and feelings). The children's interests created spaces for enquiry which connected their individual and collective funds of knowledge from their home, community and educational experiences. Their working theories incorporated mathematical skills – they used mathematics as a psychological tool (knowing mathematical concepts, rules and conventions) and as a cultural tool (using and applying mathematics in a meaningful play context). Their play shows how older children develop structure, complexity and sophistication, with integration between processes and outcomes.

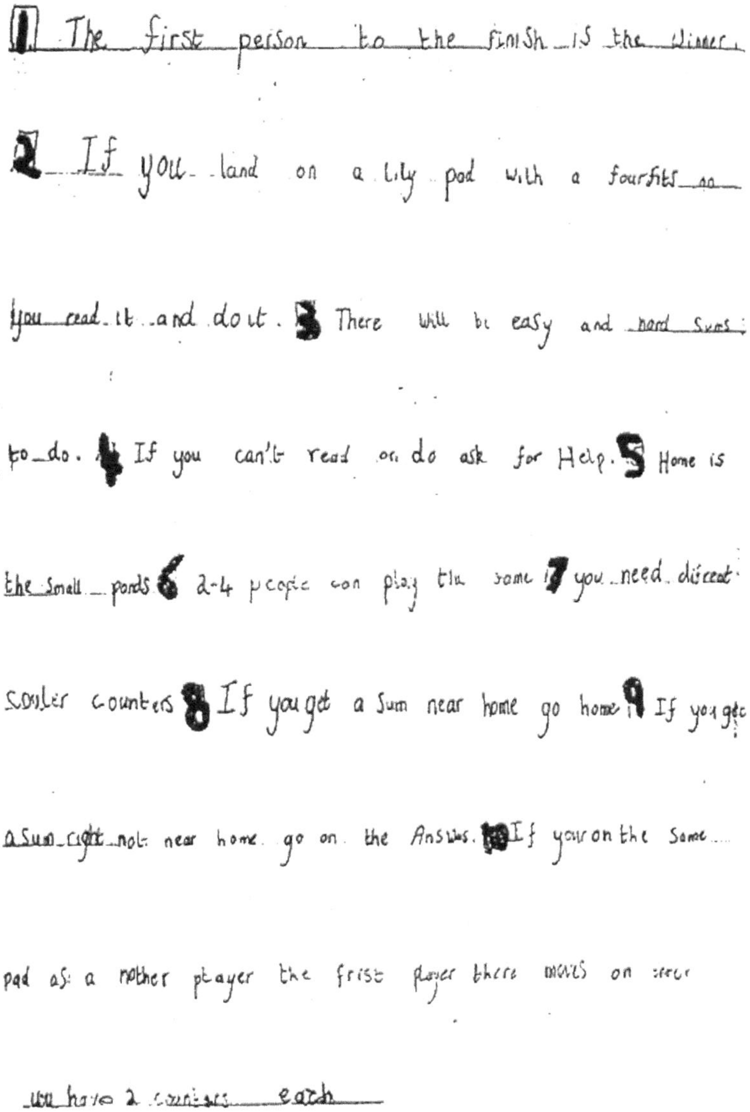

1. The first person to the finish is the winner.

2. If you land on a lily pod with a fourfits on

you read it and do it. 3. There will be easy and hard sums to do. 4. If you can't read or do ask for Help. 5. Home is

the small ponds 6. 2-4 people can play the same 7. you need diceat

souler counters 8. If you get a sum near home go home 9. If you get

a sum right not near home go on the Answs. 10. If your on the same

pad as a nother player the frist player there moves on rect

you have 2 counters each

Figure 4.9   Jenny's list of rules

Like all the subject disciplines, mathematics has its own discourse – ways of thinking, reasoning, problem-solving; methods, rules and procedures. Children's success in solving mathematical problems depends on their embeddedness in familiar, everyday practices and related discourses. Exploration and discovery are integral to children's mathematics (what does mathematics do?): the teaching of formal rules and routines enables children to think creatively within the discipline and solve problems independently and collaboratively (what can I do with mathematics?).

Play activities provide opportunities for integrating subject knowledge (scientific concepts) into everyday practices that children encounter in and out of school. The following examples show some creative pedagogical approaches that support continuity between work and play, and playful opportunities for learning.

 Case studies

Playing with ICT

Hannah had a degree in media studies: she was keen to use her skills in her mixed-age class (Reception, Years 1 and 2), and wanted to improve her provision for ICT. The project was animals; after a visit to a local farm, the children wanted to bring in their pets. She videotaped these visits to record the discussions, which often involved family members. The children were interested in the camera and wanted to learn how to use it. Hannah was surprised at how competent and responsible they were and supported their idea for a 'Pet News' programme. This involved turning the role-play area into a TV studio, with children acting as reporters and presenters. They wrote news scripts and carried out interviews with children and family members. The older children provided expert models of literacy and language for the younger children: there was much peer interaction and co-construction, as well as extension from Hannah. The children used a wide repertoire of social skills, including allocating roles, sharing ideas, organizing presentations and learning from each other about caring for pets.

Playing with history

Julie, a newly qualified teacher, worked in a small rural school, which was planning centenary celebrations that involved the whole school in the theme of the Victorians. Julie did some research in the school's old log books and discovered a story about a strict teacher who was rather harsh with the children, but also very poor at spelling. The records showed that the teacher was subsequently sacked for her spelling (but not for her harsh punishments of the children). This story provided the impetus for some teacher-directed role play with a Year 1 and 2 class. Julie prepared her children for the role play by telling them the story of the teacher, and asked the children to come dressed in costume for a Victorian school day. She hired a Victorian costume from a theatrical shop and began the day in role. She carried out hand and nail inspections and planned her lessons based on rote learning and drill, with the children using old slates and chalk. She wrote some incorrect spellings on the board, which the children spotted. The head teacher, also in role, came into the classroom and sacked Julie for her poor spellings. At this point some of the children were a little unsure about the distinction between reality and fantasy and wondered whether they would get their teacher back.

Planning for progression and continuity

While there is clear validation for play in the Foundation Stage, there remain concerns about the transition to more formal approaches in Reception and Year 1, and continuing problems with continuity in curriculum and pedagogical approaches. As discussed in Chapter 3, just as children become more skilled in their play, opportunities for play are restricted. Policy-makers assume that young children need more challenging work, whereas a consistent argument throughout this book is that children need more challenging play, along with opportunities to develop and plan some of their own activities and projects.

The examples given throughout this book indicate that children's play preferences and approaches to learning change alongside their developing skills, knowledge and dispositions. Hughes (2010) identifies the major developments beyond the pre-school phase. The child's thinking becomes more orderly, more structured and more logical. Play becomes more realistic and rule-oriented and reveals a developing need for order, a need for belonging and a need for industry. Children's play involves more cognitive activity (what can I do with this?) as opposed to sensory exploration and physical manipulation (what does this do?). Children build knowledge about play and become increasingly skilled as players. As their play skills develop, they use abstract forms of thinking: from Vygotsky's perspective (1978), action arises from ideas and symbols rather than from concrete objects.

In their need for order, children show increasing levels of competence in how they organize, structure and perform in their play-based activities (as shown in the case studies). They become less dependent on an adult for support because they are more confident about sharing ideas, allocating roles, taking risks and defining rules within a group. In terms of the need to belong, older children orientate towards peer-group affiliations and away from the family unit. Increasingly they construct their identities in relation to their peers and enjoy demonstrating skills, expertise and talents, which define their status:

the peer group is a major socializing agent in middle childhood. It is from their peers, rather than from their parents or teachers, that children learn about the culture of childhood. Peers teach a child quite effectively – and sometimes harshly – about social rules and the importance of obeying them. Peers establish a certain moral order that may differ somewhat from that established by adults. (Hughes, 2010: 134)

Hughes (2010) argues that the developing need for industry is apparent in children's work and play: they need to be productive, to achieve a sense of mastery and a feeling of accomplishment. These attitudes and dispositions are related to their social status because play can bring positive or negative validation from peers. In the gradual shift from play with objects to play that is more abstract, structured and rule-bound, children create imaginative roles. When older children engage in socio-dramatic play, they are more likely to spend time negotiating the plot and story line, defining roles and directing the action. They understand the purposes of play, which influences its content and complexity. They gradually progress from spontaneous, unconscious actions towards more structured, conscious actions: their play becomes more like a performance that incorporates well-rehearsed themes, rituals and actions, often drawn from everyday experiences, stories, films and popular culture.

Children enjoy games with rules such as board games and computer games where they compete against a partner or a character, and where success contributes to their self-esteem and status in their peer group. Children's identities become defined by their play competence and how this is perceived by their peers. Hobbies, collections and interests often structure their play: for example football cards define social status and can be used in bargaining and exchanges with their peers.

Children (and adults) do not outgrow play but their preferred modes change as they develop their skills and competences. Therefore, planning for progression in play (not just for progression in the curriculum) needs to be considered within and beyond the Foundation Stage. Children from the age of six to seven enjoy the chance to compete with adults and peers in rule-bound activities (such as board games), but may need assistance to master the rules and conventions. In constructive play, there are many opportunities for progression. Much construction equipment can be linked to computer programs and enables children to integrate playfulness and industriousness as they use their skills and knowledge to solve complex problems and extend their creativity and imagination. Children draw increasingly on disciplined ways of knowing and reasoning so that play continues to provide contexts for extending and integrating subject knowledge.

Children's patterns of development vary significantly, as do their play preferences and approaches to learning. Planning for progression should take into account differentiation for children with special educational needs so that play/learning environments, both indoors and outdoors, promote capabilities and potential.

By continuing the unity between playing, learning and teaching, opportunities for play can be extended beyond the pre-school years. To summarize, children need:

- time, space and varied, good-quality resources (these need not be expensive, because quality is related to the affordances of the resources)
- opportunities for challenge, extension, practice, mastery, consolidation and transferability
- the support of more or differently knowledgeable others – peers and adults
- opportunities to make connections between cultural funds of knowledge from home and community contexts, and to perceive relationships between areas of knowledge and experience
- opportunities to develop confidence and self-esteem, to play considerately with others and take care of their playing/learning environments
- to have their play valued, with some freedom and flexibility to plan their environments and activities.

The following chapter examines how practitioners can integrate play with their pedagogical framing, techniques and strategies.

Activity

In what ways do you aim to achieve balance between children's and adults' choices? How does 'balance' vary for children in your setting? Think about dimensions of diversity – age, culture, language, ethnicity, gender, special/additional needs.

Are there any constraints on achieving balance? In what ways might you overcome these?

Further reading

Carruthers, E. and Worthington, M. (2011) *Understanding Children's Mathematics: Beginnings in Play*, Maidenhead: Open University Press.

Goodley, D. and Runswick-Cole (2012) 'Reading Rosie: the postmodern disabled child', *Journal of Educational and Child Psychology*, 29 (2): 53–66.

Hedges, H. (2011b) 'Connecting "snippets of knowledge": teachers' understandings of the concept of working theories', *Early Years: An International Journal of Research and Practice*, 31 (3): 271–284.

Hedges, H. and Cullen, J. (2011) 'Participatory learning theories: a framework for early childhood pedagogy', *Early Child Development and Care*, 82 (7): 921–940.

Hedges, H., Cullen, J. and Jordan, B. (2011) 'Early years curriculum: funds of knowledge as a conceptual framework for children's interests', *Journal of Curriculum Studies*, 43 (2): 185–205.

Kuschner, D. (ed.) (2009) *From Children to Red Hatters®: Diverse Images and Issues of Play. Play and Culture Studies, Volume 8*, Lanham, MD: University Press of America.

Lifter, K., Mason, E.J. and Barton, E.E. (2011) 'Children's play: where we have been and where we could go', *Journal of Early Intervention*, 33 (4): 281–297, http://jei.sagepub.com/cgi/reprint/33/4/281.

Marsh, J. (2004) 'The techno-literacy practices of young children', *Journal of Early Childhood Research*, 2 (1): 51–66.

Marsh, J. (ed.) (2005) *Popular Culture, New Media and Digital Literacy in Early Childhood*, London: RoutledgeFalmer.

Saracho, O. (2012) *An Integrated Play-based Curriculum for Young Children*, New York: Routledge.

 To gain free access to specially selected SAGE journal articles related to key topics discussed in this book please visit: **www.sagepub.co.uk/wood**

CHAPTER 5

PLAY AND PEDAGOGY

The aims of this chapter are to:

- Identify some of the dilemmas and challenges of linking play and pedagogy
- Consider adults' roles in play, using the Model of Integrated Curriculum and Pedagogical Processes (Chapter 4)
- Understand children's cultures, perspectives and meanings, using the Juxtaposition Model (Broadhead and Burt, 2012)

  Case study

Mari: Asking the teacher to play

Mari, age three and a half, has been watching a group of children playing together, but does not have the skills or confidence to join in. She asks the teacher to join in her play:

Mari: You come on my bus. I'm the driver, you're the Mummy. (*Sits in driver's seat and pretends to drive the bus. Holds imaginary steering wheel and makes engine noises.*)

Teacher: Where shall we go?

Mari: Shall we go to Portland?

Teacher: Is that a long way?

Mari: Not very far, it's not very far. I've been there, we go to the zoo.

(Continued)

(Continued)

Teacher: That would be good. I'd love to go to the zoo. How long will it take to get there?

Mari: I don't know, it's not very far.

Teacher: Will it take a few minutes or half an hour?

Mari: What time is it? You look at your watch.

Teacher: Ten o' clock.

Mari: It's not very far. We go to see pandas. Oh we're there, it didn't take very long. You can come in as well.

Teacher: Do I have to pay any money to get in?

Mari: Yes.

Teacher: How much does it cost?

Mari: *(crossly)* I don't know, you've got the watch. (*Mari then turned away and lost interest in the play.*)

I have begun this chapter on play and pedagogy with an example of what not to do when playing alongside children. Mari had the confidence to approach the teacher as a play partner: she assigned roles, communicated the pretence and defined the action, showing abstract and symbolic thinking. Unfortunately the teacher was more concerned with a pedagogical gaze: eliciting Mari's concepts of space, time, distance and money. The barrage of closed questions left Mari cross and frustrated: the teacher failed to enter into role or into the spirit of the play. Based on my own experience, I always feel privileged when invited into children's play, but this demands great skill to play on children's, not the adult's terms.

Linking play and pedagogy: dilemmas and challenges

Contemporary perspectives on adults' roles in play reflect contrasting theoretical perspectives. Research shows that from birth, children are naturally active, curious and sociable, dispositions that typically provoke a synergistic response from knowledgeable others. Play is not a spontaneous, natural activity but a culturally influenced social practice: most children learn how to play with the support of skilled peers and adults, starting in their homes and communities with parents and siblings. Parents and carers are the child's first co-players and invest a great deal of time in being playful, teaching children how to play and teaching children through play (Gopnik, Meltzoff and Kuhl, 1999). Practitioners have contrasting roles in enriching and extending children's play. Structured approaches to play tutoring may be appropriate in some contexts for children with special educational needs, with English as an additional language and with diverse cultural backgrounds. Some children need support in accessing play activities and building play repertoires, but peers are also influential in these processes. Skilful practitioners nurture 'can-do' orientations to learning across the play–work continuum and help children to become master players (Jones and Reynolds, 1992). Children teach each other how to play and how to access the play cultures that they create in different spaces.

The vignette of Mari's play illustrates some of the dilemmas that practitioners face when considering their roles in play. In my work with teachers, they are often confident about creating play environments, but less so about their roles. Research evidence indicates that these concerns persist in the UK as practitioners strive to develop integrated approaches to play and pedagogy (Martlew, Stephen and Ellis, 2011; Walsh et al., 2011). In Reception classes, teachers tend to organize the play environment and control the play if it becomes too noisy and boisterous, while they get on with managing teacher-intensive group work (Rogers and Evans, 2008). In a collaborative research project focusing on adult–child interactions, Fisher and Wood (2012) document further pedagogical challenges, based on practitioners' analyses of videotaped episodes of practice and collaborative discussions. The practitioners identified episodes where they repeatedly interfered too much, as evidenced by questions and comments that were irrelevant to, and sometimes distracted children from, their thinking. Furthermore, they behaved as they do when leading an adult-focused activity: they tried to steer the conversation and frequently take it over (Fisher and Wood, 2012: 8).

Too much intervention can be as problematic as too little. Free play is seen as the private world of children, where they should have choice, ownership and control (Wood, 2013). Intervention may be intrusive, particularly where adults limit or change the direction of the play in ways not intended by the children. However, we have seen that some forms of play (especially dramatic and socio-dramatic) make high demands on children's cognitive and social competence. In the study by Bennett, Wood and Rogers (1997) the participating teachers identified many episodes of play where children would have benefited from adult involvement, because they did not always know how to enter a play situation or to solve problems as they arose. Play activities sometimes broke down because children lacked the skills of negotiation, cooperation or conflict resolution. The teachers realized that they made assumptions about children's abilities to share resources, include their peers and sustain friendships. In contrast, highly structured play, where resources and tools are used for specific purposes, allow little space for the child's creative thought and self-initiated activity. These tensions arise from ideological commitments to free play, theoretical justifications for a pedagogy of play and the ways in which play has been captured in policy sites.

Play as pedagogy in the EYFS

Validations for play as pedagogy have been influenced by Vygotsky's theories, but with contrasting interpretations of the ways in which these are used to inform policy and practice, ranging from instrumental to open-ended. The

Early Years Foundation Stage (DfE, 2012a) privileges planned and purposeful play, as described in Chapter 3. In the 'play as pedagogy' discourse play is a site for direct teaching and instruction and for 'sustained shared thinking' (SST). SST emerged as an analytical node in the EPPE and REPEY studies (Sylva et al., 2010), and is defined as:

> instances where two or more individuals 'work together' in an intellectual way to solve a problem, clarify a concept, evaluate activities or extend a narrative. (2010: 157)

SST has developed into a recommended form of pedagogy to support effective practice. Fleer (2010) draws substantially on SST in developing theories of play, learning and development, and proposes a dialectical model of conceptual play, which is informed by Vygotskian cultural–historical theories. In this model, the role of adults is to build on children's everyday working theories and emergent understanding:

> through analysing existing play activity (assessable moment) or critical moments in children's development (zones of proximal or potential development) and through using these opportunities to conceptually frame the play so that conceptual development is foregrounded and children think consciously about the concepts being privileged. (Fleer, 2010: 214)

Fleer argues that teachers should help children to build theoretical knowledge so that they learn scientific or academic concepts during play. Similar to SST, these activities result in new psychological formations and higher forms of cognition. Fleer emphasizes that conceptual play foregrounds cognition in unity with emotions and imagination, but the underpinning rationale for this model is to enable teachers to foreground conceptual learning in line with curriculum frameworks. These approaches highlight the ways in which Vygotskian theories have been aligned with dominant pedagogic discourses so that it may be adults and not children who create zones of proximal development. Holzman (2009) takes a different view and argues that the ZPD is not a zone at all, or a societal scaffold, but an activity of social creativity which is controlled by children for their own purposes. Play is revolutionary activity because children are constantly organizing and reorganizing roles, rules and relationships; they use psychological and material tools to create and invent new uses, ideas and meanings. As Henricks argues, human play should be understood as one of the special places for the conjuring of possibility (2009: 15). The conjuring of pedagogical goals through conceptual play is a far cry from these interpretations.

Although practitioners are enmeshed in the 'play as pedagogy' discourse, Martlew, Stephen and Ellis (2011) propose that a key challenge is to create more interactive and engaging pedagogical approaches. So what support can practitioners draw on in order to integrate playful pedagogies into their practice and sustain unity between playing, learning and teaching?

Practitioners' roles in play: pedagogical framing and strategies

The twin concepts of pedagogical framing and pedagogical strategies are helpful for thinking about how practitioners can support child- and adult-initiated play. *Pedagogical framing* involves making informed decisions about the structure and content of the curriculum (as described in Chapter 4). Pedagogical framing does not put the adult in control of everything that happens in the setting. Practitioners decide on the overall ethos of the setting, how the learning environment (both indoors and outdoors) will be organized, what resources will be available, where they will be located, how much choice children have, and whether materials and activities can be combined. Practitioners decide where and how they will spend their time and with what purposes. How the day, or session, is structured determines whether children have sufficient time to develop their play and build complexity.

Within this flexible structure, practitioners use a range of *pedagogical strategies* which support learning, such as working and playing alongside children, observing and assessing, introducing new themes and ideas, and demonstrating skills. Practitioners' roles include responding to children's intentions and meanings as well as allowing for unplanned developments so that the flow and spirit of play are enhanced rather than diverted to pedagogical ends. Their interactions can serve different purposes such as recognizing children's intentions and goals, responding to children's ideas, enabling them to use and apply their skills in different contexts, helping to sort out a dispute. Practitioners should tune in to the meanings that children communicate in their play and use these to inform the next cycle of planning.

Practitioners therefore need a dual perspective which involves understanding the meaning of play activities for children in the 'here and now' and deciding what are the next potential learning goals. In practice, this dual perspective may shift the emphasis towards responsive, short-term planning: children's interests and ideas can be the impetus for planning a project or informing adult-initiated activities, which helps to create the continuum between work and play, and between adult- and child-initiated activities. The immediate focus is helping children to achieve their learning goals, while the longer-term focus is on achieving the performance goals defined in curriculum frameworks such as the EYFS.

The concepts of pedagogical framing and strategies should not be seen as defining an adult-dominated approach to play as pedagogy, or privileging practitioners' plans and purposes. Broadhead and Burt (2012) outline the concepts of playful pedagogies and playful learning. They propose a 'Juxtaposition Model' which reflects adults' and children's intentions (Figure 5.1). This model respects children's cultural practices in which play has its own rules, rituals, routines and expectations, but incorporates potential for flexibility in practitioners' roles.

'Open-ended play': understanding playful pedagogies	'The whatever you want it to be place': revealing playful learning
A way for the adult to conceive of her/his own role in creating and sustaining an educational environment that is flexible enough to allow children's interests and experiences to emerge and develop; it also encompasses the adults' responsibilities in identifying, recording and planning for those interests in systematic but flexible ways and a responsibility to look for ways of extending those interests and relating them to the wider world in which the child is living and learning.	The environment and its possibilities as perceived and engaged with from the child's perspective. The child enters a space where anything is possible – whether a large or small space – and where they can engage alone or with others in exploring and exploiting that environment to match the images, plans and memories that emerge from their own minds and skills.
The early years setting becomes a space and place where adults nurture potential and push the boundaries of their personal understandings of playful learning and playful pedagogies.	The early years setting becomes a space and place where children explore their identity, potential and interests and push back the boundaries of personal possibility through playful engagement.

Figure 5.1   A Juxtaposition Model (Broadhead and Burt, 2012)

There is consistent agreement that the kinds of interactions used by adults should:

- support and respond to children's meanings and potential; enable children to elaborate and develop their interests
- support children's skills as players and learners; enrich the content of their play; challenge their own ideas and interests; and provide additional stimuli;
- plan for progression in play to develop complexity and challenge (more challenging play is as important as more challenging work).

Playful pedagogical approaches involve different modes of interaction and involvement, as described in the following sections.

1. Be a flexible planner

When developing playful pedagogical approaches to planning for child- and adult-initiated activities, a critical question is, which comes first? There is no right answer, because it depends on the flow of activities, the age and mix of the children, and dimensions of diversity. In a co-constructed, responsive curriculum (Chapter 4) practitioners pick up on children's interests, and introduce their own ideas and suggestions, which involves *sharing intentions and goals*, and planning for *intended and potential learning outcomes*. Children's *actual learning outcomes* are documented through observation and assessment (Chapter 7). Practitioners ensure that learning experiences relate to, and go beyond, the policy frameworks (teaching, learning and playing can occur 'outside the boxes'). Learning is *recursive* (children engage in a variety of activities) and *incremental* (learners become more skilled, knowledgeable, competent and confident). Gradually they extend their repertoires of participation: different play activities provide opportunities for revision, practice, challenge and extension, and the outcomes include mastery of learning and mastery of play. Planning for a pre-determined rolling programme of topics or themes is not appropriate for young children because their interests may change: some play themes last a few days, while others may span several weeks.

2. Be a skilled observer

Being a skilled observer is integral to all early childhood approaches and supports inclusive practices (Nutbrown and Clough, 2013). Observation enables practitioners to tune in to children's play activities, understand the meaning of play in their terms and identify learning potential, processes and outcomes. However, observing play raises questions about the rights of children to play without undue interference – play often becomes more interesting when it takes place outside the controlling pedagogical gaze of adults (Wood, 2013). Knowing when to stand back and allow the play to flow can be a conscious pedagogical decision. So what are the benefits of being a skilled observer?
Observation enables practitioners to:

- identify possible dangers and ensure safety; be alert to problems (children being excluded or bullied)
- ensure that all children receive attention
- be alert to new patterns and themes in play (for groups and individuals); identify ways to support and extend challenge (this may happen during or after the play)
- learn about individual children: their patterns of action and interaction, interests, agendas, dispositions, cultural approaches and play repertoires
- learn about children's meanings and intentions; show interest in, and value, children's play
- inform planning for individuals and for groups
- provide evidence to inform discussions about children's learning and play interests: share this with parents, carers and other professionals
- provide evidence for critical reflection and evaluation of the quality of the curriculum offered, make links between theory and practice, raise questions and propose solutions, support professional development.

Observation can be carried out in several ways. There is a difference between the spontaneous, ongoing observations that practitioners engage in on a daily basis, and planned, systematic observations for specific purposes. Practitioners decide:

- *who to observe*: individual child, group, adult–child or peer interactions
- *when to observe*: beginning, middle, end or whole play session
- *what to observe*: whether to follow a child through one/many activities or follow different children at one/many activities
- *how long to observe*: a general 'sweep' of the area or classroom is always useful to check on what is happening in a group or in the room. Time sampling is useful for focusing on a child/activity/routine at specific times and intervals
- *where to observe*: indoors or outdoors, in a specific area such as role play, construction, sand, water
- *how to observe*: participant or non-participant
- *how to record observations*: written notes, digital photographs or video, checklist.

Observation strategies vary according to whether practitioners want to learn more about:

- a particular child or group of children (for example, boys/girls, friendships, ability groups)
- the effectiveness of the curriculum, specific activities, routines, organization of the indoor and outdoor environments
- peer and adult–children interactions
- the value of doing observations as a research or professional development activity.

Becoming a skilled observer takes time and practice. Play-based observations should be planned into daily routines to capture the child as player/learner in the playing/learning context. *Participant observations* can be carried out during interactions with children in play activities. A notepad or checklist can be used to record information: for example, how a child enters a role-play area; communication and representation; what play choices, interests and themes are developing. Digital cameras are helpful for recording critical incidents. In participant observations, practitioners maintain an active role with the children, which is useful for tracking the effects of an interaction (for example, introducing new ideas or resources into the play), or noting teaching points to be planned into adult-directed activities. In *non-participant observations*, the practitioner is not involved in the activity, but will be placed nearby in order to record information. Using visual and digital methods captures information for subsequent reflection and discussion.

There are *ethical issues* involved in observing children (Palaiologou, 2012). All observations should be sensitive to the children: having an adult present, or nearby, can influence the flow and spirit of play. Children may play differently (in a more restrained or self-conscious way) or may not play at all. Observation can impose an unequal power relationship in that adults may intrude on aspects of play that children would prefer to remain private. Practitioners should also be mindful of how they use recorded information, particularly video and still images, and with whom the information is shared. On the positive side, children often enjoy looking at the images and may offer their perspectives on the activities. These methods are useful for observing children with special educational needs and disabilities, and sharing the information with parents and professional teams. Systematic observations can sensitize practitioners to the ways in which children master the cultural tools of school, home and society and how these are integrated in their play. These insights are integral to culturally sensitive assessment practices (Chapter 7).

3. Be a good listener

The meanings that children create in their open-ended play may not be visible to adults. A *pedagogy of listening* (Rinaldi, 2006) enables practitioners to respect and engage with children within their own frames of meanings and intentions. Respectful listening implies emotional engagement, taking an interest and being alert to children's multi-modal communication and representation. Understanding abstract and symbolic thinking can enable practitioners to understand children's playful minds and the ways in which they transform and communicate their ideas (Dowling, 2012).

Children use metacommunication in play – talking about their thinking, symbolization and actions. Referring back to Holzman's ideas (2009) about play as performance (Chapter 4) children speak and act 'as if' they are a different character, but at the same time communicate the action as they manage themselves and others. They step in and out of play in order to structure, define, negotiate and direct the sequence, which involves different modes of communication and perspective-taking. Children who are perceived as having poor listening skills in adult-directed activities often have good listening skills in play because they are more motivated and engaged. Children have to observe and listen carefully in order to filter the complex flow of information that helps to sustain the momentum and achieve the goals. For example, actions, gestures, language and symbols may be combined rapidly, with children clarifying the meaning of tools and symbols as the play progresses. Therefore 'listening to thought' aligns with observing how thought is expressed in multi-modal ways.

4. Be a good communicator

Being a skilful co-player involves understanding children's repertoires of communication: gestures, body language and facial expressions may be exaggerated as they help to signal 'this is play'. Children clarify the meaning of tools and symbols both verbally and physically. Adults need to pick up on these signals when they are invited into the play. Being a good communicator involves reciprocal engagement: commenting on action, using out-loud thinking, open-ended questioning and reasoning, pretending not to know, conveying emotions, are all useful strategies that enable practitioners go with the flow and spirit of the play. For children with special educational needs, visual and tactile modes of communication, including British Sign Language, Makaton or Braille, promote inclusion and playfulness. Being a playful communicator involves responding to children's ideas, language and actions, for example, by taking on a role, showing interest and becoming involved. 'Teachable moments' can be addressed within the play if appropriate, but should be carried into the next stage of curriculum planning to avoid taking over the play.

Given these complexities, it is difficult to apply SST as a form of pedagogy in children's play, because SST interactions are more typical in adult–child dyads or teacher-directed group activities, with clear instructional purposes based on verbal communication. These characteristics are not typical of children's collective activities in free play. In a small-scale study in German pre-schools, König (2009) develops categories for SST, to identify the key features of 'effective' pedagogic interactions in play. Through documenting classroom interaction processes between teachers and children during free play time, König's findings indicate that the teachers' interactions were highly adaptive and sensitive to the children, and mostly spontaneous, but the most frequently observed categories were 'initiate/follow-up', 'wait and listen' and 'react'. In contrast, the categories of 'motivate', 'expand/differentiate' and 'delegate/challenge' were observed infrequently (2009: 59), even though it might be assumed that this is where much pedagogic work would be necessary to advance children's learning. Similar findings are reported by Fisher and Wood (2012) and Martlew, Stephen and Ellis (2011), which suggests that caution is needed when policy frameworks rely on generalizing constructs of 'effective' pedagogic interactions to play, particularly in ways that intensify pedagogic regulation.

Ethnographic studies of play reveal the ways in which children construct their own pedagogical routines and interactions and how these operate, often around the rules which are formulated by the players (Broadhead and Burt, 2012; Cohen, 2009; Edmiston, 2008). Interactions make sense to children in the dynamic, imaginative flow of ideas and situated meanings, but may not be amenable to structured interactions such as SST, especially where children want to exclude adults or ignore rules (Wood, 2013). Wood and Cook (2009) report that two four-year-old boys, Callum and John, would often 'freeze' their play when an adult was nearby and always referred to the adults as 'trolls' (the themes of their play often centred on J.K. Rowling's Harry Potter stories, where the trolls were big and powerful, but a bit stupid and easily outwitted by the children). Children have their own ways of resisting the capture of play within a regulatory pedagogic gaze.

5. Being inspired by play

By communicating enthusiasm practitioners give powerful messages that what children are learning and doing in their play is as valuable as their 'work'. This is exemplified in the following case study.

 Case study

Box of delights

Jacqui Bamford, a Year 1 classroom assistant, worked with the class teacher to develop playful approaches to teaching literacy. They aimed to address the curriculum objectives (understanding fiction and poetry: stories with familiar settings, stories and rhymes with predictable and repeating patterns), but with more child-initiated activities and playful learning experiences which would:

- engage children's interest in reading and writing through child-initiated and practitioner-directed activities
- empower them to make choices and decisions
- encourage them to be creative and imaginative
- enable them to engage in multi-sensory and multi-modal ways (physical, cognitive, emotional and social)
- make connections across curriculum subjects.

Using traditional tales, the adult-led activities focused on discussing the plot, characters, sequence and setting for each tale. The children were organized into ability groups and each group was given three boxes to transform into miniature puppet theatres to represent the beginning, middle and end of their chosen tale. The practitioners provided assistance for the different stages of the task. The children planned and made the backdrops and scenery. Some characters were attached to the backdrop and some were made as puppets on sticks so that they that could be moved across the stage. The scenes were set for dramas to unfold.

(Continued)

(Continued)

The children were encouraged to retell the stories and make up their own versions. The adults suggested writing frames, such as retelling the story with changes to the plot and ending; writing letters (for example, from the wolf to the three little pigs); and writing scripts (for example, what Red Riding Hood said to her Mum when she got home). The boxes also provided a setting for the children to develop role play around the characters in the stories, making up dialogue, developing and changing the stories. Through their involvement as co-players the practitioners modelled taking on the role of a character, retelling the story and inviting questions from the children. In the role-play area in the classroom, links were made between adult-initiated activities and children's playful exploration of literacy and language such as:

- Goldilocks writing a letter of apology to the three bears
- taking telephone messages from Red Riding Hood to her mother
- writing a recipe for the Little Pink Pig to bake a peach tart
- directing their own play scripts and writing their own stories.

This example of a child's story, based on *Little Red Riding Hood*, shows detailed understanding of plot, sequence, script and structure:

First little red riding hode [hood] was plaing [playing] in her garden. Later on her mum calld [called] her can you take some flowers and some wine to your grandma yes she side [said]. So she got her basket and then she put her red coat on and out she went. Hello side [said] her grandma wut [what] is in ther [there] side [said] gran some wine and some flowers. Then she herd [heard] a noys [noise] saying let me out. Then she pulld [pulled] the cuther [cover] off grandma and then the big bad wolf gobard [gobbled] her up after that her dad heard a noys [noise] like a big fat wolf coming from grans house so he cwikly [quickly] ran ther and slamd [slammed] the door. Then her dad ran home and tolld [told] mum. Then mum ran to grandmas house and then thay [they] cried ther [their] eyes out. The end.

As a result of these integrated approaches, the performance goals for literacy were achieved, along with learning goals and dispositions such as enhanced confidence, competence and self-esteem. The Box of Delights project motivated children who were struggling with literacy because they could participate successfully in different ways and at different levels. The children read their own versions of the stories and performed some of their plays for the whole school.

The project integrated the subject areas across the curriculum:

- *Design and technology*: designing the boxes and puppets, physical and manipulative skills such as painting, joining, fixing, cutting out.
- *Maths*: scale and size of boxes and puppets; area; measurement; using mathematical language and concepts in storytelling.
- *Personal, social and emotional education*: collaboration, turn-taking, making group decisions; peer-group modelling and interaction; peer affiliation; empathy with characters in the stories; exploring moral issues through the stories; self-esteem.

Activity

Using the Juxtaposition Model (Broadhead and Burt, 2012), analyse the 'Box of Delights' project and consider the different contributions of the adults and the children. Think about the concepts of potential development and play as performance. In what ways do these concepts enable you to understand play from children's perspectives? How do these concepts enable you to understand your own pedagogical roles? You could analyse and share an example from your own practice for group discussion.

6. Supervise for safety, access and equal opportunities

Effective practitioners are always alert to the physical, social and emotional safety and well-being of the children. Children sometimes behave in ways that might be considered anti-social, especially where they play beyond the adult gaze. Play provides a means by which children come to understand and master the plural cultures of home, school and society. Because they play with powerful concepts such as strength and weakness, good and evil, justice and injustice, belonging and rejecting, they may convey negative or stereotypical attitudes. Discriminatory or abusive comments can occur: teasing can become bullying, for example, through name calling and exclusion. Play enables children to feel powerful in an adult-dominated world, which has both positive and negative possibilities: they may include and exclude others on the grounds of ethnicity, gender, physical appearance and capabilities. For example, Wood and Cook (2009) identified instances of individual children being excluded from play, and of boys excluding girls or disrupting their play. For older children, school playgrounds can provide ideal opportunities for bullying and aggression, especially where peer status involves challenging authority and establishing their place in the peer-group pecking order (Hughes, 2010). From a sociological perspective, Henricks (2009: 35) likens players to graffiti artists as they make their marks upon the walls of social order:

> The purpose of play, it seems, is to disturb and defile, to learn how far people can go before the world opposes and stops them.

If children's own borders and rules are transgressed, they will sometimes ask an adult to intervene to resolve a dispute. However, practitioners need to reflect on their reasons for 'managerial' interventions in play because what appear to be 'anti-social behaviours' may be part of the narrative. In Wood and Cook's (2009) study of gendered discourses and practices in play, the transcripts revealed some gender discrimination in adults' interventions. The boys' play was often energetic and boisterous, and sometimes strayed beyond the boundaries of the role-play area. Play themes included chasing, dying or being killed, rescuing and being rescued, naughty dogs, sharks and crocodiles. The teacher and classroom assistant were more likely to intervene in the noisy play of boys than in the quiet, domestic play of the girls, even where the latter was stereotypical and repetitive (cleaning, tidying and looking after the baby).

Activity

What managerial interventions are typical during play activities in your own setting? Are these interventions different according to the age/gender of the children?

All educational settings should be responsive to dimensions of social and cultural diversity (Chapter 3), and enable children to develop agency and competence to direct their own learning and development. Children's home and community cultures should be reflected in the resources of the school. This does not mean attending only to visible characteristics of cultural diversity such as food, festivals, clothing and rituals. Children should be able to co-construct learning with peers and adults through activities that integrate all aspects of their lives, including cultural approaches to learning and playing (see case studies in Chapter 8).

For children with special educational needs, ensuring access to play involves understanding their play repertoires and potential areas for development. For example, when Lina started in a nursery class, she was unwilling to speak; she had few social skills and did not know how to play. At home she was left alone for long periods of time, often in her cot and with little stimulation. She was passive and spent a long time sitting and watching the other children. The teacher and nursery nurse gradually encouraged Lina to participate in play and other activities. This involved some play tutoring, first in a one-to-one context and then gradually involving peers. Lina gradually learned to communicate and interact on her own initiative. It took about a year for her to learn the social skills for being a co-player, such as joining a game, taking on and staying in a role and being able to pretend. Children with additional or special educational needs often take small steps in their learning and playing, and take more time to build their skills and confidence, but this does not imply overly structured approaches in which children are singled out for play tutoring. O'Brien (2010) recommends naturalistic pedagogical strategies that occur in typical, everyday contexts, where adults see children as capable rather than needy and respect different approaches to learning and playing. By making appropriate adjustments, practitioners will ensure that children access indoor and outdoor play activities in their own ways and on their own terms.

Effective practitioners ensure that children feel emotionally safe. In Chapter 2 the benefits and challenges of superhero and rough-and-tumble play were discussed. Not all children engage in these forms of play, and practitioners struggle with the moral and ethical issues involved in play-fighting, especially where they strive to create a democratic, caring ethos in the setting. There are a variety of strategies to approach these issues:

- Set up discussions in which the children can state how they feel about superhero play and listen to each other's points of view.
- Explain the realities of weapons, aggression and violence in society. Preschool children are aware of conflict, violence and war from the media, which can form the basis of discussions.
- Establish what the problems are and where they are occurring – indoors and/or outdoors – and what behaviours are impacting on other children.
- Encourage the children to explore solutions to the problems.
- Engage the children in making decisions about what happens in the classroom and playground (see Chapter 6). This can be done during circle time; if the problem is more serious, dedicated time may need to be allocated.
- Implement the agreed solutions and monitor their effectiveness. Be prepared to support the children by teaching conflict-resolution strategies, developing awareness of their behaviour and sensitivity to how it affects others.
- Observe the play and discuss among the team whether there are concerns with what roles children are performing and what issues of equity and access arise – such as inclusion and exclusion, who exercises power, gender roles and relations.

7. Be a sensitive co-player

Jones and Reynolds (1992) argue that practitioners can help children to become master players. Therefore appropriate pedagogical strategies can support learning and development but should not be intrusive or domineering. Again this is a question of balance. In a predominantly *laissez-faire* environment children may miss out on adult support and guidance. In an over-structured environment, children will not learn to be resourceful or creative. Figure 5.2 lists some appropriate pedagogical strategies, with the guiding principle that all interactions should be sensitive to the child and to the play context. (It is also interesting to note that children use these skills and strategies in their peer play.)

---

observing, listening, being playful, using humour, questioning, responding to children's initiatives and directions, communicating, demonstrating, modelling, encouraging, praising, advising, guiding, suggesting, challenging, adopting a role, staying in role, playing on the children's terms, instructing, imparting new knowledge, prompting, reminding, extending, structuring, re-structuring, transforming, directing, re-directing, managing, monitoring, assessing, diagnosing

---

Figure 5.2   Pedagogical skills and strategies

It takes time for practitioners to learn when and how to engage with children in their play, how to adapt to the play context, what interactions to use in different situations and when to withdraw. Critical questions are listed in Figure 5.3:

- *When to be involved*? What assumptions does the practitioner hold – beliefs about learning, about play, about the child?
- *How to be involved*? What are the goals for the pedagogy? Whose goals are paramount? What is the purpose of the play and of the interaction?
- *With what intentions*? What are the outcomes of the pedagogical interaction for the child and for the practitioner?

Figure 5.3   Pedagogical interactions: when, how and why?

When to be involved

Many of the examples in this book show that children who are used to playful adults will readily ask them for support to solve a problem or dispute or be a co-player. With experience, children learn to identify what support they need, which shapes the interaction with adults. Skilled practitioners carry a memory bank of children's patterns and approaches to learning and playing: they can remind children of previous themes and activities, help them to extend their skills and knowledge, and make connections between areas of learning and experience. Because practitioners need to be alert to safety, they can intervene to avert problems or prevent accidents. The intervention may provide opportunities to help children to recognize the problem and learn conflict resolution or safety strategies, which they can use in other situations.

How to be involved

Practitioners adopt a variety of pedagogical roles and strategies. In child-initiated play, standing back and letting the play happen is a conscious pedagogical decision. Being a co-player should involve going with the flow of children's goals and intentions and not hijacking their thinking towards curriculum goals. Modelling is a useful pedagogical strategy because creative imitation is a powerful spur to learning in early childhood. Bruner (1991) calls this 'observational learning' and argues that it is much more complex than the term 'imitation' implies, because children are not merely 'copying' but creating their own versions of their own performances. The practitioner can actively model skills, strategies, attitudes, behaviours and learning processes by using out-loud thinking, questioning, reflection on action and feelings. This assists the process of guided reinvention in which children construct knowledge and creatively use tools for thinking and learning in their play.

Direct instruction can be skills-based and can be appropriate as long as practitioners tune their interactions with the child's interests and requests. Direct instruction may involve joint problem-solving strategies such as out-loud thinking, talking through the task, modelling skills, then checking how the child is doing. These strategies are appropriate when children need support with using tools and materials, and creating new uses and combinations. For example, in constructive play many kits are quite sophisticated and need specialized manipulative skills, technical language and understanding of concepts related to design and technology. By teaching relevant skills, concepts and knowledge, practitioners can support creativity, invention and innovation. With experience, children extend their skills in planning, designing and building, which reflect many of the processes adults use in authentic contexts. As they become more confident in problem-creating and problem-solving, they build their identities as successful players and learners, as the following case study shows.

        Case study

Art gallery

Joe, Helen, Katy and Martin (aged six to seven) are discussing their ideas for creating an art gallery and want to put up black wallpaper to display the paintings (Attfield, 1992: 66–68). They have already stripped the

(Continued)

(Continued)

walls, removed the staples and are talking about the door that is old and has several holes in it:

Joe: We could take the old door off and make a new one.

Martin: We can't do that Joe cos if we cut the old door off we won't be able to get a new one back on.

Joe: We'll put some cardboard down cos there's holes in it.

Katy: Mmm, yes, it would be stronger then.

Helen: Yes, you can put string through the holes so it will open.

Katy: There's too many holes to do that. You'll get tangled.

Joe: There's a big hole in the actual door bit. You could put a door handle there.

Martin: I know how to make a door handle. You could get those screws like you use on a bath. You could get a screw and screw it on through the other side then you'd have a handle.

Katy: There's a lot of little holes. We could cover those up with cardboard and paint over them and the big hole could be where the handle is.

Helen: Yes, and you could use string to put round the handle and it would hold the door back like the hall door. (*After this task was completed successfully, the children moved on to papering the walls.*)

Joe: We'll have to cut the shape there (*where the paper overlaps the door*), it's too big.

Teacher: Don't cut it. Instead of cutting it fold the paper under and staple it there. That will make the edges stronger than a cut edge and the edges will be smoother. If it's too big you can always fold it, if it's too small you can't make it fit.

Katy goes to stick the wallpaper up in the middle of the wall. The teacher shows her how to place it up against the corner and outside edge. Joe starts to measure the size of the paper needed by placing the one-metre ruler down the centre of the paper. The teacher shows them how to measure the outside edge. The children have measured to find the size of the wallpaper they have to cut from a roll. They measure and cut one piece and stick it on. They need three whole pieces the same size for each wall.

Martin: Start at the next bit now. It's 1 metre 55 centimetres isn't it?

Teacher: That's right. How many pieces do you think we'll need for this wall?

Helen: Two.

Joe: Um, three.

Teacher: Yes, three I think, you'll need the same piece of paper how many times?

Joe and Helen: Three.

Teacher: How about this time then we cut the next piece, then roll out the wallpaper again and lay this piece on the top, mark it and cut it to the right size?

Martin: That'll be quicker.

The children are measuring another piece of wallpaper that has to be 1 m 20 cm long. They lay down a one-metre ruler and get another one to continue measuring. The end of the second ruler gets caught on a nearby cupboard.

Teacher: Do you think we need to measure the next bit with the metre ruler? We've got 1 metre, we need our paper to be how much longer?

Katy: 1 metre 20 centimetres we said –

Joe: Twenty more.

Teacher: Yes we only need twenty centimetres more. Would it be easier to use a smaller ruler? It has centimetres the same as the metre ruler.

Helen: They'd be the same wouldn't they? (*doubtfully*)

Teacher: Let's try.

Helen picks up the metre ruler and checks to see if her measuring is the same as the teacher's and then uses the smaller ruler.

(Continued)

(Continued)

Joe: It will be the same, Helen.

Teacher: It's always a good idea to check if you're not sure.

The involvement of the teacher as mediator promotes the development of new skills, using the children's existing knowledge. This activity also demonstrates the continuum between play and work: it was child-initiated and enabled the children to follow their intentions, by transforming ideas, materials and their environment. The teacher acted as a more knowledgeable other by demonstrating skills, using out-loud thinking and prompting the children's metacognitive activity. She was responsive but not intrusive and did not take over the task or the children's thinking. The children assisted each other: they brought enthusiasm and motivation to this task because they knew that their peers were creating works of art to hang in the gallery. Play provided an integrating mechanism for their knowledge, experience and social skills and prompted further learning.

Different types of play require different forms of interaction. In order to be a successful co-player, practitioners need to observe the play and understand what the children are playing with and playing at. They need to engage on children's terms, which involves being sensitive to the themes, rules, conventions, groupings, play partners, preferences and their use of space and resources. The following example shows how a teacher engaged successfully with Jenny in her role play (Attfield, 1992).

    Case study

Ow, ow, my poor ankle

Jenny (age seven years two months) is playing as a nurse in the role-play area which was a health centre. The teacher registered as a patient with an injured ankle:

Adult: Ow, ow, my poor ankle, what shall I do nurse?

Jenny: I think that you should stay in for two days and calm yourself down and stop rubbing it.

Adult: Is it broken nurse? Can I sit down? Ow, ow.

Jenny: Yes, you'd better sit here. I'll go and get the X-ray . . . no you have sprained it. I'm going to bandage it before I water it.

Adult: You're going to water my ankle? Why are you going to water my ankle, nurse, it's not a flower?

Jenny: No I'm going to dab it and then I'll put this bandage on. (*Begins to put the bandage on over the adult's shoe.*)

Adult: Ow, ow. Do you think I should take my shoe off?

Jenny: Oh yes. Nurse come and help me (*to another child*) . . . you hold the safety pin and give it to me when I've done this.

Adult: Can I walk on my ankle or should I rest it?

Jenny: I'll give you some crutches and when you get home you've got to put it on a stool or table or something soft.

Adult: Do I have to take any tablets for the pain?

Jenny: I'll give you a 'scription (*asks for help with writing here*).

(*Later – to another child who has had a car crash.*)

Jenny: I'll put the bandage on your arm and you must never put it on the table like that or it'll get even more bad and you can still play football but try not to hit anyone with your hand and be careful you don't cut it when you're washing up. There now, come back in two weeks.

Although the dominant mode of interaction is based on adult questioning, these are at least open-ended and contextually relevant. Jenny demonstrates her skills, knowledge and understanding, including her confidence to organize her peers, her caring role as the nurse, the ability to stay in role and sustain pretence, and her enjoyment and motivation. The teacher noted that Jenny wanted to know more about X-rays and bones and how plaster is used to set broken bones.

Practitioners can find it challenging to go with the flow of children's ideas and interests and follow unplanned developments. Reflecting on the socio-cultural theories outlined in Chapters 3 and 4, practitioners can be involved in role play where the motives arise from the children and they carry out most of the negotiation and management. The adult should respond to the children's initiatives and not take over the play to the extent that it loses its spontaneity and becomes adult-led rather than child-led. They should also know when to withdraw and let the children get on with their play. As the following case study shows, these approaches require practitioners to think differently about power relationships and how they respond when children subvert or challenge classroom rules.

 Case study

Cops, robbers and guard dogs

In the study by Bennett, Wood and Rogers (1997), one Reception teacher (Gina) set up a role-play area as a shop: the children made and priced the goods and she anticipated that they would use their mathematical knowledge in buying and selling. However, the children were more interested in playing cops, robbers and guard dogs, and their play was often boisterous, noisy and disruptive. Gina believed that children should have opportunities for free play, without adult intervention. However, she acknowledged that some intervention was necessary in order to understand and support this play. Rather than banning the cops, robbers and dogs, she nurtured the children's interests during teacher-initiated activities by encouraging them to write story boards and cartoons of play scenarios, which they subsequently developed in the role-play area. On reflection, it is hardly surprising that the children wanted to enliven their shop play with cops, robbers and guard dogs: their play was much more dramatic and emotionally engaging than merely buying and selling goods. They incorporated funds of knowledge from television programmes, films and cartoons in developing their play scripts and scenarios.

8. Be a researcher

Effective practitioners are good researchers: they are alert to children's characters, dispositions and approaches to learning. They have an enquiry-based approach to improving the quality of their provision and engaging in professional development in ways that transcend narrow policy directives. Children are complex, fascinating and often enigmatic. Working and playing with children raises many questions and challenges which are not always solved in the everyday flow of activities. Being a researcher helps practitioners to become critically reflective, thoughtful and analytical, and to foreground concerns with equity and social justice in their practice (Genishi and Goodwin, 2008; Yelland, 2010). Many of the examples in this book are drawn from small-scale research studies carried out by teachers and practitioners on advanced study modules.

They often set out with burning issues, tensions between their beliefs and the demands of policy frameworks, and a genuine desire to better understand playing, learning and teaching. Studies that have engaged practitioners as researchers in their own practice have reported positive benefits:

- Taking time to stand back and think critically about what is happening in the setting
- Learning skills and strategies for observing, recording and analysing their practice
- Learning collaboratively in a community of practice
- Reflecting on their evidence and generating strategies for improvement (sometimes at whole-school level)
- Feeling empowered by developing their skills and knowledge
- Being able to challenge taken-for-granted assumptions and policy prescriptions
- Changing their theories and/or practices (Broadhead, 2004; Carr et al., 2009; Edwards and Nuttall, 2009; Fisher and Wood, 2012)

Practitioners may also learn about how their roles and practices are perceived by children. The following case study, recorded by Charlotte Rowland, provides insights into how children adapt to classroom cultures, how they set their own goals and interests, how they construct their play themes, and what forms of power and control are circulating between adults and children and between children.

 Case study

Be quiet and listen!

Context: Helen (aged five years and four months) has previously been observed playing schools on her own with imaginary pupils. Helen asked the teacher if she could play schools. She then collected the items she needed and asked two children to play with her – Khalid and Ella. Abi joined in briefly towards the end.

Helen: Do you wanna play schools?

Ella: Okay can I be Mrs F?

Khalid: I wanna be Miss R

Helen: No I'm Miss R!

Khalid: Ohhh! But . . .

(Continued)

(Continued)

Helen: We could take turns.

Khalid: Okay. (*Helen sits on chair and picks up pen and paper.*)

Helen: It's register time so you need to use your ears to listen.

Ella: I'm Mrs F.

Khalid: When's it my turn?

Helen: Be quiet and listen!

Khalid: Yes Miss R.

Helen: Now we will start, 'Good morning Khalid.'

Khalid: Good morning, Miss R.

Helen: Now we will do an activity together on the carpet. I want you to listen very, very carefully.

Khalid: But who's going to be special helper?

Helen: Oh you can be!

Ella: I'm still Mrs F.

Helen: Yes I know.

Khalid: Can I have my turn soon?

Helen: Mrs F please would you sit with Khalid because he keeps talking and he should be listening.

Ella: (*moves next to Khalid*) Yes, be quiet Khalid and listen to Miss R!

Helen: Now let's start. We are going to do some counting this morning. (*Abi comes to join play.*)

Abi: Can I play? I wanna be Miss R.

Khalid: It's my turn next.

Helen: You be you, Abi.

Abi: No I'll play later.

Helen: Let's get on now shall we, listen Khalid! We'll count to twenty.

All: Count to twenty together. (*Wind chimes – tidy up time*)

Khalid: I didn't get a turn!

Helen: You can next time.

Activity

How do you interpret this episode? What does it reveal about children's understanding of pedagogical routines? Helen has clearly internalized a 'naughty boys' discourse' as she keeps Khalid in check. What can children's play tell us about power relationships between teachers and pupils and the rules of classroom discourse?

Observations also have practical and theoretical value, in that they can enable the practitioner-as-researcher to understand children's play cultures and their systems of shared meanings (as discussed in Chapters 3 and 4). Being a researcher can also inform the processes of assessment and evaluation, which are explored in Chapter 7.

So can we define a pedagogy of play?

This chapter has shown that the practitioner's role in play can be multi-faceted and multi-layered. The guiding principle is that adult interactions should tune in to what is happening and should respect the flow and spirit of the play. Both adult- and child-initiated play can provide ideas and interests that can be developed and extended in other activities, including specific interventions to support skills and conceptual learning. This is not to claim that play is only valuable when it pays into learning outcomes and performance goals in the curriculum. Spontaneous, playful interactions can occur in adult-directed activities, just as children can be deeply engrossed and 'workful' in their play. However, play cannot be justified only as a pedagogical means for delivering performance goals in the curriculum areas of learning. Play is incredibly varied and complex and must be valued for what it means to children. Outside of the pedagogical gaze, play is done for the sake of play; children play to become better at play; mastery of play involves learning, but what is learned must be of direct use to the players. Whether play is of any use or interest to adults is beyond the concern of players.

Activity

What are parents' perceptions of play in your setting? In what ways do you communicate with parents about home-based play activities? Do you think there are cultural variations in children's choices and approaches to play? How can you use knowledge about social and cultural diversities to enrich your play provision?

Further reading

Dowling, M. (2012) *Young Children's Thinking*, London: Sage.

Nutbrown, C. and Clough, P. (2013) *Inclusion in the Early Years*, London: Sage.

Palaiologou, I. (2012) *Child Observation for the Early Years*, London: Sage.

Singh, A. and Gupta, D. (2012) 'Contexts of childhood and play: exploring parental perceptions', *Childhood*, 19 (2): 235–250, http://chd.sagepub.com/cgi/reprint/19/2/235.

Yelland, N. (ed.) (2010) *Contemporary Perspectives on Early Childhood Education*, Maidenhead: Open University Press.

 To gain free access to specially selected SAGE journal articles related to key topics discussed in this book please visit: **www.sagepub.co.uk/wood**

CHAPTER 6

PLAY AND LEARNING IN OUTDOOR ENVIRONMENTS

The aims of this chapter are to:

- Understand the principles of playing and learning in outdoor environments
- Know how to plan for inclusion, access and diversity
- Develop strategies for working with children and parents/caregivers to manage risks and hazards
- Know how to plan for play in outdoor environments, including progression and continuity with Key Stages 1 and 2

This chapter continues the theme of creating unity between playing, learning and teaching in the outdoor environment. The strategies of curriculum planning, organization and assessment outlined in Chapters 4, 5 and 7 apply equally to outdoor spaces, along with the guidance on pedagogical strategies which incorporate flexibility, observing and listening to children, and responding to their cues, invitations and enquiries. Activities should enable the children's own goals to emerge through their choices and interests, and can incorporate broad curriculum goals. The ways in which the environment is designed will make learning inevitable, because children will be engaged, involved, challenged and inspired by the possibilities offered. Taking risks and creating challenges enables children to develop mastery of play, of their environments and of themselves.

Another layer of pedagogical responsibility is added in the outdoor environment because it is in these spaces that practitioners need to exercise even more courage, trust and faith in the children and in their own decisions. This is because outdoor spaces extend affordances for choices and activities and the potential for risky play. This is not an argument for constraining children's choices, but it is an argument for attending to their understanding of risk and hazards and taking appropriate measures for health and safety. Helen Tovey has, on many occasions, made the powerful statement that 'The risk is that there is no risk.' This principle underpins this chapter.

The principles of playing and learning in outdoor environments

The last 20 years have seen a resurgence of interest in outdoor environments and I now see many settings which incorporate mini Forest Schools, natural/wildlife areas, willow structures, eco-friendly gardens including poly tunnels for growing edible plants, open-ended spaces for loose parts play, as well as the traditional fixed play equipment, sand and water. I see totem poles, sculpture trails, hay bales, rope swings and bridges, shaded spaces for 'chatting and chilling' (as a sign in one school stated), sensory spaces and musical walls. In response to requests from the children, one school has an outdoor wardrobe (large garden shed) for dressing-up clothes, with a stage nearby for impromptu performances of talent shows. The shed also contains groundsheets, waterproofs and wellingtons for 'all weather' activities. These developments have been facilitated by a policy focus on outdoor play, along with capital funding. But at the same time, many teachers report that outdoor play has become even more of a safety valve for children because there is so much sedentary activity during lessons. Outdoor play is important in its own right, not as a safety valve for the effects of inappropriate pedagogies.

As we have seen in Chapter 3 play occupies an ambiguous position in policy frameworks, because of the ways in which its value and purposes have been captured in policy sites. This is also true of outdoor play, which is credited with developing children's mental and physical well-being, fighting against childhood obesity and counterbalancing sedentary, computer-centred childhoods. Outdoor play is where we see some overlap between play in pre-school and school settings, and Playwork professionals. The work of the four UK Play Councils (Play England, Play Scotland, Playboard Northern Ireland and Play Wales) has been highly influential in advocating for play, securing funding, developing Playwork as a profession and developing play areas in schools and communities. However, as Tovey (2008) argues, Playwork has also been captured in policy sites and reflects these dominant discourses: the photographs in glossy policy documents show children playing happily, but often on fixed equipment in areas with boundary fences. These play spaces are a great improvement in terms of their size, design and variety of equipment, which reflect appropriate concerns with health and safety, but can often sustain the concept of adult surveillance and regulation of play. Recent approaches to outdoor play spaces incorporate flexible resources (such as loose parts), scope for dens and secret spaces, bare soil patches for digging and making mud and fixed structures that are open-ended and challenging (Broadhead and Burt, 2012). Beyond dominant policy discourses, outdoor play remains valuable for what players do in and with play, for their mastery of play for its own sake and for the mastery of their physical, social and emotional competence. Outdoor environments are not only about play: practitioners can develop education for conservation and sustainability by providing positive connections with nature and encouraging environmentally responsible attitudes (Wilson, 2012).

There has also been a steady growth in research with children and adults in outdoor environments. The focus is not exclusively on play, but on the range of activities in which children engage. Thus the Model of Integrated Curriculum and Pedagogical Approaches (Chapters 4 and 5) and the Juxtaposition Model (Broadhead and Burt, 2012) incorporate how children use outdoor spaces for different purposes: working, playing, learning and 'chatting and chilling'.

The concept of affordance in outdoor spaces

In outdoor spaces, children should enjoy different opportunities for 'open-ended' play activities, with access to different resources. Planning for continuous provision does not mean moving resources from indoors to outdoors. The outdoor learning environment needs to include resources that have different affordances to create challenge and extension (Bilton, 2010; Casey, 2007). Outdoor spaces can be organized to incorporate cross-curricular skills such as investigating, exploring, observing, collecting and recording data through observational drawings, charts, check lists, photographs and so forth. Curriculum (subject-based) learning activities can also be planned to develop conceptual knowledge and skills. Play continues to have a part in these structured activities because children can 'act a head taller than themselves' by being/becoming naturalists, botanists, historians, scientists, gardeners, ecologists, designers. Children enjoy working alongside adults on challenging projects. For example, in a mixed Year 1 and 2 class (aged five to seven) all the children became involved in planning a 'wild' area in the school grounds, incorporating nesting boxes, bee hives and 'bug cities'. The children became naturalists and scientists as they observed bird, insect and plant life during the year. Magnifying glasses were regularly taken outdoors and the children became skilled at trapping small insects for short spaces of time for observation on the computer screen via the electronic microscope. Paintings, sculptures and highly detailed observational drawings arose naturally from these experiences, and the practitioners found that they were never short of ideas for what to teach next because the children were full of ideas about what they wanted to learn. These open-ended activities enabled the children and adults to co-construct the curriculum, based on a combination of flexibility and structure, with playful orientations to learning, communicating and representing their knowledge.

In a study of children's secret spaces and places Moore (2010) provides compelling evidence to argue that while adults wish to design outdoor play spaces with sound theoretical playground pedagogy in mind, children have different agendas and perceptions regarding how they use the resources and create their own secret places and spaces. For children to label a place as 'secret' required the 'place' not only to be perceived as private and adult-free but uniquely constructed by the child. Sometimes this involved physical spaces such as cubbies and dens, but sometimes the secret place was in full view, but was constructed in the child's mind as secret or private because of what they chose to do there and because the adults did not know its purposes.

The outdoor environment extends affordance, and zones for potential development of children's skills and capabilities, as well as their peer cultures and private play worlds. At the same time, they offer extended scope for risk-taking, which is something that children do naturally in their play, but remains an area of great concern to adults.

Developing strategies for working with children to manage risks and hazards

Sitting outside a cafe in Akureyri, Iceland, I notice a boy of about six or seven years old, pushing his bike up a steep path that runs alongside the road and parallel to some steps that lead to the church. There are about 12 sets of steps, with eight short steps in each set, separated by one long step, and with only a short run from the bottom step to the main road that goes through the town. The boy positions his bike dead centre and rides down the steps, gathering speed, so that when he gets to the bottom, he has to execute a sharp skid to stop the bike and prevent an overshoot into the road. At the bottom he looks back up the steps and smiles, then does the same thing over again, several times. He does not wear a helmet, knee pads or any other protective gear. I am awed by his skill, confidence and competence, but disturbed by my own perceptions of risk and danger. These are the tensions that practitioners live with on a day-to-day basis, but perhaps not in such dramatic contexts. However, as Little and Wyver (2010) argue, learning to recognize risk and make their own risk judgements are vital skills as children gain greater independence and become less reliant on adults to make decisions for them.

Concerns for children's health and safety are integral to effective and ethical practice, and practitioners are required to meet standards for assessing risks on their premises and when they visit other sites. However, the concept of 'taking risks' remains fraught with fear that children will be exposed to danger and accidents. An alternative perspective is that 'taking risks' means pushing one's own boundaries, which involves recognizing potential hazards, assessing challenge and adapting one's behaviour accordingly. Taking risks safely is part of everyday life and contributes to self-efficacy and positive dispositions such as persisting with difficulty, willingness to have a go and learn from errors, mastering physical dexterity and coordination, and managing emotions such as fear and anxiety. Children rarely act in a wilfully dangerous manner for themselves or for others, although young children may not always recognize potential risks or hazards. However, many like to go to the very edge of their capabilities to see 'what happens if?' Children create imagined risks and dangers, in order to play with fear and anxiety by being fearless and brave and increasing the emotional intensity of play. As we have seen, when children are taming, controlling or killing monsters and animals they are not learning to be cruel, but are learning to test and manage emotions. However, as the case studies in this section indicate, the concepts of safety and risk involve making choices about whether to ban certain materials and activities, or work with children, parents and professionals to enable children to develop risk perception and judgements.

In Australia, Little (2010) carried out a small-scale study of the relationship between parents' beliefs about risk-taking and their response to the risk-taking behaviour of their child. The findings indicate some gender and cultural differences in allowing boys and girls to engage in risk-taking activities in outdoor play. However, the parents in the study reported that some risk-taking enables children to confront and manage risk through exercising care and control. Little (2010: 328) concludes that taking risks involves taking care, which indicates the need for healthy, positive risk-taking.

These findings are a useful counterpoint to the culture of risk-avoidance. Health and safety regulations have sometimes been over-interpreted in ways that remove rather than reduce risks and hazards. This can result in opportunities for learning being denied to children, through constraining the affordance of materials and their possible uses. Tovey (2010) and Casey (2007) concur that diminishing risk means diminishing children's experiences. This is exemplified in settings where practitioners ban large wooden blocks and hollow blocks, or provide blocks that are made from lightweight synthetic materials. I have seen children throwing these around and bashing them on hard surfaces – activities that would be difficult with heavy wooden blocks. Rules about how materials can be used can restrict children's activities and can result in their play being constructed as 'naughty' or 'disruptive', as shown in the following case study.

Case study

Constraining or enabling block play?

Outdoor play with hollow blocks: Alfie, Max, Joseph, Joel, Leanne, Henry. The large hollow blocks have been laid out in a circle by the adults, in one layer, with a small gap between them and a foam mat in the centre. The intention is for the children to develop their gross-motor and loco-motor skills (specifically balancing), sharing and cooperation, by stepping from one block to another. The activity is well within the capabilities of the children, but for the first four minutes they use the blocks as they have been laid out. Leanne pretends to wobble and 'falls' onto the mat. 'Look, I can't do it. I'll have to fall in the sea.' The children make a game of this. There is some rough-and-tumble play as they 'swim' back to the blocks and 'rescue' each other.

Max has been experimenting by jumping rather than stepping between blocks. He extends the challenge as he puts one block on top of another. This widens the gap between the blocks and Max tries to jump the gaps. Alfie, Joel and Joseph watch carefully, as if they are assessing the challenge before they join in. A new rule is invented: they jump from one block to another, then 'dive' into the 'sea' where they do forward and backward rolls. The teacher intervenes to stop their activity as it is not safe. She reminds them that they are allowed the blocks in one layer only. The children return to the stepping activity, going round in a circle, but with little interaction.

Outdoor play with hollow blocks: Joel, Alfie, Edward, Leanne. The safety rule for block play is that the children cannot build 'higher than their tummy buttons'. This episode begins with the children playing individually with the blocks, with little interaction. Alfie says, 'We've built a plane' and the play develops into making an airport with a runway, and 'a place for helicopters to land on the roof'. Leanne offers her experiences of travel; she lines up small chairs for the waiting area and lays out a piece of material for 'the place where your cases go round and round'. They start to build higher and try to get around the safety rule by standing on one, then two layers of blocks so that the top of the structure is still up to their tummy buttons. The teacher intervenes to remind them of the rule. They have to reduce the height of the airport and build only from the ground – the teacher observes until this is done, but does not ask them about their play. The play ends when the airport has been dismantled.

Activity

Do you agree or disagree with the safety rules in this setting? Think about your reasons and share these with your colleagues. What are the rules in your own setting for constructive play? Do these rules enable or constrain the play? What other strategies are available for supporting large construction play?

Tovey (2010: 80) argues that it is not just the feelings of joy that motivate children but the desire to experience the borderlines of fear and exhilaration. These borderlines are evident in the following case study.

Case study

Olympic champions on the climbing frame

In a Nursery class, there is a large climbing frame outside, with a rope and pulley at one side, fixed to the top of the platform. Jaydon, Amir, Khalid and Ashleigh are quite adventurous in their play and like to set themselves challenges. Today they industriously tie their scooters one at a time to the rope and pull them up to the platform. They are highly cooperative, and each scooter is stored in the corner, with Ashleigh excluding other children from this space, 'You can't come up here – Olympic champions only.' The next stage of the activity involves the boys riding around the platform as fast as they can in a relatively small space and trying to do skids at the corners. They seem to be in control, but they are quite competitive about speed and who does 'the best skids'. Once the teacher notices their activities, she approaches the climbing frame with a worried look.

Activity

What would you do in this context? What safety issues arise? How might you help the children to assess risks and hazards? What activities could be provided to develop the children's scooter skills and their motivation to experiment with speeding and skidding?

So what strategies can be used to maintain health and safety, but enable children to manage risks and hazards? Children need to learn to assess potential hazards in order to engage in healthy positive risk-taking (Little, 2010). Skills such as observation, care, attention and caution are necessary to feel or practice their way into a new situation. Research shows that children show care and concern for the safety of themselves and others in their play (Broadhead, 2004; Edmiston, 2008), and in outdoor activities in Forest Schools (Knight, 2011a; 2011b). Children refer to adults or older children when needed, for help in resolving disputes and managing materials, seeking advice, solving problems. Casey (2007: 71) argues that where practitioners sustain the possibility of risk in outdoor play environments children are provided with the opportunity to:

Learn to recognize and assess risks for themselves

Test and expand their own capacities

Experience the emotions associated with negotiating risk – anticipation, satisfaction, confidence, exhilaration.

Involving parents, caregivers and families helps them to appreciate the value and purposes of outdoor learning environments. Practitioners can communicate with parents and families about the benefits of the outdoor learning environment. Workshops and 'taster sessions' can enable parents to express their anxieties and fears and explore their perceptions of risk and hazard. As Tovey (2010: 81) argues, perceptions of risk may vary: what is acceptable in one context or in one culture may not be acceptable in another, and what is acceptable risk for one child may be a hazard to another. Parental and family involvement can help to address these variations and overcome anxieties, especially in Forest School environments where children use real tools, large equipment and resources, and test their physical, emotional and cognitive boundaries (Knight, 2011a; 2011b). Once parents understand that practitioners have taken safety and well-being into account, they are usually enthusiastic participants and will spread the word to other parents about the benefits of allowing children more freedom and control in outdoor spaces. They will understand that their children can enjoy these benefits by developing the know-how and competence to seek and take risks safely.

   Case study

The hanging tree

In a Primary school with a large outdoor space, five girls (aged 9 to 11) are proudly telling me about their secret den and their play activities. They have developed a complex game of chasing, which involves being naughty so that Witchy (the play leader is always Charlene) can use her magic powers to freeze you. When this happens, you have to stay still until Witchy gives you a token. (Charlene shows me a box which contains crystals of different sizes – the largest one is the most magic and it always stays with her so she keeps her magic powers.) The token releases you from the spell, depending on how naughty you have been (the more naughty you are, the longer you stay frozen). The girls then told me that if you were 'very naughty, or very, very naughty', then you would be hung from the hanging tree. Charlene then proudly pointed upwards and said, 'And that's our hanging tree, and that's the branch where I hang them from.'

At one level, this might seem to be quite a shocking theme for play. But it involved positive affect in that the girls were all smiling and laughing when they were talking to me. The hanging tree makes sense in the cultural context because this school was near Melbourne, Australia. Many of the children had learned about the history of the Ned Kelly gang; they had visited Old Melbourne gaol, where the scaffold on which Kelly was hanged remains a major visitor attraction. This episode might be seen as involving the traits of dark or cruel play described by Sutton-Smith (2001). However, children's play cultures often integrate the mythic/folkloric themes described by Edmiston (2008), Factor (2009) and Kelly-Byrne (1989). Consistent with Edmiston's (2008) research, the girls created an ethic of care in their play: involvement was consensual and not coercive; they were not 'frozen' for long periods of time; and they expressed enjoyment and even glee in these activities, especially because the game and the hanging tree were secret from adults and peers ('nobody knows it's a hanging tree, they think it's just a tree').

Activity

What is your reaction, and how do you interpret this vignette?

The following principles can be used to guide discussions about extending the affordance of activities and resources in outdoor play/learning environments.

- Understanding how to keep safe in play needs to be a co-constructive process between adults and children.
- Children take shared responsibility with adults for the care and management of resources (including tidying up).
- Dens, cubbies and secret spaces should be respected by adults, unless there are concerns with safety and hazards.

- Children can work and play safely with large equipment and resources if taught the correct strategies for moving, lifting, stacking and so forth (caring for self, others and resources).
- Parents, family members, multi-professional team members can be involved in discussions about risk and safety to ensure that all aspects are covered for children who have additional needs. These adults can also be involved as co-players.
- Play activities are fluid and potential risks can emerge 'in the moment', as children spontaneously increase the level of challenge. Children may use resources in ways that are not anticipated or intended by adults. Therefore light-touch monitoring and observation are necessary to check for any additional adjustments.

Planning for progression and continuity

A recurring theme throughout this book is that play changes with age and experience and children continue to need time and space for play that is more complex and more challenging. Simple games develop into more socially complex games where the rules are created by the players and may change over time. In Key Stage 2, children enjoy channelling their interests into projects. Therefore the concept of material affordance can be extended to consider social and intellectual affordance in the context of complexity, agency, choice and control in outdoor environments. Moore (2010) reports that the outdoor areas in her study afforded children opportunities to develop peer cultures and social competence, as well as shared and individual agency in managing and changing the environment because of the flexibility of the spaces and resources. Children have powerful drives to claim and create their own spaces, often as a response to adult surveillance and control. Outdoor play affords opportunities for children to develop a wide variety of skills and dispositions. Some children take on leadership roles and are acknowledged as the play leaders; older children teach games to younger children. Children learn to create their own cultures, as well as adjusting to school routines and cultures. It can be argued that flexibility and complexity go hand in hand, which also reflects Holzman's point that 'children are capable of doing so much more in collective activity than in individual activity' (2009: 30).

Planning for inclusion, access and diversity

In Chapter 2, the discussion on R&T and superhero play noted gender differences in how boys and girls play, how they occupy space and how play changes in the primary school (Jarvis, 2007; 2010). It would be easy just to accept that boys and girls play differently, that boys need more space because they are physically more active, and that girls are happy to hang out chilling and chatting on the peripheries. However, contemporary research urges practitioners to think differently about what is happening in play spaces and particularly outdoors. We have seen that the agreed characteristics and benefits of play include freedom, choice, control and autonomy, and the opportunities for developing agency and exercising power. From post-structural and post-developmental perspectives, play is a site in which children's identities are continually explored, negotiated, tested, including discourses of gender, sex and sexualities (Blaise, 2005; 2010; Grieshaber and McArdle, 2010). What happens in play, and what outcomes emerge, are not always knowable, because children's play cultures include their own purposes, rituals and practices. Thus the perception that boys 'need' more space can be interpreted differently: some boys learn that by choosing ball and chasing games, they are able to take up more space because they are performing valued forms of masculinity. This means that some girls and boys learn that they can only occupy the peripheral spaces that are left to them. Look at the case study in Chapter 7 of the Noah's Ark play. You will notice a girl quietly playing under a bench with a doll while some of the boys play out heroic struggles with dangerous animals. The Target Child frightens a girl when he is a fierce dog, and four children (two girls and two boys) sit on the cupboards observing the performance. It is not just that the space is used differently: there are different discourses and practices that determine who can use the space, in what ways, for what purposes and with what effects. As Blaise argues, particular forms of femininity are produced in relation to particular, and highly valued, forms of masculinity (2010: 83). Therefore, gender identity is not 'given' in the sense of being determined biologically, but is constructed and produced through social and cultural practices. Children are constantly receiving messages about what it means to be a boy/girl and how they are expected to perform gendered roles. Thus being and performing are acted out in many different ways (clothes, hair, body movements), as well as through repertoires of play, and how choices and practices are enacted through toys, games, spaces, friendships and play themes.

Gendered repertoires tend to be more evident in outdoor play where there is generally more space, more freedom and sometimes less adult surveillance (for example during break/recess). If practitioners accept that boys and girls play differently, there is a danger that they will reinforce gender stereotypes, by not contesting gendered discourses and practices. But if play is about children's freedom, choice and control, this poses the question of whether and how adults can intervene to ensure equity (equal choice of access to space, resources and activities).

Activity

Carry out some observations of children playing during break times. What do you notice about how the spaces are used and who is using them? Are there any differences in how boys and girls use the spaces? What strategies might you use to address any differences in access and opportunities to play?

Another aspect of diversity that may influence outdoor play is cultural variations in parents' and children's attitudes to risk-taking (Little, 2010). In some cultures, boys and girls experience different home-based child-rearing practices where girls are expected to be sedentary and stay close to the mother or the females in the family. Boys are allowed time and space for physical or active play. These differences transfer into early childhood settings. For example, in an action research project at Elm Primary school, the nursery practitioners noticed that many of the British Asian girls, and girls from newly arrived Somalian refugee families, chose sedentary, table-top activities where a female practitioner was present. They found it difficult to encourage the children to widen their play repertoires and in the outdoor area the girls also stayed close to an adult, wanting to hold hands and not engage in the activities. Over the course of a year, the staff worked with the English Medium Assistants to link with the local community leaders to discuss how the children could be more involved in active forms of play. Through involving parents (mostly mothers) they gradually modelled different activities and involved Reception and Year 1 children in some of their outdoor activities. This proved to be effective as the older children were more directive than the practitioners at encouraging wider participation in outdoor play, but also modelled an ethic of care.

As part of the action research project at Elm Primary School all the children were involved in making decisions about how the outdoor environment should be re-designed. One of the concerns was that boys and girls were using the space in different ways, with 'the footballers' taking up a lot of the space and impinging on other children when the balls were kicked hard or the players ran through other games. In the initial design stages, the Year 6 children (aged 10 to 11) carried out a survey of the teachers and children from Reception upwards. This involved asking them about their favourite play areas and activities and what they wanted to change or add. All the children enjoyed designing their 'dream playgrounds' which included castles, a grand prix race track and the moon complete with lunar vehicles and space station, as well as more practical suggestions.

A consensus emerged that there should be less space available for ball and chasing games, and more spaces for 'hanging out', playing games and using different sorts of equipment. This was subsequently renegotiated so that the footballers had two long playtimes on two days per week during the lunch break with more space available. The children's ideas for play activities included strings, clapping games and dancing, and play boxes.

Strings

The children wanted to design play boxes, with games and activities that could be put in a plastic container and moved easily to the outdoor space. One of the teachers suggested learning to play 'strings', based on her own love of this activity in her childhood. 'Strings' consist of a joined piece of string, long enough to loop around the hands and create different patterns (I knew this game from my childhood as 'Cat's Cradle'). The strings proved popular with girls and boys and became a regular activity with peers and adults. When the Key Stage 2 children went on a school trip, they made sure they had their strings for the journey.

Clapping games and dancing

Another popular activity during playtimes at Elm Primary School was clapping games. These appeared around the age of five among children who did not (yet) share a common language, but did share a need to connect and create friendships. Children whose heritages and community languages included Bangladeshi, Polish, Somali, Pakistani, English, Estonian, Chinese, Rwandan, Nigerian, Saudi Arabian, Egyptian and Thai were all involved: one child did the chant and actions in his/her language, and the partner held up his/her hands and tried to join in with words, shouts and physical actions. The games were so popular that the teachers liaised with parents and community support workers to video the games being played at home. Parents were delighted to add more suggestions and some came in to do demonstrations with the adults and children. The chants were recorded in English and the children's home languages as a resource.

Dancing was another cultural bridge between the children, because they incorporated their family traditions and practices. Many were also familiar with television programmes such as *Strictly Come Dancing*, and there was much interest in Bollywood dancing, which indicated shared funds of popular cultural knowledge in children's homes. The children wanted a stage for performing in the outdoor space and a karaoke machine. They used small camcorders to record their performances, discuss improvements and plan new routines. Again, once the teachers noticed the dancing during playtime, they developed their community links and asked for volunteers to come into school to teach the children and adults. The dance activities were physically energetic and proved popular with most of the boys, perhaps because they saw the potential for displaying competence and many also saw male family members dancing in their homes and communities.

The dancing led to requests for dressing-up clothes so a box was provided, which included lengths of fabric as well as a variety of donated glamorous clothes. One of the most popular items was a purple sequined dress which was almost always worn by different boys, along with scarves and jewellery. Putting on the dress was like putting on a different identity and way of being in the space. The children from British Asian cultures were used to richly coloured and decorated clothing for festivals and celebrations, so it may be that the dressing-up box afforded opportunities for them to meld different identities and practices.

Play boxes

There was a consensus in both Key Stages that the children wanted 'things to do' when they were outside. This led to the design of play boxes, which included strings and other small equipment such as ropes, bean bags and small table-top games, some of which the children designed themselves. They had to consider the longevity and robustness of their games, which engaged them in design processes. The Year 6 children sourced, costed and ordered tables and benches for 'chatting and chilling'. Another consensus was the need for shade, and the children looked at different solutions, including shade sails. However, these were outside the budget and the children decided that there were other priorities, but put them on their wish list.

Meera, aged ten, wanted to design a play box for children with disabilities. She was partially sighted and, for most of her Primary schooling, had spent her play times keeping out of the way of the footballers and chasers, and with relatively little to do. Meera's box included board games that she designed with her friends and a smaller treasure box that included 'anything that glitters'. These artefacts took on many different purposes in secret games and rituals. When Meera left to go to Secondary school, she insisted in leaving her box for other children to use. These relatively simple strategies ensured that Meera created her own places and spaces for play.

This whole school project lasted a year and was led by a play coordinator who had also done Forest School training. The school had used some of the playground space to create their own mini Forest School, which was developed by staff, family members and the Key Stage 2 children. Although the available area was not very large, the pathways were designed in curves so the distance between the gate and the central fire pit seemed quite far to the children. Dense planting intensified this effect by screening the children from the rest of the school grounds. Spaces were made available for dens and shelters, and natural materials were added on a regular basis because of the limitations of the space. Parents were asked to donate outgrown wellingtons and waterproof suits so the children got used to 'all-weather' visits. They also visited a Forest School in the countryside where they could use and apply the skills that they had learned and test their adventurousness in a much larger space.

These projects illustrate the value of whole community engagement in developing school grounds and outdoor spaces. The children's voices and perspectives were central to the design and realization of the different projects. Although their dream playgrounds included some fantastical elements, they did manage to come up with some practical solutions to the problems. They did not want much fixed equipment, and over time more loose parts were added as the teachers became more trusting and confident of the children's capabilities. Because this project took up a lot of time, curriculum goals were incorporated into many of the planning and design tasks. Also noticeable was the engagement and motivation of the children, their obvious pride in their achievements and their continued need for play.

Progression and continuity

A consistent theme throughout this book is that play does not tail off by the age of five, but develops in complexity and challenge. Understanding progression in play is a missing dimension from much research on play in educational settings, and even more so with outdoor play. For many children in the USA, recess periods (break time) have been stopped because of health and safety concerns. In the UK, playtime for older children may be fraught with difficulties as they compete for space in tarmac wastelands. Again we need to pose the question: what are we preventing children from being/becoming when we constrain or control their play?

Referring back to Chapter 2, research on children's play cultures and practices documents how children use agency and choices in their play. Children become increasingly focused on playing with their peers, and this involves establishing status, power, leadership and control. Children are often seen as good players and as play leaders. They find their own places and spaces for withdrawal, as a means of contesting adults' rules and of excluding peers. Some of these activities need to be accepted by adults within agreed limits of safety and mutual respect. Outdoor play areas that are designed collaboratively with children support continuity and progression in play where flexibility and complexity are appreciated as the drivers of creativity, invention and experimentation. Children can continue to create special places for the conjuring of possibility, for doing something unusual and for experiencing the effects (Henricks, 2009).

Further reading

Bilton, H. (2010) *Outdoor Learning in the Early Years: Management and Innovation* (3rd edn), London: Routledge.

Brown, F. (ed.) (2003) *Playwork Theory and Practice*, Buckingham: Open University Press.

Casey, T. (2007) *Environments for Outdoor Play: A Practical Guide to Making Space for Children*, London: Sage.

Knight, S. (ed.) (2011a) *Forest School for All*, London: Sage.

Knight, S. (2011b) *Risk and Adventure in Outdoor Play: Learning from Forest Schools*, London: Sage.

Little, H. (2010) 'Relationship between parents' beliefs and their responses to risk-taking behaviour during outdoor play', *Journal of Early Childhood Research*, 8 (3): 313–330.

Wilson, R. (2012) *Nature and Young Children: Encouraging Creative Play and Learning in Natural Environments* (2nd edn), Abingdon: Routledge.

 To gain free access to specially selected SAGE journal articles related to key topics discussed in this book please visit: **www.sagepub.co.uk/wood**

CHAPTER 7

ASSESSING CHILDREN'S LEARNING IN PLAY

The aims of this chapter are to:

- Outline the purposes and principles of assessment
- Describe different assessment techniques and strategies, and how these can be applied in practice
- Analyse case studies of children's play to illustrate effective assessment practices

Vygotsky (1978) argued against the pedantic intellectualization of play, but considered that only a profound internal analysis could contribute to understanding its meaning for young children. Many of the research studies discussed in previous chapters have illustrated the importance of profound analysis, particularly with regard to understanding children's motives, choices and interests, and the conditions that support play. Effective practitioners are good researchers of their practice through observing, listening, planning, interacting, evaluating and reflecting. Through critical reflection they problematize their practice, challenge assumptions and engage with equity and diversity.

This chapter demonstrates how effective assessment practices can support play provision, using the Model of Integrated Curriculum and Pedagogical Approaches described in Chapters 4 and 5. There is a dual focus on assessment for learning within and beyond curriculum policy frameworks and assessment for understanding children as players and learners.

There are ongoing concerns about the political emphasis on standards, measurement and accountability, and the ways in which assessment of individual learning outcomes can be prioritized within a narrowly focused target-setting culture (File, Mueller and Wisneski, 2012; Grieshaber and McArdle, 2010). Therefore effective assessment practices need to be 'policy-proofed' so that practitioners take account of the demands of national frameworks, but do not allow these to dominate the more sophisticated purposes that assessment serves within integrated approaches. Accordingly, the principles of assessment described here are consistent with contemporary socio-cultural theories, because assessment is not just a technical practice, but an ethical practice which is intrinsically bound with positive images of children (Carr et al., 2009; Carr and Lee, 2012). In democratic approaches to early childhood education children are seen as competent, resilient, strong and capable (Parnell, 2011); they are not seen as being in deficit against narrowly determined developmental or curriculum goals. Learning is about the transformation of participation and of children's identities (their self-image, self-concepts and self-esteem) within different communities and social practices. Case studies of children's play will demonstrate practical strategies for observing, describing, documenting and discussing evidence of children's learning, and linking assessment with critical reflection.

The principles and purposes of assessment

Assessment and evaluation are at the heart of effective teaching and learning and can be seen as complementary processes which enable practitioners to:

- understand children's characters, dispositions, identities, choices and motivations
- develop culturally situated knowledge about how children learn and develop
- make informed interpretations and assessments about children's progress and achievements, reflecting dimensions of diversity
- use assessment information to inform curriculum planning in co-constructive and responsive ways
- reflect critically on the quality and effectiveness of provision
- document information that can be discussed with families, teachers and other professionals, and make links with home and community cultures.

Assessment and evaluation contribute to critical reflection about the quality and effectiveness of provision and practice. These processes apply equally to play, because it is a leading activity that reveals children's intentions and meanings which may not be evident in formal adult-directed contexts (Edwards, 2010). Building knowledge about the child as player/learner, and the child in the playing/learning context, enables practitioners to develop cultural awareness of variations in play and among players, by:

- understanding children's interests, choices and goals
- identifying play patterns and themes and how these develop over time, for individuals and groups of children
- 'fine-tuning' their play provision and co-constructing learning activities through joint activity with children.

Forms of assessment

There are six forms of assessment, which serve different but complementary purposes:

- *formative*: practitioners develop their knowledge about children's progress and achievements and holistic understanding of children, including their identities, characteristics, dispositions, interests, play choices, patterns of learning, friendship choices and repertoires of participation. In play activities, practitioners attend to children's intentions and meanings and interpret these through discussion and reflection with children and other adults. Formative assessment informs planning the next learning activities, including space, time and resources. Children and families should be involved in these processes.
- *ipsative*: this form of assessment is referenced directly to the child rather than to external norms and expectations, with a focus on identifying small changes in learning and development. Ipsative assessment is appropriate for children with special or additional educational needs and disabilities who may appear to be underachieving or failing against developmental norms or defined learning goals. Practitioners can plan activities and interactions to support children in specific areas.
- *diagnostic*: this is a detailed form of assessment which may involve specialized tests that are administered by professionals (for example, to identify problems with hearing, developmental or language delay). Diagnostic assessment may require practitioners to observe children in specific contexts, record difficulties and challenges, plan appropriate support and liaise with professional teams. If play-based interventions are needed, the activities can be matched to the child's capabilities, dispositions and potential.
- *summative*: an overview or snapshot of progress and achievements at a specific point in time, usually referenced to curriculum goals or specific learning outcomes for individual children. Summative assessment can identify progress in children's participation across a range of contexts, to provide a holistic account of their learning and development. In the

Early Years Foundation Stage (DfE, 2012a) summative assessments occur at the age of two (the developmental check) and at the age of five (the learning goals).

- *evaluative*: assessment information is collated to provide evidence of children's progress and achievements over time, enabling practitioners to review the effectiveness of the curriculum offered and identify priorities for change and development. Assessment and evaluation can support professional learning and critical reflection.
- *informative*: assessment information is synthesized and discussed with parents, caregivers, teachers and other professionals. Areas of concern may be highlighted as the focus for further support or to inform colleagues when transitions occur.

As children learn by playing and working alongside differently knowledgeable others, they participate in increasingly complex activities, in more skilful ways and with greater levels of confidence and competence. They develop dispositions and capabilities to initiate and orchestrate their own play, revealing areas of interest and funds of knowledge. Everyday knowledge and imagination become integrated to inform and enrich their play. They use and apply their knowledge, skills and understanding, and use tools and resources in creative and flexible ways. Through the continuous processes of being and becoming (Holzman, 2009) they develop unique identities and different ways of relating to peers and adults in collective activities. Assessment practices should reflect these subtleties because learning and learner identities are always 'in the making' (Carr et al., 2009). Effective assessment is a process of building knowledge and understanding about children and about practice, which goes beyond the developmental check lists or curriculum-based 'tick boxes' which can easily dominate practice.

The assessment process

The six forms of assessment can be used as a means for understanding meanings and purposes in children's play, documenting and communicating the outcomes. However, there are a number of pedagogical dilemmas in assessing children's learning through play.

Pedagogical dilemmas

- Play may not be taken seriously if practitioners fail to realize its potential. The assessment potential is lost if play is used mainly as a reward for work or to fill 'spare time'.

- Children sometimes have to earn their play (for example in Golden Time); but this is fundamentally in opposition to children's rights to play.
- Play bears little resemblance to what it may lead to, so practitioners need to understand the immediate as well as potential outcomes.
- The skills and knowledge that children demonstrate in play may not transfer to other forms of activity (and vice versa).
- Practitioners find it difficult to demonstrate convincing evidence about the relationship between playing, learning and teaching. This evidence becomes visible over time through play choices, patterns and events.
- Because play can appear to be chaotic and unpredictable, it can be difficult to make connections between adults' and children's goals.
- Children need adequate time to develop complexity in their play.
- Adults often make judgements about what constitutes 'good play' or 'bad play', and define what forms of play are educationally worthwhile.
- It is difficult to make time for observing and interpreting children's play.

A key principle for effective assessment practice is that adults should build on children's funds of knowledge (Chapter 4) based on the cultural practices of their families and communities. Failure to do this can result in mismatches between the learner and the curriculum, which applies as much to play as to adult-directed activities. Brooker's (2010) research in culturally diverse communities shows that the problem of mismatch arises when children and their families do not understand play-based approaches. Durand (2010) also poses questions about what happens when the beliefs, values, practices and socialization goals for children are fundamentally different across home and pre-school/school settings:

> when we speak of the 'best start' for children, we have to acknowledge that the children and families we serve don't start in the same place. They come from different places. They don't look the same. They don't act the same. They don't speak or use language in the same ways. (Durand, 2010: 837)

If we add play to these concerns, mismatches can influence children's subsequent learning journeys, particularly if their home experiences, languages and cultures are not recognized. Building on children's funds of knowledge is a fundamental pedagogical principle (Hedges, 2011a; 2011b; Hedges, Cullen and Jordan, 2011), but accessing those funds is immensely challenging. This involves ongoing processes of questioning dominant universal narratives about learning, development and play, challenging personal beliefs, values and judgements, and considering cross-cultural competence as integral to ethical practice (Genishi and Goodwin, 2008).

> ## Activity
>
> Assessment in the Reggio Emilia approach is based on the concept of 'a pedagogy of listening', which is defined as 'listening to thought – the ideas and theories, questions and answers of children and adults' (Rinaldi, 2006: 15).
>
> What does this concept mean in the context of culturally sensitive assessment? How do we listen to thought? Do curriculum frameworks privilege visible 'outcomes' and underestimate the importance of listening to thought?

We have seen that play is not one activity, but many complex activities which integrate different processes. A wide range of outcomes are possible as children develop their play repertoires. The following principles underpin ethical assessment practices.

- Practitioners need sophisticated pedagogical knowledge to observe, interpret and understand play from children's perspectives.
- Practitioners should not try to control children's play according to narrowly defined curriculum outcomes.
- Practitioners need to be clear about their own goals for an activity, and the children's goals. The latter may reveal children's funds of knowledge that they integrate into their play.
- Practitioners should aim to use assessment information in co-constructive ways with children and families in order to provide challenge and extension in play. This should be a two-way process of knowledge exchange.
- The tasks of observing and documenting play should not impose inappropriate intrusion or surveillance.

Individual development and play plans

For children with additional or special educational needs and disabilities, play-based assessment can ensure an accurate match between their play preferences and the provision. Individual Play Plans (IPPs) can be developed alongside Individual Educational Plans (IEPs), with the proviso that plans can be implemented in ways that respect the child's choice of play activities, partners or groups. In Chapter 3, we noted that play can be aligned with highly structured tasks and routines that contribute to learning atomized skills and fill the missing gaps in curriculum goals. O'Brien (2010) argues that these practices do not help children to develop fully in terms of their capacities and potential. If play skills need to be taught directly by an adult, then the context should ideally include peers so that interventions are naturalistic rather than clinical. IPPs and IEPs should work naturalistically with a child's play choices and motivations as shown in Peter's case study:

Case study

Peter's motivation to plan his play

Peter, who had cerebral palsy, often made small but incremental advances in his physical development as he struggled to control his coordination and involuntary movements. He enjoyed planning layouts with the PE equipment, which enabled him to practise balancing on a plank, stepping (and attempting to jump) between boxes and climbing up ladders. These activities involved a great deal of effort and concentration. When Peter was four, his child-development profile from the hospital revealed mainly what he could not do in relation to standardized assessments based on 'developmental norms' for 'typical' four-year-olds. This was a deficit model of assessment which was inappropriate for Peter because he was not a typical four-year-old and was not developing in typical ways.

In Peter's Nursery class, the practitioners agreed to go with the flow of his motivation as much as possible. Peter wanted to walk along the plank that was balanced between two A-frame ladders. They wanted to lower the height so that, if Peter fell off, this would minimize any hurt. However, Peter was determined to walk the plank at the same height as his peers and persistently moved the plank from the lower level back to the higher level. So, after discussions with his team and parents, the practitioners placed crash mats under the plank and persuaded Peter to allow them to walk alongside him with one hand offered to help steady his balance. Peter rarely accepted help; falling off and bumping into things was part of his everyday experience which he managed with humour and resilience.

His detailed observation-based profile was supplemented by videos, and gave a balanced picture of Peter's capabilities and learning dispositions, including the strategies and willpower he used to overcome his difficulties. This was a credit model of ipsative assessment based on Peter's progress, patterns of activity and his achievements over time.

Peter's case study shows the value of a credit-based model of assessment, which focuses on children's dispositions to be ready, willing and able to participate in activities and to increase their motivation to learn (Carr et al., 2009), even though in Peter's case this seemed (at least to the adults) to involve some risks. Evidence-based discussions about children's progress and achievements can involve children, parents, caregivers and other professionals, and enable practitioners to make links between children's experiences in different contexts. Patterns of learning are not always predictable: children sometimes progress in leaps and bounds, and sometimes have difficulties and setbacks, fallow periods, or may even appear to regress, especially if they experience changes, illness or stress. Children progress at different rates across the curriculum areas, according to their interests and approaches to learning, which may be culturally influenced. If the curriculum is inappropriate (too formal, too much sedentary activity and teacher control), children may decide to switch off or change their pace and motivation, in accordance with the demands being made. Evidence of learning demonstrates to colleagues and parents the value and purposes of play from children's perspectives. So what are the guiding principles for developing inclusive assessment practices?

Guiding principles

The value of observation-based assessment is endorsed in the curriculum frameworks for the four UK countries. The three levels of understanding play presented in Chapter 4 provide a framework for examining learning processes and content. The aim is to identify patterns and interests and document actual learning outcomes (which may not be consistent with planned outcomes). Practitioners can listen to children's thinking and appreciate their capabilities and dispositions.

The strategies listed in Figure 7.1 may help to deal with the pedagogical dilemmas identified above. Practitioners should aim to focus on the child, the context and the curriculum. These strategies incorporate the 'four D's of credit-based assessment' (Carr, 2001): describing, discussing, documenting and deciding, which are outlined in the following sections.

Observing and describing

Observation is the basis for a credit-based approach to assessment across a range of play activities, both indoors and outdoors (Broadhead, 2006; Carr et al., 2009; Carr and Lee, 2012). The focus can be on children when they are:

- playing alone
- playing together (pairs or groups)
- playing with an adult.

Because play develops in complexity, effective assessment practices should reveal the value of different types of play across areas of learning and development, and

- Look at the context for assessment. What types of assessment are going to be made?
- What is the best way to gather evidence of learning? See Chapter 5 on Observation.
- What are the intended learning outcomes for the activity? Is there a match between intentions and outcomes?
- What are the potential learning outcomes? Be aware of the scope for flexibility according to the play activity, and the prior experience of the players.
- How did the activity develop and what opportunities for assessment were presented as a result?
- Document evidence of learning across different contexts in order to check how the child is using, applying and transferring knowledge and skills. Involve team members in these processes.
- Document evidence of learning over a period of time in order to understand play themes, patterns of learning, dispositions and ongoing interests.
- Discuss observations with team members, including helpers and students, to compare and challenge perceptions. Be alert to making narrow judgements about children – there may be culturally situated explanations for behaviours that do not conform to expectations within the setting. Share observations with parents and caregivers.
- Use assessments for summative, formative and diagnostic purposes: what are the child's capabilities and what are the next possible steps? Plan flexibly for challenge, extension, consolidation.
- Use assessments to inform individual education plans, and individual play plans, for children with learning difficulties and additional/special educational needs.
- Feed assessment information forward into curriculum planning (short-, medium- and long-term).

Figure 7.1   Assessment techniques and strategies

how progression through play can be supported through projects and in outdoor environments.

Discussing and documenting

Documentation can provide children with memories of their activities and can build a profile of progression over time. In Reggio Emilia and Te Whāriki, projects are documented at all stages, along with 'fragments of dialogue', to show children's working theories and funds of knowledge. Documentation provides evidence of learning in the making (Carr et al., 2009), not just the outcomes. Practitioners use this evidence to discuss projects with the children, support and extend their learning and inspire further their investigations. Children are involved in the assessment process, which enables them to develop metacognitive skills and reflect on their learning. Pedagogical documentation 'makes learning visible' and can support children's sense of mastery.

Practitioners use different strategies for documenting children's learning (see Figure 7.2).

Annotations of play document the significance of the evidence and build into more sustained learning stories (Carr et al., 2009), which provide a meaningful

> - Collect evidence over a period of time.
> - Look for patterns, meanings and interests.
> - Decide how learning can be extended through activities that challenge children's thinking.
> - Share insights with team members, parents, caregivers and other professionals involved with a child.
> - Involve children in self-assessment (for example, through the plan–do–review process, Chapter 4).
> - Provide evidence for reflection, evaluation and curriculum/staff development.

Figure 7.2   Strategies for documenting and discussing evidence

narrative rather than a snowstorm of ticks in boxes. Narratives should be specific about the learning processes and outcomes:

> Jodie investigated the water wheel. She discovered that she could make it turn fast or slow with the amount of water poured. She inquired whether it would work with sand. She tested her idea and described to the group what she had learned.
>
> Andrew enjoyed playing in the post office. He pretended to be the postman. He sorted the parcels into different sizes and learned how to weigh them. He learned that heavy parcels cost more. He decided to send letters to his friends and requested help with writing their names. He referred to the dictionary to help with spellings. He stayed in role throughout the session and identified a need for a larger post box, which he planned to make in the next session.
>
> Sean and Joanne played cooperatively with the playdough. They both rolled out sausages and used comparative mathematical language (fat/thin, fattest/ thinnest, long/short, longest/shortest). They transformed the sausages into shapes – triangle, oblong, square. Joanne said, 'This is a round.' Sean told her it was a circle and Joanne subsequently used this word. They transformed the shapes into 'wiggly worms' and decided to mould different sized 'houses'. They matched the worms to the houses and spontaneously created a story about them.

Describing children's learning in these terms can enable practitioners to avoid trivial descriptions (such as 'Joanne and Sean enjoyed playing with the dough'), and to provide accounts of complexity and diversity in children's play. Different strategies can be used for recording observations (Figure 7.3).

There are ethical considerations to assessment, because observation can be intrusive and make children self-conscious about their play. Play-based assessment should not destroy spontaneity: sensitive practitioners respect children's rights to privacy and secrecy (as long as there is no danger, risk or harm occurring). Children give clues when their play is not open for scrutiny, such as choosing silence, turning or moving away from the adult, or stopping the

- A daily diary or sticky Post-it® labels for writing down notes of significant events, which are put into children's records
- Short accounts of significant events and developments with an action plan to inform further provision
- Selected examples of the 'outcomes' of children's play – layouts, drawings, paintings, emergent writing, constructions, plans, photographs of dramatic and socio-dramatic play, both indoors and outdoors. These should be annotated to indicate their significance, and can be shared within team and family members. Examples can be collated in a child's record of achievement or in a display to show evidence of learning over time.
- Audio and video recordings can be useful for children with special educational needs where detailed evidence is needed for further reflection. Children enjoy watching videos of themselves playing and giving their own account and interpretations. Again this information can be shared with parents and caregivers.
- Check lists can identify any significant gaps in a child's experience and can inform planning for breadth and balance
- Records of planning to show how learning outcomes are integrated in adult-and child-initiated play
- Children's planning books can be annotated to document how the plans were implemented and what were the outcomes, including children's comments

Figure 7.3   Effective assessment strategies

activity. Holistic approaches to assessment enable practitioners to make connections between adult- and child-initiated activities so that work and play are not separated or differently valued. Many practitioners begin collating profiles in the Foundation Stage and transfer them into the next class or school. Parents and caregivers can contribute to the profile, thus creating links with learning and playing at home and across transition points (Brooker, 2008). These links can help to sensitize practitioners to cultural diversity in children's choices and interests.

Documenting and interpreting evidence

This section illustrates how evidence of children's play can be documented and interpreted, based on examples from research by teachers.

    Case study

Sanjiv and the Red Riding Hood puppet

Sanjiv is a first generation British–Asian child who comes from a family where the community language is spoken at home and the mother speaks no English. In his first few months at the Nursery he is mostly silent and spends a lot of time observing activities. The children have

(Continued)

(Continued)

been reading the story of Red Riding Hood and Sanjiv becomes fascinated by the puppet which is grandma at one end and the wolf at the other. He turns the puppet to show the two characters and gradually starts to approach an adult to indicate what he is doing. Over a period of weeks he starts to say the words grandma and wolf. His actions with the puppet indicate that he can act out, but not verbalize, the story. This is noted in his records and the practitioners spend time with Sanjiv and other children to re-tell the story, using mime and gestures and reinforcing the language.

The Nursery teacher liaises with the English Medium Assistant (EMA) to discuss with Sanjiv's mother if she would like to join the group of mothers who attend English classes at the school, which take place for an hour, two days a week before the end of the Nursery session. This enables the mothers to be in a safe and familiar place and to pick up their children afterwards. The EMAs also liaise with the families to communicate the purposes of play and what the children are learning in the setting. The parents are also able to express their concerns about whether and what the children are learning, and to discuss what forms of play occur in their home and community settings. Instead of the school seeking to dominate practices in the home, this ongoing work enhances cross-cultural knowledge and sensitivity.

Activity

What are your assumptions about cultural variations in play? Durand (2010: 836) argues that aspects of culture are manifested in two aspects of children's early experiences: parents' conceptions of their roles and children's language learning and use. Consider these two aspects in relation to play in your own settings. What do you know about parents' perceptions of play and their roles? What do you notice about variations in children's language use and how this influences play? Think about issues such as accessing play, inclusion, understanding play rules and routines, understanding pretence. Consider these issues in the context of Sanjiv's case study.

Assessing socio-dramatic play

Chapter 2 outlined some of the benefits of dramatic and socio-dramatic play. Children may reveal levels of competence and motivation that are not evident in other forms of play or in adult-directed activities. As Broadhead (2004) has shown, from the age of three, children make rapid progress in their ability to engage in social and cooperative play. In the 'what if' and 'as if' modes of play, children make unexpected, creative transformations: they act 'a head taller than themselves' because they are imagining possible selves and identities (Holzman, 2009).

The following example of socio-dramatic play was recorded by Cook (2003: Appendix 9), and demonstrates the value of looking closely at play in order to understand this complexity. The role-play area in the Reception classroom is Noah's Ark. The main focus is on Callum, aged five (the target child [TC]): the observation lasts ten minutes and provides an activity record (in italics) and a language record. SG denotes small group, CG and CB denote when Callum talks to a girl or boy.

    Case study

Noah's ark

Three children are in the role-play area (two boys and a girl). TC walked into the role-play area and looked inside.

TC–self: How many people are there? Three. I can play there. I can dress up.

Walked out of the area and found a friend.

TC–CB: Toby, d'you want to come and play in the home corner?

No verbal response, but CB followed TC. Both boys started to rifle through the dressing-up box for animal costumes. Two other boys were already in role, but it was difficult to ascertain their theme.

They were sitting high up on top of two cupboards. They had used a chair to get up there and were swinging their legs, watching TC and CB enter the role-play area.

CB–TC: He's scared to jump off his bed because he thinks he land in someone's kitchen.

(Continued)

(Continued)

TC had found a dog head-dress, tail and two gloves. His friend helped him put these on.

CB–TC: Hello doggy.

TC–CB: Ruff ruff.

TC crawled away on all fours. No-one followed him so he started to take off his dressing-up clothes. Another CB spoke:

CB–TC: I'm going to be a Daddy.

TC–CB: I'm going to be a bamboo. It's wild and very very fierce. It's like Tarzan and an elephant talks.

It later became clear that he meant a baboon ... TC tried to pick up the dog costume and put it all back on again. Spoke to SG.

TC–SG: I'm a fierce dog.

TC then ran around the outside of the screen, frightening a CG in the process. She replied:

CG–TC: Bad doggy. No, bad doggy.

TC continued to chase. CG ran and hid under the bench.

TC–CG: I'm scaring you.

TC took off his outfit and wandered over to another CB who was putting on a monkey outfit.

TC–CB: I'm going to be what you are. I'm gonna be a gorilla.

TC ran around beating his chest. Two girls and another boy joined the group and all the children decided to use a chair to get up to sit on the work bench area.

TC–SG: Who wants to be Noah?

CB–SG: Who wants to see what you look like?

TC–SG: We're looking for sharks. I'm going to save everyone.

CB jumped down and followed TC holding a plastic asparagus.

CB–TC: This is what kills sharks. I'm going to smack them on the head.

The two boys continue this theme on their own. TC and CB pretend to swim around the side of the play area. Another CB joins them.

TC–CB: Anyone who can swim can kill sharks. Quick, there's a shark.

(Continued)

TC found a skipping rope and began swinging it around his head. He picked up a teapot and spoke to the two boys.

TC–SG: Sharks hate tea. That's why I'm holding a teapot.

TC pretended to pour tea everywhere.

TC–SG: I'll pour it all over the sea I would.

CB–TC: I can't stand up on water.

TC–CB: Let's fill it up again.

CB found a plastic kettle and pretended to pour it everywhere.

CB–TC: This one's full up.

TC–SG: There's a shark inside (*in a very loud voice*).

TC ran into the role-play area and hit the floor with his teapot (imagining a shark). All the children ran inside and jumped onto the bench.

TC–SG: The shark's eating your legs.

CB tried to carry on a different theme and fell onto the floor.

CB–SG: I'm a crocodile.

CB–CG: The crocodile's dead. Let's tickle him.

CB–CG: I'm alive.

TC tries to intervene and change the plot again.

TC–SG: I can hear a roar in that place. Can you help me find him?

TC picked up his teapot again and started making sweeping motions under the work bench.

TC–SG: Swipe swipe, I'm still looking for sharks (*loudly*).

TC fell to the floor laughing to himself.

TC–CB: You throw it and the sharks can't sleep (*refers to his teapot*).

TC got up and ran around the outside of the play area, shouting to the SG.

TC–SG: There's some sharks down there.

He picked up a piece of cloth which was lying on the floor.

TC–SG: I'll use my dusters and then they'll go.

TC ran screaming back into the role-play area.

TC–SG: Run. You nearly got blown up by that thing.

Under the work bench a girl was sitting holding a doll.

TC–CG: I'm a goody.

Activity

There are different ways of analysing and interpreting this episode. Looking at this episode from the perspective of the EYFS, it is possible to identify some learning goals in personal, social and emotional development, language and communication, and knowledge and understanding of the world. But this would provide a partial and limited understanding of the play.

So how can we develop a deeper understanding of the social and symbolic complexity of this episode? Read the episode and make notes on events that grab your attention or raise questions for you. Discuss these with a colleague or in a group. Now look at the characteristics and qualities of play (see Appendix), and identify the children's competences.

Think about developing a critical perspective: are there any issues about power, choice and inclusion here? How are these children performing gender roles, particularly the target child? Who dominates the play and with what purposes? What roles do the animals play and what behaviours and responses do they provoke?

Discuss your responses in a group and consider what implications this episode has for how you understand the complexities of play.

Developing individual play plans

The Code of Practice for children with special educational needs (DfEE, 2001) recommends that children should have Individual Education Plans (IEPs), which provide a clear statement of their needs and how these can be met. Sayeed and Guerin (2000) developed the idea of IPPs, which can help practitioners to ensure that their provision includes play for children with additional or special educational needs and disabilities, based on:

- high expectations
- careful planning
- quality provision
- potential reached.

The practitioner uses play-based assessment to:

- establish new expectations for the child as player/learner
- identify specific needs and interests
- support long-term goals and short-term targets.

Children with SEN may have general and/or specific learning difficulties; however, many will develop their play skills along the same continuum as their peers, but in different ways. Checklists for children's progress tend to be based on developmental norms – what is typically expected for children of a similar age and background. The learning goals and outcomes in curriculum policies such as the EYFS and Key Stage 1 present a hierarchical framework of skills, knowledge and understanding, but the sequences in which these are learned will differ among children. Therefore, it is all too easy for practitioners to develop deficit, rather than credit, perceptions about the progress and achievements of children with SEN and disabilities, which may influence their access to play and to a broad and balanced curriculum.

The Model of Integrated Curriculum and Pedagogical Approaches (Chapters 4 and 5) is equally applicable, with the addition of techniques and strategies to enable children to access play and to participate successfully in different activities. Practitioners need to take into account:

- specialized knowledge about the child and about specific syndromes (such as Autistic Spectrum Disorder, Down's Syndrome, Attention Deficit and Hyperactivity Disorder)
- knowledge about the nature and effects of any impairments (auditory, visual, speech, language, communication, social, physical)
- children's perspectives on their abilities and potential.

Norwich and Kelly (2004) argue that, in the context of research with children who have special educational needs and disabilities, eliciting their perspectives is not just a technical matter, it also involves complex ethical considerations and contextual factors. These principles can be applied to assessment in early years settings. Eliciting children's perspectives on their play should take into account:

1   the child's and young person's competences and characteristics;

2   the questioner's competences and characteristics;

3   the purpose and use made of eliciting child and young person's views;

4   the setting and context: power, relationships and emotional factors;

5   ethical and human rights considerations. (Norwich and Kelly, 2004: 45)

Communication and collaboration are integral to effective provision, and the best sources of information come from parents, caregivers and the professionals involved with the child/family. Play-based assessment can enable all those involved to contribute their observations and knowledge about a child, to work together towards common goals and to ensure access and inclusion (see Em's story in Chapter 8). If a child is having difficulty in a specific area of play, it may not be the child, but the provision, the resources or the practitioner's images of the child that need to be modified, as shown in Peter's case study. Nutbrown and Clough (2013) report an action research study with early years practitioners, which documents that children's views of inclusion and belonging were often different from those of adults. In response to the children's views, the practitioners planned specific changes and interventions, which led to more inclusive polices and pedagogies.

Assessment and evaluation as ethical practice

Assessment and evaluation can be used by practitioners for auditing their provision, in order to develop insights into the patterns of learning for each child, their progress, capabilities and achievements over time. However, assessment is not simply a technical process of mapping children's progress against curriculum goals or learning outcomes: auditing from a technical perspective will provide limited information that allows practitioners to solve problems that are related to national policy frameworks, and in ways that are consistent with policy aspirations (such as 'raising standards' in literacy, motivating 'underachieving boys' or solving the 'obesity crisis'). In England, four versions of the Foundation Stage have been implemented between 1999 and 2012, which reflects shifting influences such as political ideologies, media panics and knee-jerk reactions to spurious comparisons of performance in international league tables.

An alternative perspective is that assessment is an ethical practice. Practitioners can build professional knowledge and capacity for critical reflection which informs their ability to mediate policy frameworks in ways that respond creatively to dimensions of diversity in children's lives. In the approaches to assessment that are described in this chapter, children's perspectives are included, because they can best interpret their ways of knowing and understanding their social and cultural experiences. Again, this reflects commitments to inclusive, democratic and participatory approaches to early childhood education, which are evident in the principles that underpin curriculum models described in Chapter 4. However, practitioners must be prepared for the fact that understanding children's perspectives can challenge dominant policy discourses and practices in pedagogy, curriculum planning and assessment (Wood, 2010c). While policy frameworks define quality and effectiveness, these can result in cultural distance and dissonance, because universal discourses are privileged. The principles of believing in children's rights and competence need to be informed by critical, reflective engagement with institutional cultures and practices, and with personal judgements and biases. Quality and effectiveness can then be understood in ways that are locally situated and responsive to diversities among children, families and communities.

Can auditing and knowledge-building work in harmony? Many practitioners use an on-line version of the Early Years Foundation Stage Profile which tracks children's progress in the learning goals. The data can be used to analyse patterns of progress and achievement across the whole class or for specific groups of children.

 Case study

Interrogating the data

Jo, an experienced early years teacher (also the school's assessment and SEN coordinator) became highly skilled at interrogating the data to address her own concerns about differences in achievement between children, and particularly between boys and girls. The data showed her that the patterns existed, but not *why*: the explanations were more complex and needed further analysis and discussion with the EYFS and Key Stage 1/2 teams. Jo also used the Profile data to discuss with senior management her concerns about the differences in performance between the boys and girls, particularly in writing. It is tempting to use this type of data to identify children's deficits (poor hand coordination; lack of attention; inability to memorize phonic blends). However, Jo and the team critically examined their provision and pedagogies, focusing on whether their literacy activities were contextually relevant and stimulating for children's engagement, involvement and interest. Reasons and explanations were discussed, followed by significant changes to their provision and practice to ensure that all children were experiencing more child-initiated activities, more time outdoors, with opportunities for using and applying literacy skills in a range of contexts.

The recursive and integrated processes of assessment and evaluation should enable practitioners to engage critically with play. Effective practitioners are good researchers and are not afraid to address controversial issues, whether these arise from their own beliefs and values, from their engagement with children and families, and from their wider reading and research. Rather than accepting romantic or idealized versions of play, it is essential to engage with difficult and discomforting questions about children's choices, power relationships, inclusion and exclusion, risky and adventure play, and play as sites for subversion of adults' rules and purposes. Contemporary play scholarship is viewing these issues through different theoretical and methodological lenses, and approaches them by researching *with* rather than *on* children. We can continue to learn from and with children, because they are the skilled players and can teach us about the power of play throughout our lives.

Activity

Critically examine the curriculum frameworks that you are working with in your setting. What are the purposes of assessment and the expectations for your roles and responsibilities? Contrast the guidelines on assessment in the policy framework with your approaches to assessment. From reading this chapter, what areas do you think you need to improve or change?

Further reading

Brooker, L. (2008) *Supporting Transitions in the Early Years*, Maidenhead: Open University Press.

Carr, M. (2001) *Assessment in Early Childhood Settings: Learning Stories*, London: Paul Chapman.

Carr, M. and Lee, W. (2012) *Learning Stories: Constructing Learner Identities in Early Education*, London: Sage.

Carr, M., Smith, A.B., Duncan, J., Jones, C., Lee, W. and Marshall, K. (2009) *Learning in the Making: Disposition and Design in Early Education*, Rotterdam: Sense Publishers.

Genishi, C. and Goodwin, A. Lin (2008) *Diversities in Early Childhood Education: Rethinking and Doing*, New York: Routledge.

Lifter, K., Mason, E.J. and Barton, E.E. (2011) 'Children's play: where we have been and where we could go', *Journal of Early Intervention*, 33 (4): 281–297, http://jei.sagepub.com/cgi/reprint/33/4/281.

Vallberg Roth, A. and Månsson, A. (2011) 'Individual development plans from a critical didactic perspective: focusing on Montessori- and Reggio Emilia-profiled preschools in Sweden', *Journal of Early Childhood Research*, 9 (3): 247–261, http://ecr.sagepub.com/content/early/2011/04/22/1476718X10389148.full.pdf.

 To gain free access to specially selected SAGE journal articles related to key topics discussed in this book please visit: **www.sagepub.co.uk/wood**

CHAPTER 8

DEVELOPING PLAY

The aim of this concluding chapter is to support professional development activities in your settings. You will develop your skills of critical reflection by engaging with:

- pedagogical dilemmas
- change processes
- personal values, beliefs and attitudes

Although play is not the only means of learning in early childhood, there are many benefits for children, including positive dispositions and 'can-do' orientations to learning. These benefits can be developed through the Model of Integrated Curriculum and Pedagogical Approaches that has been used in this book. The final chapter presents activities and case studies that can be used to inform professional development. The case studies have been developed in a range of settings, based on practitioners' involvement in collaborative research projects. These provide examples of change and innovation, based on practitioners identifying their own principles and addressing problems or challenges in their practice. Each of the case studies can be used for discussion and critical reflection. Being a critically reflective practitioner involves challenging values, beliefs and assumptions, and a willingness to engage critically with issues of equity, diversity and social justice.

Knowledge bases for teaching and learning

International research studies emphasize the complexity of the knowledge bases that underpin practice in early childhood settings. Practitioners need deep understanding of the structures of the subject areas of the curriculum – the concepts, skills, tools for enquiry and investigation, and distinctive ways of thinking and reasoning. They need to understand the integrated nature of learning/teaching, how connections can be made between areas of learning and what connections children make through their own activities.

Professional knowledge encompasses shared as well as individual values, principles, visions and beliefs that influence the ethos of the setting. Professional knowledge is not static: skilled practitioners reflect critically on their provision and are willing to improve their practice. They use evidence from their own evaluations, from their peers and from research studies to support their development and to ensure that curriculum frameworks do not become straitjackets. They draw inspiration from children's lives as they bring new ideas and competences into the setting. Very young children are already skilled at using touch-screen computers and older children are more technologically adept than many adults. They are bringing their educational and play futures into early years settings, and practitioners must be ready, willing and able to respond (Yelland, 2010). The following section focuses on integrated approaches to playing, learning and teaching, building on the main principles and theories outlined in previous chapters.

Learning to play: Em's story

Em's story is taken from a research study carried out by Diann Cudmore (1996). Diann was home visitor with the Portage programme, which is an early intervention programme for children with special educational needs. The role of the home visitor is to work and play alongside parents, who are recognized as the child's first, and most important, teachers. Parents and Portage visitors work collaboratively to promote learning and development and enable children to achieve their potential. Learning and teaching through play are integral to the programme and the children's individual plans will incorporate objectives that can be achieved through a wide range of play activities. The Portage Programme is based on a two-way flow of information between the practitioner and the child's family so that interactions are co-constructed around shared observations and teaching strategies.

Diann based her Master's dissertation on Em, a two-year-old girl with Down's syndrome. This decision was informed in part by Diann's dissatisfaction with the assumptions that children with special educational needs learn from self-directed free play. From her experience, Diann had noticed the role of the adult is crucial in helping children to learn how to play and supporting their play-based learning. Em's story illustrates mediated learning experiences (MLE) (Sayeed and Guerin, 2000), in which the adult uses scaffolding strategies to support play and learning. Interactions remain sensitive to the child's observed responses, so that the adult mediates meaning and significance, feelings of competence, shared participation and control of behaviour (Sayeed and Guerin, 2000: 82–83). Em's story therefore illustrates socio-cultural theories of learning and shows how flexibility and structure need to be carefully balanced.

Diann decided to focus on supporting Em's pretend play. She began her study with the understanding that children with learning difficulties are typically described as having developmental delay rather than developmental differences. This enabled Diann to look at Em in terms of her differences and potential rather than deficits against developmental norms. Em's difficulties were multiple: language, speech, hearing, memory, cognitive processing and physical coordination. Em, Diann and Mum were learning Makaton sign language, which combines a gesture with the spoken word and helps children to communicate through acts of shared meaning. Diann also identified that Em needed lots of opportunities to practise and consolidate new skills, using sensory stimulation and scaffolding strategies to encourage Em to participate in play. Episodes of joint play were video-recorded and were shared with Em's Mum to discuss progress and achievements and make decisions about future activities.

In the first episode, Mum introduced a doll to Em, and modelled the actions for putting the doll to bed and covering her with a blanket, drawing attention to her activities through language. Em imitated this activity, but then moved on to another activity. She took the doll out of bed and dropped it in front of Mum with a face cloth (small towel). Mum thought that Em wanted to wash the doll's face and modelled the actions.

However, Em had a different agenda, but found it difficult to convey her meanings. She put the doll back on the bed and covered her with the blanket and the face cloth. Later in the episode, a similar event occurred. Em picked up the doll's nappy and shook it at her Mum, who thought that Em wanted to put the nappy on the doll. Em immediately pulled the nappy off the doll and used it as a cover.

Diann identified some pedagogical dilemmas in the early play episodes. Both adults used a range of resources and techniques to engage Em in pretend play. However, because Em could not verbalize her intentions, it was often difficult for them to tune in to her play agenda. To support Em's learning, photographs were taken of play events such as washing the doll, brushing hair, feeding and drinking, and putting the doll to bed. One photograph showed a spoon, bowl and some chocolate buttons (Em's favourite sweets, which were given as a reward when she used signs to communicate with others). The photographs were laminated and put into a book as a shared resource to help Em with her Makaton signing, using the pictures as additional clues to convey meaning and intentions. Sometimes the photographs were helpful and at other times they were a distraction. In the second videotape, Em had made significant progress in her signing and communication skills, but occasionally became frustrated with the book. She pointed to the picture of the spoon, bowl and chocolate buttons and seemed to indicate that she wanted some buttons to eat, thus distracting her from the dramatic play. This shows that even the best intentions for supporting learning can go astray. For Diann and Mum, understanding Em's meanings became a focus of their play activities, as they gradually shifted from their own agendas of what they wanted to teach Em.

Over a period of three months, Em made significant progress in playing and learning. She communicated more easily as she learned to use signs in context and to express her own intentions:

> During the following play session, there are several incidents where Em uses the sign for 'bed' ... and signs 'drink' in imitation, followed by a more successful episode when Em pretends to drink herself, offers me the cup and then, with a prompt from me, gives the doll a drink. Other brief successes are when Em brushes the doll's hair in imitation, and washes the doll in imitation.
>
> Mismatches also occur; one specific incident showing Em's apparent refusal to switch her attention from the bedding she is holding and shaking to my asking her 'who is this' and showing her the doll.
>
> Although Em looks at the doll and looks at me she ignores my question. She persists in her own intentions, making it very clear that she wants the doll on the bed by vocalizing insistently and pointing to the bed vigorously, saying 'bed' through her use of sign. (Cudmore, 1996: 57)

These mismatches proved to be valuable learning experiences because they provided insights into Em's patterns of learning and highlighted effective interactions as well as breakdowns in communication:

> Problems arise for the adults during the play when attention-switching strategies fail to distract Em from her own intentions. Successful communication occurs most frequently when the adults follow Em's lead, matching their comments, questions and actions towards the toy or game that Em was already engaged with and that had been chosen by her. (Cudmore, 1996: 58)

This practice-based evidence was valuable for challenging assumptions, designing play experiences and informing more finely tuned interactions which could be used by Diann and Mum to support continuity of experience. The study also shows the value of *ipsative assessment* (Chapter 7), which enables adults to plan the next steps in learning based on observed patterns of play and the dispositions of the child (rather than only on defined teaching objectives). On the basis of her research, Diann developed a dramatic play checklist which identified 30 different types of behaviour across four stages:

1   Self-pretending and object–person pretending.
2   Object pretending.
3   Sequence pretending action/objects.
4   Role play.

Diann and Mum used the checklist, not as a hierarchy of skills and competences, but as a typical range of behaviours that could be identified in the context of playing alongside Em. This enabled them to track Em's development and to plan their activities in response to her interests and play choices. While MLE can be a valuable pedagogical approach for children with special educational needs, a key principle for mediating play is maintaining a focus on the child's motives and intentions. For Em, mediated playing and learning experiences supported her communication skills, imaginative use of symbols and tools, and her skills as a player.

Plan–do–review: Amanda's story

Inspired by Julie Fisher's work (see Chapter 3), Amanda Kersey decided to use the plan–do–review (PDR) approach with her Reception/Year 1 children. As a newly qualified teacher, Amanda aimed to align her own values and beliefs with her practice, and considered that PDR would enable her to support children's autonomy, independence and self-initiated activity. Because of other curriculum demands, Amanda decided that she could not use this approach every day with the whole class. It was too time-consuming and, at a pragmatic level, she could not be sure that children would cover all curriculum areas in their planning. She used the class groups for developing PDR so that each group had a turn at planning each afternoon. Amanda organized an adult to be available to help the children with their plans and provide support. Review time was carried out with the whole group so that children could talk about and show what they had been doing. PDR is not an easy option in the early stages: the first half-term was taken up with teaching children planning skills, routines and expectations. Amanda organized the layout of the classroom to ensure open access to good-quality resources (tools, materials and play equipment). For example, in the writing area children had access to materials for making books, which linked with Amanda's approach to teaching literacy.

Amanda decided to use planning sheets to record the children's plans and feedback. Later these were changed to planning books, which served as a record of the children's activities. The planning sheet enabled the children to plan two activities and provided space for feedback to supplement discussion at review time. Perry's plans have been chosen to show evidence of progression in his planning skills over time and to show how Amanda documented evidence of the children's learning.

Perry – October

At the beginning of the Reception year, Perry is able to represent his plans by drawing pictures of blocks. Amanda records his plan (Figure 8.1).

In March, he is able to write his name and has become more skilled at representing what he wants do in his plans (make a tower with the bricks and make a map of the bricks at the writing table – Figure 8.2). Perry made boxes, which he took to the writing table, and put in some plastic letter shapes. In review time, Amanda records his comments:

> I made a good tower. I used a flat piece of wood at the bottom so I could stand on it and make it taller.

> Fine – I made a book. You had to find out what was in the boxes.

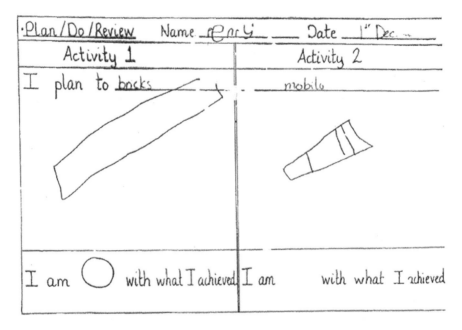

Figure 8.1   Perry's planning sheet 1

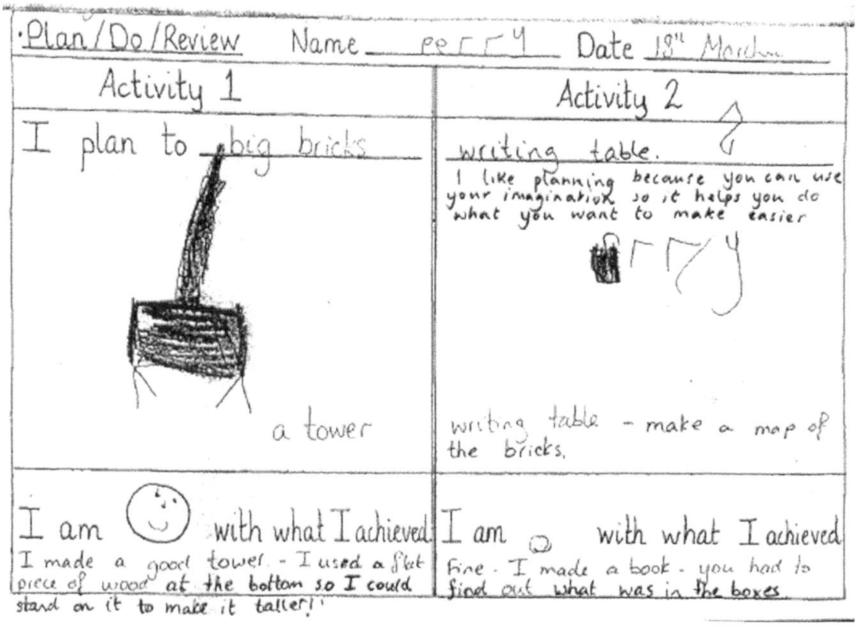

Figure 8.2   Perry's planning sheet 2

By the end of the year, Perry was more ambitious in his plans, and more sophisticated in his representation. Perry planned to make a puppet theatre with a friend. In his drawing (Figure 8.3), he shows them standing either side of the box, holding the pole that raises the curtain. Perry had seen a puppet show and wanted to make the curtain himself. This was a self-initiated activity that involved some complex problem-solving skills: how to make the curtain, fix the pole to the front of the box and raise the curtain at the start of the show.

After making the puppet theatre, Perry developed play scripts with his friends, based on the theme of Bears. At review time, Perry described their play:

> A crocodile came along and ate all the bears' food. The crocodile went upstairs and ate all their beds. The bears came home and saw the crocodile eat all their things. The bears whacked the crocodile on the nose with their paws. The crocodile went back to the water to swim away. Naughty crocodile!

Through this self-initiated activity, Amanda was able to make informed assessments of Perry's progress and achievements. His account shows that he is able to sequence and structure a story, with a beginning, middle and end. He has a good understanding of plot and makes novel connections between the story of the three bears, but replacing Goldilocks with the naughty crocodile. Perry creatively transforms the traditional tale and invents new meanings and roles.

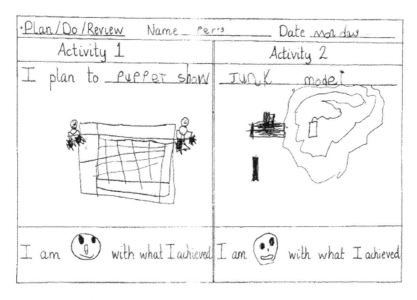

Figure 8.3   Perry's planning sheet 3

Lucy, Kate and Kirsty also became involved in the writing area, making books and puppets related to the theme of bears and writing stories about them. Their feedback at review time provides evidence of their learning and activities and some metacognitive skills.

Lucy made a book about teddy bears (Figure 8.4)

The bears lived in the forest. They saw a house and the bear went in the house then went upstairs and went to sleep in the bed. I dressed up as a bear. I was a koala bear from the North Pole. I put lots of clothes on because it could be cold up there.

Kirsty made a house and a book (Figure 8.5)

I made a teddy bear's house. I needed five squares for the outside and four triangles for the roof. The three bears live in the house. Next time I would make the house bigger so it is nicer for the bears.

I made some teddy bear books for my mum. I found the writing easy but the pictures were hard because they are a bit difficult.

Kate made a bear and a book (Figure 8.6)

I found it hard to put the fingers on. I made the head with bits of plastic. I made the legs with toilet rolls. When I made the body I had to use bits of circles. I stuck these things with glue. You must only use a little bit of glue because otherwise it won't stick. I like my bear. Next time I will paint my bear. I made a book about bears. I found it easy to draw the pictures. I found it hard to do the right words. I will give it to you to read.

These examples show what children can achieve when they are encouraged to plan and reflect on their learning and self-initiated activities. Lucy demonstrates emerging geographical knowledge, even though she located koala bears in the wrong hemisphere. Kirsty and Kate are competent technologists and designers. They use precise mathematical language and are able to use and apply mathematical knowledge. They also indicate their abilities to reflect on their learning and consider how they would do things differently in future. The plan–do–review approach creates time and opportunities for encouraging self-assessment and teaching children language about learning. The examples above show children's ability to sequence events, reflect on action using the past tense, link cause and effect and plan further activities. The children also integrate discipline-based knowledge in technology, mathematics, geography and literacy.

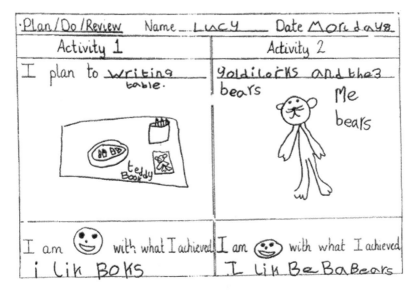

Figure 8.4   Lucy's planning sheet

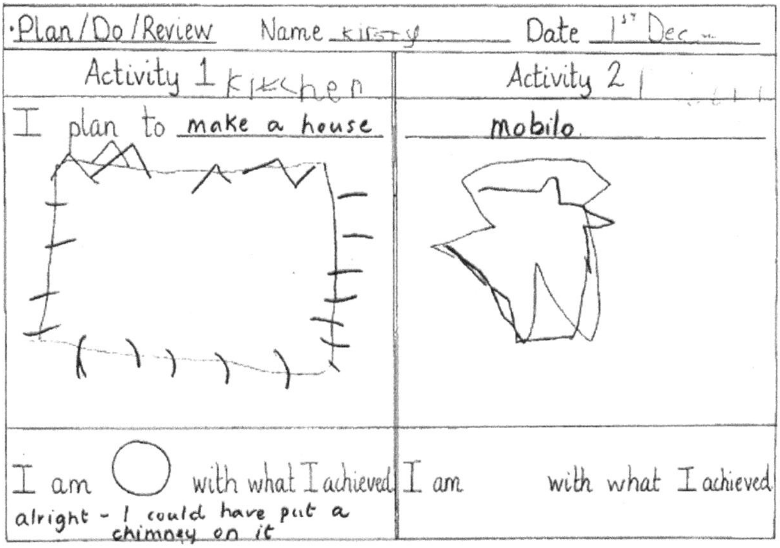

Figure 8.5   Kirsty's planning sheet

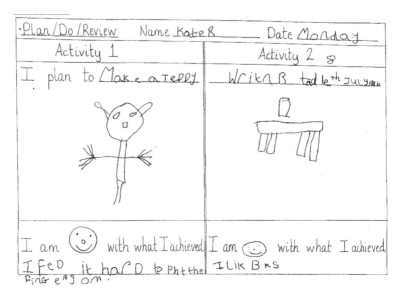

Figure 8.6   Kate's planning sheet

Creativity in a nursery class: Cathie's story

Cathie was inspired by the Reggio Emilia approach (Chapter 3) and wanted to stimulate the children's creativity through a wide variety of media. Materials and resources were made accessible to the children, including different kinds of paints, pencils, chalks and crayons, sizes of brushes, types of paper, equipment for printing, glues, tools and a wide range of collage materials. The team planned some experiences where the children were taught how to use the materials and tools as well as specific techniques, which they then developed in their self-initiated activities. These included observational drawing, mixing paints, selecting tools, media and equipment to create different effects, combining media and learning specific skills such as sewing and weaving. The children also looked at works of art, and regular exhibitions were held in the school, which combined children's, teachers' and parents' contributions. The children's work was displayed well but it was not 'edited' by the adults. The children were also responsible for taking care of the tools and resources and tidying up after themselves.

Through these processes the children were encouraged to explore the materials, play with ideas, make novel combinations, represent their ideas and experiences, learn to use and apply techniques and skills, and value their own and each other's creativity. They had opportunities to work at easels, on flat surfaces and on the floor for larger projects. They worked individually, in pairs, in groups and occasionally produced pieces involving the whole class. The children's work was valued and displayed sensitively and there were no adults' representations in the room. The children were inspired by the quality of the materials available, their freedom to choose, their ability to play with materials and ideas, and the support provided through sensitive interactions with the practitioners. They combined work with playfulness in these experiences and learned that creativity is not the preserve of the gifted few.

Developing a playful school

A primary school appointed a curriculum coordinator for play across the 3–11 age range. She gave advice and support for developing a whole-school approach and identified the teachers' requirements. She drew up a rolling programme of resource acquisitions over a three-year period and was allocated time to play alongside the children to model her role and support the children with some of the more demanding technical and constructive equipment. The older children were encouraged to play with the younger ones on a regular weekly basis and they enjoyed their roles as play tutors. A further spin-off from this whole-school approach was the redesign of the outdoor play environment, again with additional resources, delineated areas for ball games, chasing games and for sitting. The teachers, mealtime assistants and children learned traditional games and, within a short space of time, these approaches eradicated behaviour problems: the daily lines of 'naughty children' outside the headteacher's office became a thing of the past.

In each of these examples, the practitioners conceptualized play as an integral part of the school culture and ethos. They provided enabling conditions to improve the quality of play. They were prepared to change or adapt the indoor and outdoor learning environments, provide appropriate resources and support and make time available for different kinds of play tutoring. Their approaches indicated their values and beliefs about the role of play: they had the confidence and expertise to implement these and, to a certain extent, to take risks in their practice.

Funds of knowledge

This extract illustrates the pedagogical concept of funds of knowledge (Chapters 4 and 5), drawing on research in the experimental Raleigh School, which was based on the work of Susan Isaacs (Boyce, 1946). The school was attended mostly by children from poor homes and communities (low socio-economic status in contemporary terms). Miss Boyce (1946) exemplified how practitioners need to be tuned in to the culturally situated nature of children's learning, and the funds of knowledge that they bring from their experiences in their homes and communities. She provided detailed insights into children's home-based mathematical knowledge, which was also influenced by their social class (in pre-decimal currency, 12 pennies made one shilling, which is the contemporary equivalent of five pence):

> Mathematics was easy for us to teach, since their home and street experiences were rich in mathematical content. Some children almost fed themselves on six days of the week. They had a free breakfast at a charitable institution; with a few coppers [pennies] bought their own dinner (this usually consisted of chips, cakes or a penny pie), coerced their parents into giving them another copper to buy cakes for tea, and finished with bread and margarine. They also brought a halfpenny to school for their daily milk …
>
> Even the more cared-for children heard a great deal about economic situations. They knew the day on which the rent was due and the means of avoiding payment. Most of them ran errands and were successful shoppers although the food was invariably bought in pennyworths. Every outing and all new clothes meant saving up or weekly payments. We had a penny bank into which the children paid their parents' savings in pennies and sixpences; they watched the procedure with interest and could follow the entries in their 'paying in' books … They took themselves, as well as their younger brothers and sisters, to the 'Penny Pictures'. These and other first-hand experiences gave them a background of utilitarian knowledge which the child in the more comfortable home does not acquire. (Boyce, 1946: 157–158)

Miss Boyce documents many play activities in which the children used their 'home and street' experiences, thus demonstrating the important principle that practitioners' understanding of children's funds of knowledge should be socially and culturally sensitive. What is taught in school may not always be part of children's everyday experiences. For example, a Reception class teacher wanted to know how much mathematical knowledge about money the children were using in the role-play area, which was a supermarket. Close observations and transcripts of the play revealed little mathematical content, because the transactions were made using a credit card (the till had a space for 'swiping' cards). So there was no transfer between adult-directed teaching of concepts about money and the children's play activities. Using their observations as points of assessment and evaluation, the teachers speculated whether children today (unlike Miss Boyce's children) hear and see fewer transactions that involve counting out payment or change, because these activities are done technologically, with cards and electronic displays.

Activity

How do funds of knowledge change over time and in different contexts?

Does provision for play reflect children's contemporary knowledge and experiences, and especially the technological practices they encounter in everyday contexts?

In what ways are new technologies changing children's play?

Play memories

The concepts of fear, anxiety, danger and uncertainty are familiar themes in children's play. These emotions can be created imaginatively 'inside the mind' as well as in physical contexts. Between the ages of around four and seven my child-centred world included two ghosts, one in the coal cellar and one in the attic. If I climbed the stairs to the attic without treading on the squeaky step, then the ghost stayed asleep and I got to play with my older brothers' Scalextric and listen to the latest pop records. How the ghost stayed asleep though this racket escaped my attention (the triumph of imagination over reason). The task of missing the squeaky step involved much physical contortion and climbing along the staircase – part of the ritual necessary for defying the ghost. I avoided the coal cellar unless I was helping to fill a scuttle, because ghosts never came out when adults were around. The ghosts were often joined at night by the skeletons that could crawl out of the broken tombs in the local graveyard. Fairies lived in the garden and needed to be given 'perfume' – concoctions of rose petals and water – to protect me from the ghosts and skeletons. I got into trouble for taking the petals from the roses, but my need to placate my tormentors overrode an occasional telling off.

Activity

My play memories often make me think about the meaning of child-centredness and whether we understand this concept from adults' rather than children's perspectives. What play themes, characters and rituals did your child-centred world contain? Did anyone share this world with you and did you keep it secret from adults? What imagined 'risks' did you create? Compare these with actual risks that you took in your play lives, and what were the outcomes?

Improving the quality of provision for play

Practitioners, not policy-makers, are at the heart of improving the quality of teaching and learning in educational settings. Practitioners are in a powerful position to create detailed pedagogical knowledge through engaging critically with educational practices and the theories that inform them. Most of the practical examples given throughout this book have arisen from practice-based research, where early childhood specialists have worked collaboratively on problems and challenges in their own settings, and created their own 'designer versions' of integrating play into their provision. The following two tasks are designed to stimulate critical engagement with beliefs, values and assumptions about play.

Activity

Sharing values, beliefs and attitudes about play

This activity can be carried out in a team or in collaboration with parents and caregivers. Each member of staff should write a short account of an episode of good-quality play. The episode can be indoors or outdoors; solitary, parallel or cooperative; with or without an adult present. Members of staff should work together in small groups to discuss the characteristics of good-quality play. The following framework can be used for analysis:

- The type of play observed
- Number of children
- Resources available and how they were used
- Whether an adult was present and what role the adult played
- Time available, layout of the classroom/play area
- What happened in the play – how did it develop, was it 'successful', who were the leaders/followers, what did you learn about the children?

The outcomes of the analysis should be written on a large sheet of paper and shared/contrasted with another group. If the activity is used as part of a whole-school focus on play, the analysis could inform the development of a policy on play, taking into account continuity and progression across the Foundation Stage and Key Stages 1 and 2.

Activity

Personal beliefs and theories about play

Drawing on your knowledge and experience, and the analyses of play in practice, discuss the following questions:

- Are there differences between your idealized vision of the value of play and what actually happens in your practice?
- Can you identify what constraints there are in your practice and how these impact on the quality of your provision for play? Think about rules and how these operate to constrain or enable play.

- How might some of the constraints/rules you have identified be changed?
- What areas do you need to focus on in order to improve the quality of provision for play?

Discuss and share your ideas within a group. You could use some of the examples and transcripts of play in this book, or carry out and analyse your own observations. A ten-minute episode can provide much valuable information for analysis and critical reflection.

Future directions

Improving the quality of provision for play in pre-school and school settings is a continuing concern. Creating unity between playing, learning and teaching remains a significant challenge for early childhood specialists. Finding spaces for play remains a significant challenge for young people. Although the United Nations Convention on the Rights of the Child recognizes play as a fundamental human right, those rights can be impeded or ignored. In a study of children's accounts of their experience of the right to play, Davey and Lundy (2011) identified many constraints to play opportunities including issues of safety, access, supervision, distance from home and the occupation of local streets by cars.

I hope that this book inspires practitioners and students to think critically and creatively about play and about their provision. Policy-defined versions of educational play represent a technical approach to managing play into some semblance of order and predictability. But play will always elude whatever utilitarian structures and boundaries we create, including policies, academic theories and expectations for what play is and what play does. Returning to Henricks' philosophical notion that play is the laboratory of the possible (2006: 1) we must remain open to the possibilities that children create for themselves, and that we help to create through our professional practice.

Further reading

Markström, A. (2010) 'Talking about children's resistance to the institutional order and teachers in preschool', *Journal of Early Childhood Research*, 8 (3): 303–314, http://ecr.sagepub.com/content/8/3/303.

 To gain free access to specially selected SAGE journal articles related to key topics discussed in this book please visit: **www.sagepub.co.uk/wood**

APPENDIX

UNDERSTANDING THE COMPLEXITIES OF PLAY

I have attempted to describe some of the qualities of play that indicate its complexity (especially dramatic and socio-dramatic play). These are not criteria, but are characteristics of play that can be seen when we look closely at children's actions and interactions. These can be used as a pedagogical tool and as a research tool for analysing play, but with the proviso that by looking and listening carefully, we develop our understanding of children's meanings and purposes.

Play skills and knowledge

- Uses memory and recall strategies
- Defines a theme – plot, characters and sequence (play text)
- Negotiates a play frame and establishes rules (play context)
- Uses own ideas and listens to others
- Able to negotiate and cooperate towards agreed ends
- Transforms objects, materials, environment and actions
- Communicates through language, signs, symbols and gestures (representational thinking)
- Communicates the pretence, defines roles and actions. Conveys meanings and intentions (metacommunication)
- Steps in and out of the play (distancing)
- Rehearses roles and actions, directs or manages the play
- Can be directed and managed by others
- Can maintain and develop a role
- Uses imagination and creativity to combine and re-combine ideas

- Empathizes/understands the perspective of others
- Creates, identifies and solves problems
- Reveals motives, needs and interests
- Listens, cooperates, revises and extends ideas
- Uses metacognitive strategies – predicts, monitors, checks, reflects, evaluates

Socio-affective and communicative skills and processes

- Communicates with peers and adults in small and large groups
- Engages in conversations with peers/adults
- Conveys ideas, comments on actions, gives directions
- Joins in a game or activity
- Assigns roles, takes on roles, stays in role
- Negotiates rules, abides by rules
- Plays alone/in parallel/collaboratively in pairs/in groups
- Uses props/assigns meaning to objects
- Uses abstract thinking to convey meaning and pretence
- Offers alternative suggestions
- Manages self and others in play
- Understands own and others' emotions
- Regulates own feelings and emotions
- Distances self to direct, negotiate, develop and extend the play
- Establishes friendships – same and opposite sex
- Uses conflict resolution strategies
- Listens to others/understands perspective of others

Investigation, exploration and problem-solving skills and processes

- Creates, recognizes and solves problems
- Observes closely and carefully
- Asks and answers questions
- Uses sensory exploration in investigating the properties and behaviour of materials
- Uses fine motor skills in investigating, controlling and manipulating materials
- Uses a variety of tools to assist investigation
- Notices and communicates causes and effects
- Uses descriptive language to convey experience, feelings and ideas, to organize, persuade and report accurately
- Represents ideas through different media
- Uses specific terms to describe and analyse experience (e.g. mathematical, scientific, technological)

- Perceives and describes relationships
- Perceives and describes classifications
- Makes connections between existing and new knowledge
- Makes predictions, tests ideas/hypotheses
- Describes activities and conveys information
- Collaborates with others towards agreed ends
- Seeks help from peers/adults

Creative and imaginative skills and processes

- Understands the what if/as if nature of pretend play
- Able to pretend, conveys pretence, develops the pretence
- Distinguishes fantasy and reality
- Combines fantasy and reality
- Generates and communicates ideas and imagination through language and different media – drawing, painting, modelling, writing, collage, printing, constructions and layouts
- Combines materials and resources
- Transforms materials and resources (making one thing stand for another)
- Enjoys sensory experiences
- Takes risks, refines ideas, edits work/products
- Conveys abstract ideas verbally and through different media
- Responds emotionally to experiences and expresses emotions verbally and through different media

BIBLIOGRAPHY

Alcock, S. (2010) 'Young children's playfully complex communication: distributed imagination', *European Early Childhood Education Research Journal*, 18 (2): 215–228.

Anning, A. and Ring, K. (2004) *Making Sense of Children's Drawings*, London: Sage.

Attfield, J. (1992) 'The possibilities and value of assessing children's learning through play at Key Stage 1', unpublished MEd thesis, University of Exeter.

Bennett, N., Wood, E. and Rogers, S. (1997) *Teaching Through Play: Teachers' Thinking and Classroom Practice*, Buckingham: Open University Press.

Bilton, H. (2010) *Outdoor Learning in the Early Years: Management and Innovation* (3rd edn), London: Routledge.

Blaise, M. (2005) 'A feminist poststructuralist study of children "doing" gender in an urban kindergarten classroom', *Early Childhood Research Quarterly*, 20: 85–108. doi: 10.1016/j.ecresq.2005.01.002.

Blaise, M. (2010) 'Creating a postdevelopmental logic for mapping gender and sexuality in early childhood', in L. Brooker and S. Edwards (eds), *Engaging Play*, Maidenhead: Open University Press, pp. 209–219.

Bodrova, E. (2008) 'Make-believe play versus academic skills: a Vygotskian approach to today's dilemma of early childhood education', *European Early Childhood Education Research Journal*, 16 (3): 357–369.

Booth, D. (1994) *Story Drama: Reading, Writing and Roleplaying Across the Curriculum*, London: Pembroke Publishers.

Boyce, E.R. (1946) *Play in the Infants' School* (2nd edn), London: Methuen.

Brady, L.-M., Gibb, J., Henshall, A. and Lewis, J. (2008) *Play and Exercise in the Early Years: Physically Active Play in Early Childhood Provision*, London: Department for Culture, Media and Sport.

Bredekamp, S. and Copple, S. (eds) (1997) *Developmentally Appropriate Practice in Early Childhood Programs Serving Children from Birth Through 8* (revised edn), Washington, DC: National Association for the Education of Young Children.

Broadhead, P. (2004) *Early Years Play and Learning: Developing Social Skills and Co-operation*, London: RoutledgeFalmer.

Broadhead, P. (2006) 'Developing an understanding of young children's learning through play: the place of observation, interaction and reflection', *British Educational Research Journal*, 32 (2): 191–207. doi: 10.1080/01411920600568976.

Broadhead, P. (2010) 'Cooperative play and learning from Nursery to Year One', in P. Broadhead, J. Howard and E. Wood (eds), *Play and Learning in the Early Years: From Research to Practice*, London: Sage, pp. 43–59.

Broadhead, P. and Burt, A. (2012) *Understanding Young Children's Learning Through Play: Building Playful Pedagogies*, Abingdon: Routledge.

Broadhead, P., Howard, J. and Wood, E. (2010) (eds) *Play and Learning in the Early Years: From Research to Practice*, London: Sage.

Brooker, L. (2006) 'From home to home corner: observing children's identity maintenance in early childhood settings', *Children and Society*, 20: 116–127.

Brooker, L. (2008) *Supporting Transitions in the Early Years*, Maidenhead: Open University Press.

Brooker, L. (2010) 'Learning to play, or playing to learn? Children's participation in the cultures of homes and settings', in L. Brooker and S. Edwards (eds), *Engaging Play*, Maidenhead: Open University Press, pp. 39–53.

Brooker, L. (2011) 'Taking children seriously: an alternative agenda for research?', *Journal of Early Childhood Research*, 9 (2): 137–149.

Brooker, L. and Edwards, S. (eds) (2010) *Engaging Play*, Maidenhead: Open University Press.

Brown, F. (ed.) (2003), *Playwork Theory and Practice*, Buckingham: Open University Press.

Bruner, J. (1991) 'The nature and uses of immaturity', in M. Woodhead, R. Carr and P. Light (eds), *Becoming a Person*, London: Routledge/Open University Press.

Bruner, J.S., Jolly, A. and Sylva, K. (eds) (1976), *Play: Its Role in Development and Evolution*, London: Penguin.

Carr, M. (2000) 'Technological affordance, social practice and learning narratives in an early childhood setting', *International Journal of Technology and Design*, 10: 61–79.

Carr, M. (2001) *Assessment in Early Childhood Settings: Learning Stories*, London: Paul Chapman.

Carr, M. and Lee, W. (2012) *Learning Stories: Constructing Learner Identities in Early Education*, London: Sage.

Carr, M., Smith, A.B., Duncan, J., Jones, C., Lee, W. and Marshall, K. (2009) *Learning in the Making: Disposition and Design in Early Education*, Rotterdam: Sense Publishers.

Carruthers, E. and Worthington, M. (2011) *Understanding Children's Mathematics: Beginnings in Play*, Maidenhead: Open University Press.

Casey, T. (2007) *Environments for Outdoor Play: A Practical Guide to Making Space for Children*, London: Sage.

Chazan, S. (2002) *Profiles of Play*, London: Jessica Kingsley.

Chen, J.-Q., Masur, A. and McNamee, G. (2011) 'Young children's approaches to learning: a socio-cultural perspective', *Early Child Development and Care*, 181 (8): 1137–1152. doi: 10.1080/03004430.

Christman, D. (2010) 'Creating social justice in early childhood education: a case study in equity and context', *Journal of Research on Leadership Education*, 5 (3): 107–137.

Cohen, D. (1993) *The Development of Play* (2nd edn), London: Croom Helm.

Cohen, D. and MacKeith, S.A. (1991) *The Development of Imagination: The Private Worlds of Childhood*, London: Routledge.

Cohen, L. (2009) 'The heteroglossic world of preschoolers' pretend play', *Contemporary Issues in Early Childhood*, 10 (4), 331–342. doi.org/10.2304/ciec.2009.10.4.331

Cook, J.S. (2003) 'Progression and continuity in role play in the Foundation Stage', unpublished MEd thesis, University of Exeter.

Corsaro, W.A. (2004) *The Sociology of Childhood*, Thousand Oaks, CA: Pine Forge Press.

Cowie, B. and Carr, M. (2004) 'The consequences of socio-cultural assessment', in A. Anning, J. Cullen and M. Fleer (eds), *Early Childhood Education: Society and Culture*, London: Sage, pp. 95–106.

Cudmore, D. (1996) *Developing Dramatic Play in the Portage Programme*, unpublished MEd thesis, University of Exeter.

Davey, C. and Lundy, L. (2011) 'Towards greater recognition of the right to play: an analysis of Article 31 of the UNCRC', *Children and Society*, 25: 3–14. doi: 10.1111/j.1099-0860.2009.00256.x.

DCELLS (Department for Children, Education, Lifelong Learning and Skills) (2008a) *Framework for Children's Learning for 3–7 Year Olds in Wales*, Crown Copyright, www.wales.gov.uk (accessed 7 November 2011).

DCELLS (Department for Children, Education, Lifelong Learning and Skills) (2008b) *Play/Active Learning Overview for 3–7 Year Olds*, Crown Copyright, www.wales.gov.uk (accessed 7 November 2011).

DeVries, R. (1997) 'Piaget's social theory', *Educational Researcher*, 26 (2): 4–17.

DfE (Department for Education) (2011) *The Early Years: Foundations for Life, Health and Learning. An Independent Report on the Early Years Foundation Stage to Her Majesty's Government*, www.dfe.gov.uk (accessed 15 April 2011).

DfE (Department for Education) (2012a) *The Statutory Framework for the Early Years Foundation Stage. Setting the Standards for Learning, Development and Care for Children from Birth to Five*, www.education.gov.uk/publications/standard/AllPublications/Page1/DFE-00023-2012 (accessed 15 April 2012).

DfE (Department for Education) (2012b) *Foundations for Quality. The Independent Review of Early Education and Childcare Qualifications. Final Report (The Nutbrown Review)*, www.education.gov.uk/nutbrownreview (accessed 15 July 2012).

DfEE (Department for Education and Employment) (2001) *Code of Practice for the Identification and Assessment of Special Educational Needs* (revised), London: DfEE.

Dockett, S. and Meckley, A. (2007) 'What young children say about play at school: United States and Australia comparisons', in D.J. Sluss and O.S. Jarrett (eds), *Investigating Play in the 21st Century. Play and Culture Studies, Volume 7*, Lanham, MD: University Press of America, pp. 88–113.

Dowling, M. (2010) *Young Children's Personal, Social and Emotional Development* (3rd edn), London: Sage.

Dowling, M. (2012) *Young Children's Thinking*, London: Sage.

Dunn, J. (2004) *Children's Friendships: The Beginnings of Intimacy*, Oxford: Blackwell Publishing.

du Pré, H. and du Pré, P. (1997) *A Genius in the Family: An Intimate Memoir of Jacqueline du Pré*, London: Vintage.

Durand, T.M. (2010) 'Celebrating diversity in early care and education settings: moving beyond the margins', *Early Child Development and Care*, 180 (7): 835–848. doi: 10.1080/03004430802466226.

Edmiston, B. (2008) *Forming Ethical Identities in Play*, Abingdon: Routledge.

Edwards, S. (2007) 'From developmental-constructivism to socio-cultural theory and practice: an expansive analysis of teachers' professional learning in early childhood education', *Journal of Early Childhood Research*, 5 (1): 83–106.

Edwards, S. (2010) 'Numberjacks are on their way! A cultural historical reflection on contemporary society and the early childhood curriculum', *Pedagogy, Culture & Society*, 18 (3): 261–272. doi: 10.1080/14681366.2010.504649.

Edwards, S. (2011) 'Lessons from "a really useful engine"™: using Thomas the Tank Engine™ to examine the relationship between play as a leading activity, imagination and reality in children's contemporary play worlds', *Cambridge Journal of Education*, 41 (2): 195–210.

Edwards, S. and Nuttall, J. (2009) *Professional Learning in Early Childhood Settings*, Rotterdam: SensePublishers.

Engdahl, I. (2011) 'Toddler interaction during play in the Swedish preschool', *Early Child Development and Care*, 181(10): 1421–1439.

Factor, J. (2009) '"It's only play if you get to choose": children's perceptions of play and adult intentions', in C. Dell Clarke (ed.), *Transactions at Play. Play and Culture Studies, Volume 9*, Lanham, MD: University Press of America, pp. 129–146.

File, N., Mueller, J. and Wisneski, D. (eds) (2012) *Curriculum in Early Childhood Education: Re-examined, Rediscovered, Renewed*, New York: Routledge.

Fisher, J. (2013) *Starting from the Child?* (4th edn), Maidenhead: Open University Press.

Fisher, J. and Wood, E. (2012) 'Changing educational practice in the early years through practitioner-led action research: an adult–child interaction project',

International Journal of Early Years Education, 20(2), 114–129. doi: 10.1080/09669760.2012.715400.

Fleer, M. (2010) *Early Learning and Development: Cultural-historical Concepts in Play,* Cambridge: Cambridge University Press.

Fromberg, D. (1987) 'Play', in P. Monighan-Nourot, B. Scales, J. VanHoorn and M. Almy (eds), *Looking at Children's Play,* New York: Teachers College Press.

Fromberg, D.P. and Bergen, D. (2006) *Play from Birth to Twelve: Contexts, Perspectives, and Meanings* (2nd edn), New York: Routledge.

Frost, J.L., Wortham, S.C. and Reifel, R.S. (2005) *Play and Child Development,* Upper Saddle River, NJ: Prentice-Hall.

Garvey, C. (1991) *Play* (2nd edn), London: Fontana.

Genishi, C. and Goodwin, A. Lin (2008) *Diversities in Early Childhood Education: Rethinking and Doing,* New York: Routledge.

González, N., Moll, L.C., and Amanti, C. (eds) (2005) *Funds of Knowledge: Theorizing Practices in Households, Communities, and Classrooms,* Mahwah, NJ: Lawrence Erlbaum.

Goodley, D. and Runswick-Cole, K. (2012) 'Reading Rosie: the postmodern disabled child', *Journal of Educational and Child Psychology,* 29 (2): 53–66.

Gopnik, A., Meltzoff, A.N. and Kuhl, P.K. (1999) *The Scientist in the Crib: Minds, Brains, and How Children Learn,* New York: William Morrow and Company.

Grieshaber, S. and McArdle, F. (2010) *The Trouble with Play,* Maidenhead: Open University Press.

Guttiérez, K.D. and Rogoff, B. (2003) 'Cultural ways of learning: individual traits or repertoires of practice', *Educational Researcher,* 32 (5): 19–25.

Hall, E. (2010) 'Identity in young children's drawings: power, agency, control, and transformation', in P. Broadhead, J. Howard and E. Wood (eds), *Play and Learning in the Early Years: From Research to Practice,* London: Sage, pp. 95–112.

Hedges, H. (2010) 'Whose goals and interests?', in L. Brooker and S. Edwards (eds), *Engaging Play,* Maidenhead: McGrawHill/Open University Press, pp. 25–38.

Hedges, H. (2011a) 'Rethinking SpongeBob and Ninja Turtles: popular culture as funds of knowledge for curriculum co-construction', *Australasian Journal of Early Childhood,* 36 (1), 25–29.

Hedges, H. (2011b) 'Connecting "snippets of knowledge": teachers' understandings of the concept of working theories', *Early Years: An International Journal of Research and Practice,* 31 (3), 271–284.

Hedges, H. and Cullen, J. (2011) 'Participatory learning theories: a framework for early childhood pedagogy', *Early Child Development and Care,* 82 (7): 921–940. doi: 10.1080/03004430.2011.597504.

Hedges, H., Cullen, J. and Jordan, B. (2011) 'Early years curriculum: funds of knowledge as a conceptual framework for children's interests', *Journal of Curriculum Studies,* 43 (2): 185–205. doi: 10.1080/00220272.2010.511275.

Henricks, T.S. (2006) *Play Reconsidered: Sociological Perspectives on Human Expression*, Urbana, IL: University of Illinois Press.

Henricks, T.S. (2009) 'Play and the rhetorics of time: progress, regression, and the meanings of the present', in D. Kuschner (ed.), *From Children to Red Hatters®: Diverse Images and Issues of Play. Play and Culture Studies, Volume 8*, Lanham, MD: University Press of America, pp. 14–38.

Henricks, T.S. (2010) 'Play as ascending meaning revisited: four types of assertive play', in E.E. Nwokah (ed.), *Play as Engagement and Communication. Play and Culture Studies, Volume 10*, Lanham, MD: University Press of America, pp. 189–216.

Henricks, T.S. (2011) 'Play as deconstruction', in C. Lobman and B.E. O'Neill (eds), *Play and Performance: Play and Culture Studies, Volume 11*, Lanham, MD: University Press of America, pp. 201–236.

Holland, P. (2003) *We Don't Play with Guns Here: War, Weapon and Superhero Play in the Early Years*, Maidenhead: Open University Press.

Holzman, L. (2009) *Vygotsky at Work and Play*, East Sussex: Routledge.

Howard, J. (2010) 'Making the most of play in the early years: the importance of children's perceptions', in P. Broadhead, J. Howard and E. Wood (2010) (eds), *Play and Learning in the Early Years: From Research to Practice*, London: Sage.

Hughes, F.P. (2010) *Children, Play, and Development* (4th edn), Thousand Oaks, CA: Sage.

Hutt, S.J., Tyler, C., Hutt, C. and Christopherson, H. (1989) *Play, Exploration and Learning*, London: Routledge.

Hyder, T. (2005) *War, Conflict and Play*, Maidenhead: Open University Press.

Jarvis, P. (2007) 'Monsters, magic and Mr Psycho: a biocultural approach to rough and tumble play in the early years of primary school', *Early Years*, 27 (2): 171–188.

Jarvis, P. (2010) '"Born to play": the biocultural roots of rough and tumble play, and its impact upon young children's learning and development', in P. Broadhead, J. Howard and E. Wood (2010) (eds), *Play and Learning in the Early Years: From Research to Practice*, London: Sage, pp. 61–77.

Johansson, E. and Emilson, A. (2010) 'Toddlers' life in Swedish preschool', *International Journal of Early Childhood*, 42 (2): 165–179.

Johnson, J.E., Christie, J.F. and Wardle, F. (2005) *Play, Development, and Early Education*, New York: Pearson/Allyn and Bacon.

Jones, E. and Reynolds, G. (1992) *The Play's the Thing: Teachers' Roles in Children's Play*, New York: Teachers College Press.

Kangas, S., Määttä, K. and Uusiautti, S. (2012) 'Ethnographic research on autistic children's play', *International Journal of Play*, 1 (1): 37–50.

Kapasi, H. and Gleave, J. (2009) *Because It's Freedom: Children's Views on their Time to Play*, Play England/Inspire, www.playday.org.uk.

Kelly-Byrne, D. (1989) *A Child's Play Life: An Ethnographic Study*, New York: Teachers College Press.

Knight, S. (ed.) (2011a) *Forest School for All*, London: Sage.

Knight, S. (2011b) *Risk and Adventure in Outdoor Play: Learning from Forest Schools*, London: Sage.

König, A. (2009) 'Observed classroom interaction processes between pre-school teachers and children: results of a video study during free-play time in German pre-schools', *Educational and Child Psychology*, 26 (2): 53–65.

Kuschner, D. (ed.) (2009) *From Children to Red Hatters®: Diverse Images and Issues of Play. Play and Culture Studies, Volume 8*, Lanham, MD: University Press of America.

Levinson, M.P. (2005) 'The role of play in the formation and maintenance of cultural identity: gypsy children in home and school contexts', *Journal of Contemporary Ethnography*, 34 (5): 499–532. doi: 10.1177/0891241605279018.

Lifter, K., Mason, E.J. and Barton, E.E. (2011) 'Children's play: where we have been and where we could go', *Journal of Early Intervention*, 33 (4): 281–297.

Lillemyr, O.F. (2009) *Taking Play Seriously: Children and Play in Early Childhood Education – An Exciting Challenge*, Charlotte NC: Information Age Publishing.

Little, H. (2010) 'Relationship between parents' beliefs and their responses to risk-taking behaviour during outdoor play', *Journal of Early Childhood Research*, 8 (3): 313–330.

Little, H. and Wyver, S. (2010) 'Individual differences in children's risk perceptions and appraisals in outdoor learning environments', *International Journal of Early Years Education*, 18 (4): 297–313.

Löfdahl, A. (2006) 'Children's play and peer-cultures in preschool', *Journal of Early Childhood Research*, 4 (10): 77–88.

Lowenstein, A.E. (2011) 'Early care and education as educational panacea: what do we really know about its effectiveness?', *Educational Policy*, 25 (92): 93–114. doi: 10.1177/0895904810387790.

Macintyre, C. (2001) *Enhancing Learning Through Play: A Developmental Perspective in Early Years Settings*, London: David Fulton.

MacLure, M., Jones, L., Holmes, R. and MacRae, C. (2012) 'Becoming a problem: behaviour and reputation in the early years classroom', *British Educational Research Journal*, 38 (3): 447–471. doi: 10.1080/01411926.2011.552709.

MacNaughton, G. (2009) 'Exploring critical constructivist perspectives on children's learning', in A. Anning, J. Cullen and M. Fleer (eds), *Early Childhood Education: Society and Culture* (2nd edn), London: Sage, pp. 53–63.

Malaguzzi, L. (1993) 'For an education based on relationships', *Young Children*, November, 9–13.

Markström, A. (2010) 'Talking about children's resistance to the institutional order and teachers in preschool', *Journal of Early Childhood Research*, 8 (3): 303–314.

Marsh, J. (2004) 'The techno-literacy practices of young children', *Journal of Early Childhood Research*, 2 (1): 51–66.

Marsh, J. (ed.) (2005) *Popular Culture, New Media and Digital Literacy in Early Childhood*, London: RoutledgeFalmer.

Marsh, J. (2010) 'Young children's play in online virtual worlds', *Journal of Early Childhood Research*, 8 (1): 23–29. doi: 10.1177/1476718X09345406.

Marsh, J. (2012) 'Purposes for literacy in children's use of the online virtual world *Club Penguin*', *Journal of Research in Reading*. doi: 10.1111/j.1467-9817.2012.01530.x.

Marsh, J. and Millard, E. (2000) *Literacy and Popular Culture: Using Children's Culture in the Classroom*, London: Paul Chapman.

Martlew, J., Stephen, C. and Ellis, J. (2011) 'Play in the primary school classroom? The experience of teachers supporting children's learning through a new pedagogy', *Early Years: an International Journal of Research and Development*, 31 (1): 71–83. doi: 10.1080/09575146.2010.529425.

Meade, A. and Cubey, P. (2008) *Thinking Children, Learning About Schemas*, Maidenhead: Open University Press.

Meadows, S. (2006) *The Child As Thinker*, London: Routledge.

Meadows, S. (2010) *The Child as Social Person*, London: Routledge.

Meckley, A. (1994) 'Disappearing pegs in the road: discovering meaning in young children's social play', paper presented to the American Educational Research Association Conference, 6 April.

Meckley, A. (2002) 'Observing children's play: mindful methods', paper presented to the International Toy Research Association, London, 12 August.

Moll, L., Amanti, C., Neff, D. and González, N. (1992) 'Funds of knowledge for teaching: using a qualitative approach to connect homes and classrooms', *Theory into Practice*, 31 (2): 132–141. doi: 10.1080/00405849209543534.

Moore, D. (2010) 'Only children can make secret places: children's secret business of place', unpublished MEd thesis, Monash University, Victoria, Australia.

Naerland, T. and Martinsen, H. (2011) 'Child–child interactions and positive social focus among preschool children', *Early Child Development and Care*, 181 (3): 361–370. doi: 10.1080/03004430903387701.

New Zealand Ministry of Education (1996) *Te Whāriki. He whāriki matauranga mā ngā mokopuna o Aotearoa: Early Childhood Curriculum*, Wellington: Learning Media Ltd. Available from www.educate.ece.govt.nz/learning/curriculumAndLearning/TeWhariki.aspx.

New Zealand Ministry of Education (2007) *New Zealand Curriculum Framework for Primary Education*, Wellington: Learning Media Ltd.

Newton, E. and Jenvey, V. (2011) 'Play and theory of mind: associations with social competence in young children', *Early Child Development and Care*, 181 (6): 761–773. doi: 10.1080/03004430.2010.486898.

Norwich, B. and Kelly, N. (2004) 'Pupils' views on inclusion: moderate learning difficulties and bullying in mainstream and special schools', *British Educational Research Journal*, 30 (1): 43–65.

Nutbrown, C. (2011) *Threads of Thinking: Young Children Learning and the Role of Early Education* (4th edn), London: Sage.

Nutbrown, C. and Clough, P. (2013) *Inclusion in the Early Years*, London: Sage.

Nuttall, J. (ed.) (2013) *Weaving Te Whāriki, Ten Years On* (2nd edn), Rotterdam: Sense Publishers.

O'Brien, L.M. (2010) 'Let the wild rumpus begin! The radical possibilities of play for young children with disabilities', in L. Brooker and S. Edwards (eds), *Engaging Play*, Maidenhead: Open University Press, pp. 182–194.

Palaiologou, I. (2012) *Child Observation for the Early Years*, London: Sage.

Parker, C. (2001) '"She's back!" The impact of my visit to Reggio Emilia on a group of 3- and 4-year-olds', in L. Abbott and C. Nutbrown (eds), *Experiencing Reggio Emilia: Implications for Pre-school Provision*, Buckingham: Open University Press, pp. 80–92.

Parnell, W. (2011) 'Revealing the experience of children and teachers even in their absence: documenting in the early childhood studio', *Journal of Early Childhood Research*, 9 (3): 291–307.

Pearce, G. and Bailey, R.P. (2011) 'Football pitches and Barbie dolls: young children's perceptions of their school playground', *Early Child Development and Care*, 181 (10): 1361–1379.

Pellegrini, A.D. (1991) *Applied Child Study: A Developmental Approach*, Hillsdale, NJ: Lawrence Erlbaum.

Pellegrini, A.D. and Blatchford, P. (2000) *The Child at School: Interactions with Peers and Teachers*, London: Arnold.

Piaget, J. (1962) *Play, Dreams and Imitation in Childhood*, New York: Norton.

Pramling Samuelsson, I. and Fleer, M. (2009) *Play and Learning in Early Childhood Settings: International Perspectives*, New York: Springer.

Rinaldi, C. (2006) *In Dialogue with Reggio Emilia: Listening, Researching and Learning*, New York: Routledge.

Roberts-Holmes, G. (2012) '"It's the bread and butter of our practice": experiencing the Early Years Foundation Stage', *International Journal of Early Years Education*, 20 (1): 31–42.

Rogers, S. and Evans, J. (2008) *Inside Role-play in Early Childhood Education: Researching Young Children's Perspectives*, Abingdon: Routledge.

Rogoff, B. (2003) *The Cultural Nature of Human Development*, Oxford: Oxford University Press.

Rutanen, M. (2007) 'Two-year-old children as co-constructors of culture', *European Early Childhood Education Research Journal*, 15 (1): 59–69.

Ryan, S. (2005) 'Freedom to choose: examining children's experiences in choice time', in N. Yelland (ed.), *Critical Issues in Early Childhood*, Maidenhead: Open University Press, pp. 99–114.

Sandberg, A. and Ärlemalm-Hagsér, E. (2011) 'The Swedish National Curriculum: play and learning with fundamental values in focus', *Australasian Journal of Early Childhood*, 36 (1): 44–50.

Saracho, O. (1991) 'The role of play in the early childhood curriculum', in B. Spodek and O. Saracho (eds), *Issues in Early Childhood Curriculum*, New York: Teachers College Press.

Saracho, O. (2010) 'Children's play in the visual arts and literature', *Early Child Development and Care*, 180 (7): 947–956. doi: 10.1080/03004430802556356.

Saracho, O. (2012) *An Integrated Play-based Curriculum for Young Children*, New York: Routledge.

Sawyer, R.K. (2003) 'Levels of analysis in pretend play discourse: metacommunication in conversational routines', in D.E. Lytle (ed.), *Play and Educational Theory and Practice. Play and Culture Studies, Volume 5*, Westport, CT: Praeger, pp. 137–157.

Sayeed, Z. and Guerin, E. (2000) *Early Years Play: A Happy Medium for Assessment and Intervention*, London: David Fulton.

Sendak, M. (1963) *Where the Wild Things Are*, London: Red Fox Books.

Sherwood, A.S. and Reifel, S. (2010) 'The multiple meanings of play: exploring preservice teachers' beliefs about a central element of early childhood education', *Journal of Early Childhood Teacher Education*, 31 (4): 322–343.

Singh, A. and Gupta, D. (2012) 'Contexts of childhood and play: exploring parental perceptions', *Childhood*, 19 (2): 235–250.

Siraj-Blatchford, I. (2009) 'Conceptualising progression in the pedagogy of play and sustained shared thinking in early childhood education: a Vygotskian perspective', *Educational and Child Psychology*, 26 (20): 77–89.

Siraj-Blatchford, I. and Sylva, K. (2004) 'Researching pedagogy in English pre-schools', *British Educational Research Journal*, 30 (5): 713–730.

Siraj-Blatchford, I., Sylva, K., Muttock, S., Gilden, R. and Bell, D. (2002) *Researching Effective Pedagogy in the Early Years*, Research Report No. 356, DfES, London: HMSO.

Skånfors, L., Löfdahl, A. and Hägglund, S. (2009) 'Hidden spaces and places in the preschool: withdrawal strategies in preschool children's peer cultures', *Journal of Early Childhood Research*, 7 (1): 94–109. doi: 10.1177/1476718X08098356.

Smidt, S. (2006) *The Developing Child in the 21st Century: A Global Perspective on Child Development*, Abingdon: Routledge.

Smilansky, S. (1990) 'Sociodramatic play: its relevance to behaviour and achievement in school', in E. Klugman and S. Smilansky (eds), *Children's Play and Learning: Perspectives and Policy Implications*, New York: Teachers College Press.

Smith, P.K. (2010) *Children and Play*, Oxford: Wiley-Blackwell.

Stephen, C. (2010) 'Pedagogy: the silent partner in early years learning', *Early Years: An International Journal of Research and Development*, 30 (1): 15–28. doi: 10.1080/09575140903402881.

Sutton-Smith, B. (1997) *The Ambiguity of Play*, Cambridge, MA: Harvard University Press.

Sutton-Smith, B. (2001) *The Ambiguity of Play* (2nd edn), Cambridge, MA: Harvard University Press.

Sylva, K., Melhuish, E., Sammons, P., Siraj-Blatchford, I. and Taggart, B. (2010) *Early Childhood Matters: Evidence from the Effective Pre-school and Primary Education Project*, London: Routledge.

Thornton, L. and Brunton, P. (2007) *Bringing the Reggio Approach to Your Early Years Practice*, Abingdon: Routledge.

Tovey, H. (2008) *Playing Outdoors: Spaces and Places, Risk and Challenge*, Maidenhead: Open University Press.

Tovey, H. (2010) 'Playing on the edge: perceptions of risk and danger in outdoor play', in P. Broadhead, J. Howard and E. Wood (2010) (eds), *Play and Learning in the Early Years: From Research to Practice*, London: Sage, pp. 79–94.

Vallberg Roth, A. and Månsson, A. (2011) 'Individual development plans from a critical didactic perspective: focusing on Montessori- and Reggio Emilia-profiled pre schools in Sweden', *Journal of Early Childhood Research*, 9 (3): 247–261.

Vygotsky, L.S. (1978) *Mind in Society* (translated and edited by M. Cole, V. John-Steiner, S. Scribner and E. Souberman), Cambridge, MA: Harvard University Press.

Walsh, G., Sproule, L., McGuinness, C. and Trew, K. (2011) 'Playful structure: a novel image of early years pedagogy for primary school classrooms', *Early Years: An International Journal of Research and Development*, 31 (2): 107–119.

White, E.J. (2009) 'A Bakhtinian homecoming: operationalizing dialogism in the context of an early childhood education centre in Wellington, New Zealand', *Journal of Early Childhood Research*, 7 (3): 299–323. doi: 10.1177/1476718X09336972.

Whitebread, D. (2010) 'Play, metacognition and self-regulation', in P. Broadhead, J. Howard and E. Wood (eds), *Play and Learning in the Early Years: From Research to Practice*, London: Sage, pp. 161–176.

Wilson, R. (2012) *Nature and Young Children: Encouraging Creative Play and Learning in Natural Environments* (2nd edn), Abingdon: Routledge.

Wisneski, D. and Reifel, S. (2012) 'The place of play in early childhood curriculum', in N. File, J. Mueller and D. Basler Wisneski (eds), *Curriculum in Early Childhood Education: Re-examined, Rediscovered, Renewed*, New York: Routledge, pp. 175–187.

Wohlwend, K.E. (2009) 'Early adopters: playing new literacies in pretending new technologies in print-centric classrooms', *Journal of Early Childhood Literacy*, 9 (2): 117–140. doi: 10.1177/1468798409105583.

Wohlwend, K.E. (2011) *Playing Their Way into Literacies: Reading, Writing, and Belonging in the Early Childhood Classroom*, Language & Literacy Series, New York: Teachers College Press.

Wolfe, S. and Flewitt, R. (2010) 'New technologies, new multimodal literacy practices and young children's metacognitive development', *Cambridge Journal of Education*, 40 (4): 387–399. doi: 10.1080/0305764X.2010.526589.

Wood, E. (2010a) 'Reconceptualising the play–pedagogy relationship: from control to complexity', in L. Brooker and S. Edwards (eds), *Engaging Play*, Maidenhead: Open University Press, pp. 11–24.

Wood, E. (2010b) 'Developing integrated approaches to play and learning', in P. Broadhead, J. Howard and E. Wood (eds), *Play and Learning in the Early Years: From Research to Practice*, London: Sage, pp. 9–26.

Wood, E. (2010c) 'Listening to young children: multiple voices, meanings and understandings', in A. Paige-Smith and A. Craft (eds), *Developing Reflective Practice in the* Early *Years* (2nd edn), Maidenhead: Open University Press.

Wood, E. (2013) 'Free play and free choice in early childhood education: troubling the discourse', *International Journal of Early Years Education*, in press.

Wood, E. and Cook, J. (2009) 'Gendered discourses and practices in role play activities: a case study of young children in the English Foundation Stage', *Educational and Child Psychology*, 26 (2): 19–30.

Wood, E. and Hall, E. (2011) 'Drawings as spaces for intellectual play', *International Journal of Early Years Education*, 267–281. doi: 10.1080/09669760.2011.642253.

Worthington, M. (2010) 'Play as a complex landscape', in P. Broadhead, J. Howard and E. Wood (eds), *Play and Learning in the Early Years: From Research to Practice*, London: Sage, pp. 127–144.

Worthington, M. and Carruthers, E. (2003) *Children's Mathematics: Making Marks, Making Meaning*, London: Paul Chapman.

Yelland, N. (ed.) (2010) *Contemporary Perspectives on Early Childhood Education*, Maidenhead: Open University Press.

AUTHOR INDEX

SUBJECT INDEX